THE
Seasons *of*
Change

Using Nature's Wisdom
to Grow Through Life's
Inevitable Ups and Downs

CAROL L. MCCLELLAND, PH.D.

FOREWORD BY PAUL PEARSALL, PH.D.

CONARI PRESS

First published in 1998 by Conari Press
an imprint of Red Wheel/Weiser, LLC
with offices at:
665 Third Street,Suite 400
San Francisco, CA 94107
www.redwheelweiser.com

Paraphrased elements from "The Handless Maiden" a literary version by Clarissa Pinkola
Estés, Ph.D., in *Women Who Run With the Wolves,* copyright © 1992, 1995 by Clarissa
Pinkola Estés, Ph.D. Used by kind permission of the author, Dr. Estés, and her publisher,
Ballantine Books, a division of Random House, Inc.

ISBN: 978-1-57324-078-9

Cover photo by Joshua Sheldon, courtesy of Photonica
Cover design by Ame Beanland
Book design by Jennifer Brontsema
Charts and worksheets by Ellen Margaret Silva

Library of Congress Cataloging-in-Publication Data
McCclelland, Carol L., 1960–
     The seasons of change: using nature's wisdom to grow through life's inevitable ups
and downs / Carol L. McClelland.
          p.   cm.
     Includes bibliographical references and index.
     ISBN 1-57324-078-8 (pbk.)
     1. Life change events.   I. Title.
     BF637.L53M374   1998
     155.2'4—dc21   97-53277

Printed in the United States of America

10 9 8 7 6 5 4 3

THE
Seasons *of*

Dad, I've taken your advice to heart.
I'm happy and having fun. Hope you are too!
Thanks for everything.

August 22, 1932 – December 11, 1986

The goal of life is living in agreement with nature.

—Zeno, 335 B.C.

Contents

Foreword

Everyone faces change—whether it's the heart-wrenching loss of a child, a partner, or a home or the dull ache that accompanies a questionable medical test, a rumor at work, or an inner knowing that an intimate relationship is in trouble—there's really no way around it. The only choice you have is how you're going to approach the changes that are staring you in the face.

You can connect with your situation with a quiet, open heart, ready and willing to receive the wisdom that comes from the spontaneous insights and cellular memories you receive when you are alert to the lessons of the heart's code and its dance with the subtle energies of nature.

Or, you can enhance your struggle and suffering by trying to avoid your plight—trying to rationalize, deny, or escape whatever you can, even if such approaches are only the brain's way of self-protection that ultimately fail and can result in more physical, mental, and spiritual pain.

Although there is certainly pain to be experienced in either scenario, I think most of us would choose the first option if only we knew how!

In *The Seasons of Change*, Carol L. McClelland, Ph.D. helps us tremendously by teaching us how to navigate life's ups and downs using, as a model, the inevitable, yet graceful, way nature has changed with the seasons for all of time. The insights we gain from nature's tried and true wisdom of constant change and renewal can help us muster the courage we need to make our way through changes that are happening to us and inspire us to discover within ourselves the faith and patience to create the changes we desire.

Whether you're suffering through your current transition or you've begun to sense the glimmers of new revelations on the horizon, Carol's rich nature images, touching anecdotes, perceptive activities, and heart-felt guidance will awaken your Seventh Sense to lead you toward a new place of wholeness and joy. Then the next time you're faced with change, you will have the skills you need to approach your situation, not with dread and despair, but with the anticipation and hope of a wiser, lighter, healthier, and connected heart.

Paul Pearsall, Ph.D.
Author of *The Heart's Code* and *The Pleasure Prescription*

Part I

Discovering the Healing Power of Nature's Wisdom

After creating the Heavens and the Earth, the Great Goddess realized she was lonely. So she looked within, into the darkness of her heart, to find an answer, and there she saw the image of a face. She knew instinctively that although it was not her face, it was possible for her to give birth to it and love it.

After the gestation period, she went into labor, sending a jarring vibration around the world. The instant she gave birth to her "Sun," she knew happiness and a surge of energy.

As the "Sun" developed, he began wandering over the earth, gracing her with his light. Over time, his light illuminated the universe and made his mother, the Great Goddess, proud.

Sometime later, as the Great Goddess was wandering in her garden, she stopped to look in a pond. And there, reflected on the surface, was an image of the "Sun." By now, her "Sun" had reached manhood and she felt the stirrings of love within her.

As they spent time together, wandering through the fields hand in hand, they both experienced great joy and passion for each other and for the earth that brought them together.

Ultimately, they married and consummated their union under the shade of a giant oak in the garden where they'd met. Neither had ever felt such fulfillment and contentment.

They took the fullness they felt and enjoyed every day they spent together. Gradually, though it was barely noticeable at first, the Lord grew older and his light began to fade. With this change, the Great Goddess felt sorrow arise within her.

When it became clear that his life was fading, the Lord exclaimed to the Great Goddess that she had brought him great happiness. He asked her to remember the love and joy they'd experienced in their time together. Although she felt great sorrow as she watched her Lord become weak and pale, the Great Goddess honored his request and said a prayer of thanksgiving.

Not long afterwards, the Lord breathed his last breath. As her Lord journeyed into the realms of death, she mourned her loss and knew once again that she must look within at the void in her heart. And, just as she'd lost all hope, she saw again a glimmer of light within her. Over the years, the Great Goddess and her Lord, the "Sun," have reunited time and time again, each time with the same intensity and wonder as the first.

According to Kisma Stepanich, author of *The Gaia Tradition*, ancient cultures used stories like this one to help their people understand, trust, and honor the cycles of nature: birth, life, death, and rebirth. This truth—that everything is born, lives, dies, and is then born again in a new form—is at the core of all that we experience, whether it plays out in the microcosm of an event or in the macrocosm of an entire life.

We are each somewhere in the midst of this cycle right now, as we handle the changes, both large and small, that are occurring in our lives. By learning from nature's wisdom, we can come to a new understanding of how change really works and how to use change to lift our lives to a new level.

I tapped into this wisdom myself over ten years ago after I experienced a series of intense transitions, including the death of my father. It brings me great joy to be able to share this encouraging, positive approach to change with you, after all these years. I know my father has contributed as much to this work as I have, for he has been with me every step of the way. I hope our joint effort gives you the strength and faith to move through your changes mindfully and gracefully.

To illustrate the ways of change, I've included a number of anecdotes I've collected over the years. In each case, I've changed the names and certain identifying details to protect the anonymity of those involved. In some cases, I've taken the liberty to combine the stories of various people to demonstrate several points at once.

One

When Changes Get Personal: From Denial to Awakening

June sat in my office, her eyes glistening with unshed tears. She told me that just as she'd decided to sell her business of fifteen years she'd been blindsided by her brother's death and, two weeks later, by the news of an unexpected though welcome pregnancy.

As tears spilled down her cheeks, she whispered, "I'm so confused, I can't seem to make sense of anything right now. What I really want to do is spend some time alone, but no one will let me. They all want me to cheer up and get my mind off my worries."

You might be experiencing something similar as you deal with whatever change has brought you to read this book. "Your desire to go within is perfectly natural," I gently said to June, "and probably one of the best things you can do for yourself right now."

She took a full, deep breath, let out a huge sigh, and said, "You mean . . . I'm not going crazy?!?"

I've heard this sigh many times from clients as they discovered, for the first time, that there really *is* some rhyme and reason to how they feel as they face life's inevitable changes. I want to offer you the same comfort. Knowing my work brings people hope gives meaning to all the dark, scary nights I spent wondering if I myself was going crazy.

Will I Ever Feel Okay Again?

For the first twenty-five years of my life, I took great pride in the fact that my life seemed to unfold like clockwork. I grew up in a comfortable, suburban area of California, part of a happy family of four. We had two cars, a dog, and took family vacations every summer. The only big changes I experienced were the anticipated moves as I climbed the academic ladder.

Then one muggy summer day, the stability of my life was irrevocably shattered during a phone conversation with my parents. Although they were only informing me that my father's biopsy looked a bit questionable, I knew in a heartbeat that he was going to die as a result. And soon. All my life, I'd never known anything that completely. As I stared at the shiny eggshell-colored enamel on the doorjamb next to the phone, I tried to make sense of what my parents were saying. Somehow, I managed to hold myself together while we talked, but as soon as we hung up, I started crying hysterically.

I had next to no experience dealing with emotions of such magnitude, with death, or with how to continue my life when everything I'd ever known was crumbling. To make matters worse, I was halfway across the country in the midst of a summer internship. All of my friends were hundreds or thousands of miles away. I'd never felt so alone in my life. In the months that followed, I often wondered if I'd ever feel okay again.

By the time my father died, eighteen months later, I'd finished graduate school, gotten a corporate job, and had begun to reestablish my life in California. Talk about a time of transition! At least now I was only an hour away from home when the phone call came, so I was able to be there to support my mother and to receive the comfort of family and friends. Given my father's deteriorating condition, the biggest shock was not his death but the strong feeling of rightness that settled, within twelve hours, over my mother and me. We both sensed that his passing would be an important catalyst for each of us—a feeling that was haunting and reassuring at the same time. For about a month, I was "fine," but numb. Then, the waves of grief started to hit. Although the quality and intensity of the waves changed over time, they continued for several years.

Ironically, a few years before he died, Dad loaned me his copy of *Transitions: Making Sense of Life Changes* by William Bridges, the first book on the market to define the stages underlying all transitions. My familiarity with that book allowed me to realize that what I was experiencing was normal and that I could use my process as a catalyst for personal growth. Although those years of grief were the toughest I've ever experienced, some of my most poignant and meaningful memories come from that period.

Then, just as I was beginning to make sense of my father's death, life handed me a number of other intense issues to work through: my mother's bout with cancer, the deaths of three grandparents, my own physical and mental burnout. Each of those experiences woke me up to the reality of life's changes.

Somehow, in the depths of my despair, I realized that by experiencing my own grief process, I would learn how to help others move through the often treacherous journey associated with life changes. That knowing became the light at the end of a very long tunnel for me. I immediately became very conscious of my own process, paying particular attention to how I felt, what I was going through, and what helped ease my pain and anguish. I gleaned information from any source I could find—books, workshops, talks, conversations.

Then as the space between the waves of grief lengthened, my interest in navigating life's transitions moved beyond the purely personal. My role in a large corporation put me in an ideal position to observe a wide variety of changes at both the organizational and individual levels. Everywhere I went, inside and outside of the company, I heard people talking about the changes they were struggling with: downsizing, relocating, a child leaving home, aging, divorcing. As I listened to them talk, I took note of the kinds of support they were or were not receiving and began to get a feel for what might assist them in moving through their transitions more gracefully.

Through my observations, I became more and more fascinated with the *process* of change. I began to see that when people understand and go through a natural progression of feelings and behaviors in dealing with life changes, they can arrive, more easily, at a new, happier, and healthier place. The process certainly isn't free of pain—I could attest to that—but the potential for growth that comes *with* change is phenomenal. Learning to tap this potential is vital to the health and well-being of everyone alive, because no matter who you are, there is no escaping change.

The Ubiquitous Nature of Change

It doesn't take a rocket scientist to figure out that change is everywhere these days. Indeed, paradoxically perhaps, change is the only constant in life. As Alvin Toffler stated in *Future Shock*, "Change is avalanching upon our heads." One might think he wrote that sentence today, for it certainly feels true, but he actually published it in 1970. Just think of all the shifts, expansions, and inventions that have occurred since then!

It's definitely no secret that computers have had a tremendous impact on our society. The creation of microchip technology has had a profound impact on even our most basic appliances and vehicles. The rate at which this kind of technology changes means that by the time you get your computer set up it's already practically obsolete. When it breaks down, it's often cheaper to replace it than to invest in fixing it.

With computer and other technological advances has come the information explosion. In the opening paragraph of his book *Escape Velocity*, cultural critic Mark Dery quotes Marshall McLuhan's *1967* pronouncement that "electronic media have spun us into a blurred, breathless 'world of allatonceness' where information 'pours upon us, instantaneously and continuously,' sometimes overwhelming us." Looking back from where we are now, the volume of information has increased so much that the '70s and '80s look like a lazy day in the park.

In 1990, in their book *Megatrends 2000*, futurists John Naisbitt and Patricia Aburdene noted the startling expansion in the sources of media we must contend with on a daily basis—television networks, news shows, magazines. Since that statement, the availability of satellite dishes and access to the Internet have increased the options yet again a thousandfold. Unfortunately, Naisbitt's statement in his 1982 book *Megatrends* that "we are drowning in information and starved for knowledge" is more true now than ever before. If people in the '60s, '70s, and '80s felt overloaded with information, how can we possibly assimilate all that comes our way each day in the '90s?

This information overload has everything to do with our feeling overwhelmed by change. It used to be that you were primarily impacted by the changes that happened within a day's horse ride from your homestead. It might have taken weeks, months, or even years to discover a loved one had died, a revolution had taken place, or the steam engine had been invented. Now everything that happens all over the world also happens in your living room, your car, your office—instantaneously. As transition consultant William Bridges notes in *JobShift*, "time and distance no longer buffer us against the effects of change." While in the past we may have been affected by four or five of the changes happening worldwide, now we experience hundreds of them. It's no wonder everyone's talking about change these days.

Technology has also changed the way we communicate. We can now "talk" with friends and colleagues around the world via phone, fax, e-mail, beeper, or video conferencing, essentially instantaneously and sometimes for no more than the cost of a local phone call. Although these new forms of communication make it possible for us to telecommute, connect with people when we're stuck in traffic, and stay in touch with loved ones at the touch of a key, they also blur the boundaries between our professional and personal lives and between night and day. Now, thanks to whizzy technological inventions, our bosses can page us in our bedrooms, call us by cell-phone on the ski slopes, and e-mail us on our laptops at the lake.

Work *can* literally happen anytime, anywhere, these days and our bosses, our customers, and our gotta-get-it-done selves all try their best to convince us that it should. In fact, in the book *Thriving in Transition*, career consultant Marcia Perkins-Reed notes that "we are working more than ever before." She cited statistics from Juliet Schor's *The Overworked American* to demonstrate that in 1989 the average American worked 158 hours (approximately one month) more than in 1969, while the amount of time the average woman worked increased by 287 hours over the same period.

Another area of great change is how and where we work. Not only has the emphasis of the economy shifted from smokestack industries and manufacturing to information and services, the actual number of jobs available through traditional sources is decreasing due to automation, closures, downsizing, consolidations, and reengineering. In fact, white-collar jobs are decreasing even faster than blue-collar jobs. Another significant trend is the ever-increasing reliance on temporary, contract, part-time, freelance, and leased employees. Toffler spotted this trend in 1970 when he noted there were 500 temporary agencies placing 750,000 short-term employees in jobs ranging from secretaries to engineers. In 1994, Bridges reported that there had been a 60 percent increase in the use of temporary employees since 1980. Quite a significant jump! It's also interesting to realize that temporary jobs aren't just for technical and clerical work anymore. Now executives and project managers are also among the ranks of the temporarily employed.

On top of all these changes in the workplace, and maybe because of them, those of us who are currently employed can expect, according to the United States Department of Labor, to have *three* to *six* careers in our lifetime, and the next generation can expect to have between *six* and *ten* careers in theirs. And we question why we're reeling from change and having a hard time dealing with it?

All these technological and work changes have a definite impact on the family in terms of the time we have at home, how we play, how we learn, where we live, and how often we move. The trend toward dual career couples also changes the landscape of the family, bringing childcare issues and concern for family time to the fore. Furthermore, the divorce rate, now over 50 percent in the United States, takes its toll on all of us as family units are dissolved and reformed on a regular basis. We have yet to see the full ramifications all these changes have on the family and on our lives.

There are also major political shifts happening worldwide (the fall of the Berlin Wall, the dissolution of the Soviet Union, Hong Kong reverting back to Chinese rule) and environmental changes occurring as a result of our consumption-based, technology-hungry culture (clearcutting of the old-growth forests and rainforests, disposal of toxic waste, increasingly resistant strains of bacteria, viruses, and insects to medications and pesticides). Most of us try to ignore these changes because the ramifications are so huge and overwhelming that we can't predict their impact, let alone find ways we as individuals can address them. But they affect us nonetheless, whether we're consciously aware of them or not.

Even in 1970, Alvin Toffler was commenting on the impact such changes have on individuals—decision stress, information overload, the assault on our senses, an accelerated pace of life, an awareness of the temporariness of it all. He felt that all these changes would lead to "future shock"—"the shattering stress and disorientation" of being "subjected to too much change in too short a time." His thought at that time was that "unless man quickly learns to control the rate of change . . . we are doomed to the massive adaptational breakdown." From where we sit today, it's clear that we can't control the rate or range of the changes we experience. Nor can we just ignore the reality of change. We must find a way to accept that change is a part of our lives and learn to relate to it differently.

This can be very difficult because we lack adequate language to have meaningful discussions about change. I think Jungian analyst Robert Johnson said it best, in *The Fisher King and the Handless Maiden*, when he claimed, "Where there is no terminology, there is no consciousness. A poverty-stricken vocabulary for any subject is an immediate admission that the subject is inferior or depreciated in that society."

Let's take a quick look at how individuals are affected when a culture doesn't have an adequate word for an important concept. Take a moment to imagine what would happen if we didn't have a word for the act of thinking. "Thinking" is something that can't be seen, touched, smelled, heard, tasted, or sensed. And, in this scenario, it can't be discussed either. What would happen if you started thinking one day? Would you be able to describe your experience to others? Would they have any way to understand you? How would you feel if you knew what you were experiencing was not only real, but very important, and yet you had no way to get others to believe you? My guess is you'd feel discounted and possibly even crazy. You might even talk yourself into believing that "thinking" doesn't exist, even though you know you've just experienced it.

This is the situation many of us face when we go through big transitions. We know we're in the midst of powerful shifts, but we don't have the words to validate, for ourselves or others, what we're going through. As a result, we question ourselves and our sanity. This is tragic, for we desperately need to make peace with the process of change.

How We Handle Change

In *Future Shock,* Toffler noted with despair that "most people are grotesquely unprepared to cope" with change. In fact, for most of us our first line of defense is to avoid change whenever and wherever we can. We see it as a threat to our carefully choreographed lives, something to be staved off at all costs: "This isn't really happening so I won't worry" or "It's not *going* to happen because I've got everything under control."

I'll never forget the conversation I had with a man at a networking fair not long after I started my consulting business helping people through life transitions. As soon as I introduced myself, he stated emphatically that he had no need for my services and never would, because his life wasn't ever going to change. He claimed to know that for a fact. I sometimes wonder how long his life cooperated with his vision.

When we *are* dumped into change, our favorite strategy is to try to recover our lives as quickly as possible: "Oh yes, my marriage broke up, but I'm fine now" or "I had hepatitis for a week and the doctor ordered limited work for three months, but I'm too busy to slow down." Because there's a part of us that feels we've failed when life takes an unexpected (or even expected) turn, we really don't want others to know what we're going through—an abusive relationship, an illness, an unsuccessful job search—so we gloss over details, put a smile on, and do what we can to make our lives look good while we try to get things back on track.

Society's general lack of support during times of change reinforces our feelings that change is bad and that we're failing in some way if our lives are in flux. Whether we're negotiating the vast cultural shifts of our time or making personal changes that are a natural and unavoidable part of being human, we tend to get the same message from the media, corporate America, and even our families and friends: Fix it immediately and get your life back to normal so you don't get stuck in the morass of confusion you're in now. In this scenario, there's no room for difficult emotions, little encouragement to find the best, most fitting solution, no opportunity for healing the wounds that are inevitable in any kind of change, and no understanding that true change takes time—sometimes a long time.

In many families, there's also a very powerful unwritten rule that lurks around the dinner table, bedroom, and car: Don't rock the boat. This often translates to: Don't threaten our carefully guarded existence by springing bad news on us that might cause us to get emotional. If this is a strongly held agreement, family members in the midst of a difficult situation may go to great lengths to "protect" the family. Over the years, I've run across situations in which a mother held off telling her children about a cancer diagnosis; a father failed to inform his daughter of her mother's impending death until it was almost too late for her to say good-bye, a fiancé hid information about a large debt; a daughter sheltered her parents from news of her layoff.

In the end, this "don't rock the boat" environment impacts everyone adversely. The people going through the transition feel isolated, and don't receive the practical help and emotional support they desperately need from their loved ones. Then, on top of that, the family members who've been shut out actually end up having a *more* difficult time with the transition because instead of having a chance to come to terms with the change as it happens, they must then try to integrate all the information at once—no small feat in any situation.

In corporate America the lack of support for people in transition shows up in written or unwritten office protocol that says "leave your problems at the door." I've seen instances in which employees in transition don't have any access to a phone so they can't communicate with their lawyer or get results from a doctor during working hours; they're penalized if they take longer than their prescribed break to make a call or run an errand to sign papers; they're reprimanded or even sent home for displaying emotions. In one large company, renowned for their employee-centered management style, managers are trained *not* to offer any support to employees coping with life changes, no matter whether the employee is battling AIDS, going through a divorce, or having discipline problems with their children. Empathetic comments, suggestions about support resources outside the company, and problem solving with employees are discouraged for fear that the company might be held liable in case of a lawsuit. Employees who experience this kind of treatment when they're already feeling vulnerable also feel abandoned and unvalued by their employers. If companies do provide any support, it tends to be short-lived. Employees are usually expected to get back on their feet and return to being full corporate citizens in short order.

The way corporations handle in-house change is not any better. Employees are often kept in the dark about pending changes, told not to worry when there is obviously plenty to worry about, and expected to assimilate any news, good or bad, instantly. Furthermore, employees are often required to keep up full levels of production amid the chaos. Since some kind of major change always seems to be on the horizon in the form of possible layoffs, new technologies, vast job redesigns, or the merging of units, departments, or even entire companies, it's extremely unfortunate that employers and employees handle change so poorly.

Models for Change

To make any headway in understanding change, we must begin by looking at how we view change. Typically, we see it in three ways.

1. Change by Replacement

Our most common experience of change comes from our daily activities and the material goods we use. As we change our shoes, clothes, sheets, oil, tires, and vacuum bags, we replace the old with the new by simply making the decision, gathering the necessary supplies, and doing it. Then, when we get holes in our shoes, our cars don't start, and our vacuum cleaners lose their ability to suck up dirt, we make the decision to fix the item, pitch it, or buy a new one.

From these experiences, we believe:

- We're in control of the changes we make in our lives.
- Change happens at the flip of a switch.
- We always have the option to fix what is broken or dispose of it if it can't be fixed.

Although these beliefs may be very efficient when faced with a broken appliance or vehicle, they fall flat when you try to use them to "fix" your broken heart or broken spirit. In the complex world of human emotions and thoughts, "flipping a switch," "installing a new part," or "getting a replacement model" are detrimental at best.

When we rely on this approach to make changes, we often come up against the fear that if we do decide to make a change, the life we've known will be replaced—completely—in a heartbeat. For instance, I've had clients hesitate to start a career *discovery* process with me for fear that just by *starting* the process they'll *have to* make a career change, whether they want to or not. For them, beginning the process means they've flipped that switch and there's no turning back. This "all or nothing" mentality tends to paralyze us, preventing us from making the much needed changes in our lives.

2. Change by Formula

When we do find ourselves in a pickle that requires more than replacing one thing with another, we typically ask around to see if we can find a quick, easy way to solve the problem. As a result, we usually end up with one kind of formula or another: old wives' tales about how to conceive, fad diets to lose weight, a how-to book to build self-esteem, or the ten steps guaranteed to land a job. Then, like a good student, you take what you've been told and dive into the process, following the gospel to the letter. With a bit of luck and perseverance, you may get the results you're looking for.

On the other hand, you may not. Therein lies the rub. If you believe with all your heart (or your pocketbook) that this or that formula will be the answer to your prayers, and it isn't, what will you do then? Depending on your personality, you may find fault with the formula or with yourself for buying into such a load of crock. Or you may blame yourself for failing to follow the formula correctly. Certainly, this last scenario has the most detrimental effects.

Working through this filter, we get a slightly different perspective of change.

- Although we have some control over the actions we take in response to a change, we can't control the outcome.
- Change happens after we take the steps defined by the formula. Depending on the complexity of the formula, this may take some time.
- If we don't complete the formula properly, we won't see results.

This formulaic approach to change can be quite useful when there really are specific steps you need to take to accomplish your goals (getting into shape, expanding your social circle) or when you need some guidelines on how to approach a situation for the first time. The trouble occurs when you rely too much on formulas to resolve the complex, emotional issues you're facing or you have too much faith in what they can do for you.

Sometimes the replacement approach to life leads us to believe that if we follow the formula correctly, we will, by definition, get the results we were promised. What we discount in this case is that things like timing, other people's actions, bureaucratic systems, and other, better opportunities also play a part in whether our formulas produce the results we're looking for.

The other thing we may tend to forget when using a formula is that whenever we put new plans into motion, it takes *time* to complete the steps and *time* for the results to show up. If you walk away too soon, you may never know if your efforts amounted to anything. You must give your actions time to take hold.

3. Change by Magic

Sometimes, when we're really in the thick of it and need a quick solution to our woes, we reach deep into our unconscious and reconnect with the part of our minds that marveled at the way Cinderella's Fairy Godmother magically fashioned her transportation to the ball from a pumpkin, some mice, and a rat. Then we find ourselves praying that we too will wake up one day, as Psyche did, to find ourselves in a huge castle full of exquisitely beautiful things. After "coming to our senses" we realize how ridiculous it is to rely on a Fairy Godmother or a powerful god, so instead we pin our hopes on winning the lottery, meeting our dream partner, or finding *the* perfect job, all the while visualizing what life will be like when our wishes are granted.

These are the conclusions we reach about change when we employ magical thinking:

- A force outside of us makes change happen—Fairy Godmother, God, the state lottery, or Mother Nature.
- Change happens almost instantaneously.
- When it happens, the change is so complete that nothing is left of the old.
- There's as much chance the results will be spectacular as devastating.

There certainly are occasions when the storybook plot does happen: two people fall in love at first sight, someone inherits a sizable estate, you build your dream home overlooking the lake. And, sometimes, when life is really depressing, the dream is the *only* thing that keeps us pushing forward.

Difficulties arise, however, when we rely on magic to solve our problems. That is when we abdicate our power to someone or something else and forget to take care of ourselves and our day-to-day lives. The longer we wait for our dreams to come true, the more disillusioned we become, until we're so out of touch with reality that we can't begin to understand that we're doing anything wrong or that we've given away or lost our power.

Under the sparkle and glitter of this approach to change, we may feel a tinge of terror as we come to terms with the fact that we have absolutely no control over when, where, or how the magical change will happen. We can become slightly paralyzed when we realize that one day we could wake up and our lives could be completely, irrevocably different. This scenario is unsettling whether the change is a good one—sudden wealth, marriage, relocation—or a bad one—a tornado, layoff, an accident.

As it turns out, not all fairy tales rely on magic to solve the problems of the day. In fact, in the book *Once upon a Midlife*, Allan Chinen used "middle tales" (fairy tales in which the main characters are working adults dealing with life's challenges) to illustrate why adults must let go of their reliance on external magic and apply the magic that comes from within—creativity, focus, intuition, and perseverance—to solve their problems.

The True Nature of Change

As we look at these three models of change, we can see why our culture has so little understanding of change and how that affects people. If we're to learn how to make change our ally instead of our enemy, we must find a more appropriate model for change, one that reflects what we truly experience. But where can we turn for a richer set of images, stories, and experiences to guide us? Actually, the answer is within our bodies and right outside our front doors.

4. Change as Growth

One kind of natural change is so subtle we tend to forget about it unless we're around young children, puppies, or seedlings. The constant incremental growth that occurs in every living animal and plant, including ourselves, provides a very gentle model of constant, continuous change.

When we look at this kind of change at a broader level, we see the seasons change. Hours turn to days, days turn to months, months to seasons, and gradually the world changes before our eyes. Because our experience of the seasons varies by year and by location, it proves, as we'll soon see, to be a very rich metaphor for change.

As the seasons pass, we see the ultimate cycle play out in nature: birth-life-death-rebirth. We watch as a plant breaks through the soil, growing daily to produce buds which blossom, dry up, and drop seeds to the ground. These seeds come to life once again when the conditions are right. We also see the cycle occur in our neighborhoods as a neighbor gives birth to a baby, a child becomes an adult, a good friend passes on, and another child is born.

This natural approach to change provides us with an entirely different view:

- Consistent changes occur from inside out.
- Change takes time and happens gradually.
- Change may come in the form of growth or decay.

Although this perspective on change doesn't apply when you're dealing with changes of a mechanical nature, it's very appropriate when you're dealing with issues associated with being human. Here we have the opportunity to marvel at the constant change that occurs with growth, and we can take our time, experiment with our options, and *allow* a natural sort of change to occur.

Of course, it's important to note that we must do our part in keeping the change alive. We must feed it, nurture it, love it, touch it, play with it, and attend to it. If we give away our part by expecting someone else to do it for us, the glimmers of change are likely to begin to fade.

The other piece of this puzzle is that, although we must participate, we can't for a minute believe that we control the growth. We don't. In fact, we can't, because natural growth is part of a much larger mystery. On some occasions, things beyond our control might occur that cause decay rather than growth. The key is to take responsibility for our part of the puzzle and no more.

5. Change by Metamorphosis

Another powerful metaphor for change is symbolized by the butterfly—an insect that begins as a tiny egg, become a landlocked caterpillar, lies dormant in a cocoon, and emerges as a beautiful winged creature. This is an awe-inspiring process because it's hard for us to grasp how such profound changes in form can happen so gracefully. It's much different from watching a puppy turning into a big adult dog; the process of metamorphosis is that of a being going through a transformation in which, over time, it takes a series of distinctly different forms.

From this metaphor, we learn that:

- Transformative changes can occur naturally.
- Change takes time.
- Gradual change can culminate in abrupt shifts in form and function.
- The being experiencing a change may not be able to project just what it or life will be like after the shift.

This view of change is incredibly helpful for people who are experiencing a series of changes, who need to know that even if today they're a caterpillar munching on leaves, they have the ultimate potential to fly free. Such a transformation is a complete rebirth of sorts. Because we have models of this in nature, it allows us to trust the process and the greater mystery. We know that all we can do is participate with and learn from the natural states of life.

Weaving it All Together

Now let's look at all the models for change together, for there's a time and a place for each of them. As you can see in Figures A and B, they fall along a continuum defined by three factors:

- The first factor, represented by the lightly shaded area in Figure A, is the amount of control you have over the change. This includes the degree to which you control the actions that lead to the change, you participate in the process, and you are responsible for the results.

- The second factor is the degree to which someone or something (indicated by the darkly shaded area), controls the change. Depending on your situation and your beliefs, the other force might be one or more of the following: God, Goddess, Mother Nature, the Universe, Lady Luck, angelic forces, chaos, circumstances, other people. As you wrestle with your changes, your understanding of how these factors influence your life are likely to change. As you can see by the chart, the degree to which someone or something controls change in the five models is inversely related to the amount of control you have. For example, with Change by Replacement, other forces have little impact

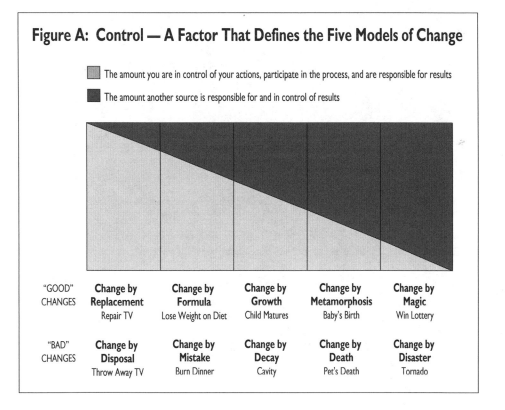

Figure A: Control — A Factor That Defines the Five Models of Change

☐ The amount you are in control of your actions, participate in the process, and are responsible for results

■ The amount another source is responsible for and in control of results

"GOOD" CHANGES	Change by Replacement	Change by Formula	Change by Growth	Change by Metamorphosis	Change by Magic
	Repair TV	Lose Weight on Diet	Child Matures	Baby's Birth	Win Lottery
"BAD" CHANGES	Change by Disposal	Change by Mistake	Change by Decay	Change by Death	Change by Disaster
	Throw Away TV	Burn Dinner	Cavity	Pet's Death	Tornado

on the results, while in the Change by Magic category, others have complete control. In the natural forms of change, both contribute to the results.

- Each model also varies in terms of the amount of time required to make a change. The U-shaped curve in Figure B indicates that the models at each end of the spectrum tend to expect instantaneous results, while the models in the middle acknowledge that change takes time to occur.

Up until now, we've been focusing on change as a positive event, bringing good results, but we all know that this is not always the case. Sometimes changes occur because we dispose of something, we make a mistake, something decays, something dies, or a disaster strikes. These represent the shadow, or unpleasant side, of change. Examples of these forms of change are also shown in Figures A and B.

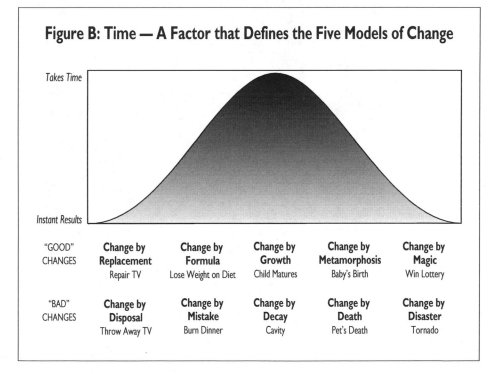

Figure B: Time — A Factor that Defines the Five Models of Change

Takes Time					
Instant Results					
"GOOD" CHANGES	**Change by Replacement** Repair TV	**Change by Formula** Lose Weight on Diet	**Change by Growth** Child Matures	**Change by Metamorphosis** Baby's Birth	**Change by Magic** Win Lottery
"BAD" CHANGES	**Change by Disposal** Throw Away TV	**Change by Mistake** Burn Dinner	**Change by Decay** Cavity	**Change by Death** Pet's Death	**Change by Disaster** Tornado

To give you an idea about the different ways the five models work, I've laid out examples of how each might be applied in three common transitions: changing relationships, finding a new career, and dealing with a broken-down car. As you'll see, each model is more appropriate for some situations than for others.

Applying the Models of Change to Three Transitions

	Change Your Relationship	Change Your Career	Fix Your Car
Change by Replacement	Order Spouse from a Catalog	Take the First Job You Find	Take Car to Shop to Have it Fixed
Change by Formula	Follow "The Rules" to Find a Spouse	Use Self-assessment Survey to Find Career	Use Auto Manual to Fix Problem
Change by Growth	Allow Relationship to Deepen Gradually	Allow Career Ideas to Germinate Before You Act	See if You Can "Grow" the Part You Need
Change by Metamorphosis	Go from Dating to Engaged in Weeks	Transform from Computer Analyst to Artist in a Month	Leave Car in Garage Until it Becomes a Classic
Change by Magic	Love at First Sight	Get Discovered	Pray Your Car Will Start

Because we've lost touch with the natural world and have relied for so long on the models of change at the two extremes, it's time to learn more about the insights nature has to offer us. It is here we will find deep wisdom for dealing, in the most positive and healthy ways, with the changes life will inevitably bring.

The Natural Approach to Change

I've always been an avid observer of nature. As a child, I collected caterpillars and tadpoles to watch them emerge as butterflies and toads. After a visit to the local tidepools, I was so enchanted with sea anemones that, while the rest of my Brownie troop argued over who got to be the princess in our puppet show, I demanded that I play a sea anemone.

(Goodness knows how the plot for that puppet show worked out!) And to this day, I remember the hospitals I'd set up in shoe boxes lined with grass to save earthworms that had come between my mother's trowel and the dirt. Even my favorite children's books had to do with nature in some way.

Of course, growing up in Northern California gave me a rather skewed view of the seasons. The first year I attended graduate school in the Midwest, I started searching for signs of spring in February, the time our mild spring arrived in California! I had a long wait, because the plants didn't begin to get green until the middle of May. Each year I was there, I reveled in nature's stunning display of the four distinct seasons. In fact, my walk to class each day felt like a field trip. Little did I know that the hours I spent observing nature were preparing me for my future work.

When my father died, I often found myself turning to nature for comfort. As I watched trees blossom several months after his death, I remember saying to myself, although I feel like a barren tree today, I know I'll blossom again someday. Everywhere I looked, I saw scenes in nature that mirrored my own transition.

It wasn't until 1991, however, when I started supporting others in the midst of life transitions, including career changes, relocations, relationship changes, illnesses, spiritual awakenings, and deaths, that I began drawing upon nature to describe the processes people were experiencing.

At that point, I had a set of nature images I used on a regular basis, but they weren't in a cohesive package that anyone else could use. Encouraged by a friend, I sorted through my analogies, and over several days developed a cohesive way to view life's changes, which I call The Seasons of Change. In many ways, this model is intuitively obvious; we're all in our own personal cycle of seasons, continuously moving through the cycle as we experience changes in our lives. Sometimes, we're even in different seasons at the same time—in the spring of becoming a parent, for example, while at the same time in the winter of a dying career. To flesh out my ideas even more, I spent time consciously observing and thinking about how animals and plants move naturally through the changing seasons. Their methods of surviving and growing through change, year in and year out, added even more depth to this approach.

As I began to use this model in my practice, I was amazed at the transformation people went through when I drew images from nature to explain where they were in their transition. "This is the part where you are barren like a tree in winter," I would say. "But, in time, you will turn green and lush again." Tapping into nature's wisdom provided people with a gentle and hopeful way to look at the chaos and pain they were experiencing.

Nature as Teacher

Using nature as a teacher is certainly not a new concept. Through the ages, many cultures, including Native American, Australian Aborigine, and Celtic, used their knowledge of nature to make sense of their lives through vision quests, walkabouts, and seasonal celebrations.

In earlier times, all peoples were so aware of the earth, its cycles, and the delicate balance between human beings and nature that they formally acknowledged and celebrated their connection eight times a year with seasonal festivities. Four of the ceremonies coincided with the beginning of each season at the solstice and equinox points on the calendar, while the other four occurred at the halfway marks between the seasons (in our culture, we have the vestiges of these rites on only three dates: Groundhog Day, May Day, and Halloween).

Of all the celebrations, the winter solstice was probably the most poignant. As the days became shorter, people literally feared that the sun would continue to fade until only darkness remained. Because they depended so much on the earth for survival, they knew their existence was completely linked with that of the sun and believed that only their prayers and carefully orchestrated actions could bring the sun back. By celebrating the cycle of the seasons as a unified group, as Kisma Stepanich noted in *The Gaia Tradition,* each community became aligned with the "natural order of this great planet and flow[ed] with its energy instead of against it."

Human beings' strong connection with nature and its cycles allowed them to work *with* natural forces to plant and harvest food, protect themselves from the elements, and heal ailments. Being able to anticipate and prepare for seasonal changes increased their chances of thriving and left them no room to be detached from or disrespectful of the inherent cycles of nature.

As our world has become more and more industrialized and we've come to believe only scientific explanations for how the world works, we've also become divorced from the wisdom and power inherent in nature. We no longer connect with the natural rhythms of life because we're so caught up in the mechanical order we've established through clocks, structured work schedules, freeway systems, and highrise office buildings. Furthermore, we've become so busy with our "time-saving devices"—computers, faxes, express mail, microwaves, e-mail—that we no longer have (or take) the time to smell the roses, watch the sunset, look at the stars, or notice the land around us changing with the seasons.

The first major sign of this separation came in the seventeenth century. As organizational consultant Margaret Wheatley noted in "The Heart of Organizations," "We came to believe not only that the world is a machine but that people can best be understood as machines." In fact, we've been using technology as a metaphor for our own brains since the mid-1800s.

Is it possible that our confusion about and pain over change stems from our detachment from the natural rhythms of the earth? How can we possibly embrace the natural cycles of birth and death in our own lives when our scientifically based, results-oriented worldview sees change only as an event to be mastered? To accept and move with change, we need to recognize that even though we've overlaid our own notions of order onto our lives, we live on the Planet Earth and are still subject to its laws of nature. We must unearth our innate knowledge that change is a process, as natural as sunrise and sunset, the passage of the seasons, and the phases of the moon.

Nature's wisdom is never far away if you take the time to look around you. Notice your surroundings as you drive from place to place. Experience the transformation your yard and neighborhood go through each year. Open your windows so you can hear the wind, see the birds, and smell the fragrance of the flowers. The more you reconnect with the miraculous rhythms and cycles of our planet, the more at home you'll be with change.

Two

What Does Change Mean to You: Failure or Opportunity

If you've had a traumatic event occur in your life, you're probably reading this book to help make sense of what you're experiencing. If, on top of that, you've lived a life in which success is your highest goal, your philosophy of life is probably being stretched to the limit right about now. One part of you wants to keep up appearances and proceed as if nothing's happened, while another part wants to stop and heal. You're stuck between the proverbial rock and a hard place, unable to move in any direction.

The only way you can move forward and become whole is to shift how you view the ups and downs of your life. Over the years, I've discovered that the way we deal with change is dictated by how we view success and failure. So if you want to learn how to make healthy transitions, you must begin by changing the way you view success.

Life as Continuous Expansion

Most of us, especially those of the Baby Boomer generation, grew up with the idea that life would just get better and better over time. In his book *Success!*, Michael Korda describes it this way, "You'll know success when you've gone that one step further in wealth, fame, or achievement than you ever dreamed was possible." Amy Saltzman notes in *Down-Shifting* that we are not successful, according to fast-trackers, "unless one is consistently moving up the ladder in some clearly definable way." We all understood, of course, that it would take lots of effort and hard work to achieve this kind of success, but we also believed that if we just worked hard enough and followed the formula of success, we'd get all that we wanted—a strong career, a happy family, a good home. Furthermore, we were confident that the results gained would far outweigh the sacrifices we'd have to make along the way. In this model, our most sought after goal, no matter how well we were doing, was to become well-established enough that we could ultimately retire and live happily ever after.

We also believed that once we'd acquired our "goodies" they'd never go away. To put it another way, as anthropologist Mary Catherine Bateson does in her introduction to *Composing a Life*, "the real success stories are supposed to be permanent and monogamous." She's referring here to both marriages and careers, and to the belief that we're supposed to find the one perfect job and the one perfect spouse to fulfill us, and then grow upward with them from that time forward. The movement we crave is ever onward and upward to greater success.

After all, there's no room in the American Dream for loss, mistakes, or failure. This idea is so ingrained in us, we don't even feel comfortable taking a step back in order to move forward in a new direction. Frequently when clients first talk to me they'll say, "I want to change my career, but I certainly can't take a step down to do it." They definitely want—and need—to keep their upward-moving trend alive and well in order to maintain their sense of status, their identity, and, of course, their paycheck.

Even when our situations don't live up to this scenario, we still hold this picture in our heads as the ideal and we do our best to keep up appearances so others will at least *think* we're climbing the ladder and doing well.

This picture of success is very common among the cultural group referred to as "Moderns" in Paul Ray's research report, *The Integral Culture Survey.* A researcher studying values and lifestyles over the last ten years, Ray discovered that the United States is divided into three distinct groups: Heartlanders, Moderns, and Cultural Creatives. The Moderns, currently seen as the predominant group in our culture, accounting for 47 percent of the population, emphasize success in terms of climbing the corporate ladder and collecting status symbols in the form of material goods. They tend to have a mechanistic view of nature, their bodies, and life itself. It is within this group that we find the "replacement" model of change at work: Marriage broken? Just get a new wife. Body broken? Get your heart valve replaced. Then just keep on keepin' on, up the ladder.

Although this phase of Modernism began in the 1920s, the earliest threads of this perspective can be traced to the end of the Renaissance period, 500 years ago. Our country's notions of progress, for instance, have certainly been aligned with this perspective throughout its history. Expanding the territory, building the railroad, and growing our cities are all cultural manifestations of the Modernistic worldview. The axioms of the Moderns, as described by Sam Keen in *Fire in the Belly,* include "more is better, the latest is the greatest, speed increases efficiency, yesterday's limit is today's challenge."

Our views of success can also be traced to the fairy tales we heard as children. In these stories, as you well know, a young hero or heroine either chooses to leave home or is forced to by an evil (usually older) character. As these tales unfold, the hero/heroine struggles against great odds and accomplishes nearly impossible tasks to prove themselves. Then, as a result of fulfilling all their obligations, the prince and the princess find each other, marry, claim their riches, and live happily ever after. After reading approximately 5,000 fairy tales, mythologist Allan Chinen concluded that 85 percent followed this same basic plot. Since most of us were weaned on these so called "youth tales" (Snow White,

Aladdin, Cinderella, and the like), their messages became deeply ingrained in our psyches. We learned from reading and hearing about these characters that we too "must be kind, compassionate, honest, and hardworking to succeed." In teaching us this view of success, these myths have also done much to instill in us a preference for change by magic. Furthermore, they have contributed to our belief that once you have success, you never lose it, because once the prince and princess achieve their success, the story ends—we never hear about Snow White's breast cancer, Aladdin's lost job, or Cinderella's unhappy marriage.

When people talk about this kind of success, I see them climbing a staircase with each step representing another accomplishment—a promotion, a new home, the birth of a child—that takes them closer to their ultimate goal. Notice that the only changes embraced by this view of success are those that prove we're moving up the line and are therefore becoming more and more successful.

What's Wrong with This Picture?

In his book *Celebrate the Solstice*, Richard Heinberg writes, "in many areas of human affairs we have convinced ourselves that there should be only constant, unending growth." In the '80s, we saw this in the corporate world with businesses growing by leaps and bounds. Now we see it most clearly in technology where there's always a faster chip or a more efficient way of transmitting data on the horizon. When you think about it, there was a time not so long ago when our hard drives were "only" forty megabytes. Now most of us wouldn't dream of getting a computer system with a hard drive that holds less than a gigabyte (1,000 megabytes) of data.

Yet unfettered growth is not natural. Imagine, for a moment, what your life would be like if there were daylight twenty-four hours a day, 365 days a year. You could never sleep. There would never be a chance to rest, never an opportunity to shut down and turn inward. As research has shown, you would go crazy—the human body and mind require sleep—a mini-death—in order to remain healthy and sane. Or what if you lived in a land of perpetual summer? It would always be hot, the plants would die, the water would evaporate, and you'd become exhausted from constant activity.

Allan Chinen shared a myth from Japan called "The Man Who Did Not Wish to Die," which warns against everlasting life. In the story, a very wealthy man realized he couldn't stand the thought of dying and losing his fortune. So he searched and searched for the Elixir of Life that would allow him to live forever. Although the gods didn't think he'd done enough to deserve the potion, they did allow him to ride upon the back of a crane to the land of perpetual life. The wealthy man was ecstatic until he noticed the odd behavior of the residents. They spent all their time collecting and eating poisonous mushrooms and playing with dangerous snakes—all in an effort to die so they could leave their boring existence. He watched with curiosity but couldn't understand these people, until centuries had passed and he too wished he could leave that place. Luckily for him, his entire experience was just a dream created by the gods. He eventually woke up and saw the value of living life fully—*today!*

This myth points out how boring an eternal existence would be. Other myths illustrate the dangers of constant expansion. In the "Mortal King," a myth told in China, another rich man realized that he too would lose all he'd created if he were to die. He reveled in the idea of living forever—enjoying great feasts and great happiness until the end of time. One of his noblemen, however, had a broader picture of perpetual life, which he shared with the king. "If everyone continued to live, then all the heroes who'd lived before you would still be alive and you'd be relegated—for all time—to the status of clerk." The king quickly saw the wisdom in this reasoning and changed his tune. The moral of the story is that we must look beyond our own life to see the big picture and the importance of passing on our riches to those coming after us.

Other myths warn of the impact continuous life and growth would have on the planet. In "The Origins of Death," told among the Siksika, or Blackfeet, tribe of Montana, shared in the book *Keeper of the Earth*, an old woman decreed that people shouldn't come back to life after they die. She said, "If people lived forever, the earth would be too crowded. There would not be enough food." This teaches us that the earth has a carrying capacity that we must respect. Italo Calvino shares an Italian tale in which a man corked Death inside a magic bottle. This story tells of the ramifications of this action—the number of old and infirm people skyrocketed, the sick suffered. Eventually Christ and Saint Peter came to ask the man to release Death, because Death plays too important a role to be incapacitated.

The fact that these stories, from so many different cultures, speak of the need to balance the desire for continual growth with its impact on the earth and human beings, tells us we must begin to look at how our own mythology of constant expansion hinders our existence. As theologian Matthew Fox points out in *Original Blessing,* one of the reasons we hold so fast to a mentality of continuous expansion is that we are a "light-oriented" society. We crave positive good, life, and constant growth. Inherent in this perspective, however, is a fear of darkness that leads us to deem each contraction, death, or downturn a failure.

Our culture's insistence on perpetual growth and our fear of death have a tremendous impact on how we live and die. One of the places this fear is most evident is in the extreme heroic efforts we take to keep someone alive even when their quality of life is so diminished that they "live" like vegetables. Its prevalence is also demonstrated when we hear medical professionals lamenting a patient's death as a "failure." But this fear extends far past the death of the body and shows up every time we experience a "death" in our lives—a business downturn, a job loss or layoff, a chronic illness, the end of a relationship, a child leaving home. Just like doctors who speak of "losing" a patient, we see all the changes in our lives as personal failures that shouldn't have happened, but did because we did something wrong. With this perspective, it's no wonder we're so afraid of change!

What we tend to forget in all this is that there are forces at work in our lives that we can't fully understand, let alone control. With the help of a natural model of change, we can begin to see that death is not a failure, but a crucial part of the life-cycle. In fact, *without* death, we can't continue to live, breathe, grow, and blossom, because it is death itself that allows for rebirth. We see this cycle come to life in nature each time a plant decays, providing nutrients for the soil so that new plants can grow; each time day turns to night, allowing us time for rest and repose; each time a Giant Sequoia seed resting on the forest floor is stimulated to sprout by the heat and destruction of a forest fire. When we have the strength to view our own lives in this way, we can see the same dynamic at work: breaking off a dissatisfying relationship allows space for a fulfilling one to begin; deciding to leave a job brings new leads and opportunities; allowing adult children to spread their wings stimulates a new space for creativity within you. Whether we like it or not, we're a part of this cycle.

As an integral part of the natural world, it's high time we learn to revere all phases of the cycle of life. Given our slant in this culture, I have no doubt that you celebrate births and the good parts of life easily. Now it's time to lift the filters we've put in place to avoid seeing death and decay. Take a day or two to notice death around you in a non-morbid way. You'll notice that they're easier to spot in some settings than others. In a wilderness forest, for instance, seeing signs of decay—a fallen tree, a crumbling stump, rotting leaves—is easy because in purely natural settings there are just as many signs of life as there are of death. In and around your own home, you may notice a fly on your windowsill, an insect in a spider's web, a lifeless leaf on your plant, or a dead branch on the tree outside your window. In an even broader sense, start catching yourself when you lament a cloudy day, the shortening of daylight as the seasons change, or the death of a person who has lived a good, full life. Really look at how each of these spots of darkness is a part of the natural cycle of life.

Remember, I'm not asking you to love or even like death, but to revere it—to honor it. Loss, in any form, is hard—and always will be—but when loss is seen in the context of the cycle of life, it has a poignancy that can often soften the despair. I sometimes wonder if the increased portrayal of death and destruction in the media is an unconscious attempt to get us to wake up and acknowledge the dark side of life on earth.

By not being attuned to notice decline of any sort, folks with the

Modern perspective—about 50 percent of those living in the United States—have a tendency to press their bodies, marriages, jobs, finances, and emotional well-being to the limit and beyond before they recognize that something isn't working in their lives. When they do finally notice a problem, they do all they can to avoid, deny, gloss over, and downplay it, because within the Modern's model of success there's absolutely no room for crises—the dozens of unpredictable, sometimes devastating, changes that move us off the ladder of success.

In the short run, we may succeed in our denial because our efforts to push beyond our difficulties often take us up to the next rung of the ladder. But ignoring these "deaths" is dangerous. Unhealed traumas don't disappear; they fester like wounds that haven't been properly tended. Eventually—whether it's weeks, months, or even decades later—we must acknowledge our losses and face the truth about the situations that caused us pain in the first place. Only then can we truly live again. Because our wounds have often accumulated over the span of several decades, it's no wonder it can take substantial amounts of time to complete this healing process.

Success as Authenticity

Beginning in the 1970s, more and more people began seeing life and, in particular, success in a new way. Cultural Creatives, as Paul Ray called this group, have rejected the Modernist views of the world as a machine and of success as a climb up some externally defined ladder. Rather, they see the world in a holistic way, with humans as part of, not separate from, nature. This group, currently about one-quarter of the population, or 44 million people, is drawn to spirituality, conscious relationships, altruistic endeavors, and ecologically sound causes. They see the purpose of life as the continuous process of discovering who they are at the deepest levels. And to this end, they strive to be "authentic" in all that they do—their work, relationships, lifestyles, purchases, spiritual practices, homes—and to align their actions, choices, and words with their values and beliefs. As Jan, one of my clients, puts it, they "want to be 'real.' " As a result, they don't succumb to pressures to do or be something they aren't in response to societal norms, office politics, or family dynamics.

At first glance, this approach to life may seem rather selfish, but when you stop to think about it, you really are here to live *your* life. If you're more inclined to act in ways to please or protect others, you're actually placing a higher value on *their* happiness than on your own. Although this shift takes a bit of getting used to, you'll find that when you act in alignment with your values, you're even more open and available to support those you love. Furthermore, they'll benefit more from being around you in your strength than they would if you were martyring yourself for their benefit.

In this model, change is not seen as an error or mistake that knocks you off the ladder of success, but rather as an opportunity—an invitation—to deepen your connection to yourself, to other people, to nature, and to life itself.

By moving through a series of stages, similar to the cycle of life, you gain more clarity about what's important to you and make adjustments so your life is increasingly in alignment with your highest and truest self. In this way, change acts as a catalyst to move you to new levels of authenticity and is, therefore, to be valued and honored.

This is not to say that change is easy. But simply recognizing that change is a natural process that takes time and requires an equal measure of faith and perseverance along the way will help you go through the process more gracefully. By participating with the various phases of this process, you'll have more options and will reach new planes of healing and awareness more easily than if you were to dig in your heels and resist.

When I think of the process of becoming more authentic, I don't envision it as moving straight up a ladder, but moving around and gradually up a spiral. The shape of the spiral suggests continuous growth as well as subtle changes in direction along the way.

A crisis of some kind often provides the impetus for people to make the commitment to live authentically. Chances are if you're reading this book some change has come to rattle your world view and perhaps, your life circumstances. Perhaps now that you've begun to see that such change is a part of nature, and not something to be faulted for, you're ready to restructure the way you interact with change. But how do you actually go about living life in this way?

The Transition Journey

In simple terms, the purpose of any transition is to move from Point A to Point B. This is true whether we're changing jobs, moving to a new town, coming to a new understanding of a relationship, or becoming more authentic in who we are.

Although we always learned in school that the shortest path between two points is a straight line, we know from experience that a direct linear path isn't always possible when it comes to moving through a transition. We now know we can't rely on the "Beam me up, Scotty" approach (Magic), the "ready, aim, fire" philosophy (Replacement), or the "guaranteed or your money back" packaged deals (Formula) to get us where we want to go. We must look beyond these quick fixes and find a new way to envision the process of getting from where we are now to where we want to be.

Another common way to get from Point A to Point B is to travel. Whether we're taking a trip to our grandmother's house, traveling between states of health, immigrating to a new country, or transversing the ups and downs of welcoming a newborn into our lives, the journey metaphor provides us with the guidance, insight, and direction we need right now.

From our own travels, we know that preparing for and completing a journey of any kind takes time, energy, and resources. Sometimes the going is easy and straightforward, while other times it's fraught with delays, detours, and distractions. The farther you travel, the longer the trip, the more likely you are to end up in a land with a different culture and language. Although this can bring homesickness, it increases the likelihood that you'll come home with an entirely new sense of yourself and perspective on life.

Of course, we're not the first to have discovered this metaphor.

Mythological tales, past and present, have taken this metaphor and parlayed it into very rich tales about both heroes (Ulysses, "Jason and the Argonaut," *City Slickers*) and heroines ("The Handless Maiden," "Vasalisa the Wise," Persephone) who embark on journeys and return home with new wisdom and strength. When we first meet the main characters in such tales they're usually just about to leave the world they've known to enter into the depths of the unknown—a forest, a dungeon, a desert, a cave, or the sea. In the darkness and chaos of the journey, they discover that the answer they've been searching for all along is within. Having made this discovery, the characters begin the second part of their journey—returning home to discover a way to be part of their old world in their new form. According to Joseph Campbell, author of *The Hero with a Thousand Faces*, the "hero's journey" is undertaken by people of all cultures, in all walks of life, and across many periods of history.

Chances are good that you're on such a journey right now. Just as there are numerous reasons, good and bad, to travel, there are also many kinds of events that can trigger us to embark on a transition journey.

What's Rocking Your Boat?

You were sailing along doing just fine when all of a sudden your boat started to rock and roll. In an instant, your life was no longer what you'd known, and whether you were prepared for it or not, you began one of life's transition journeys. Describing the hero's adventure to Bill Moyers in *The Power of Myth*, Joseph Campbell said that a person begins a journey for one of two reasons: something has been taken from them, or they feel "there's something lacking in the normal experiences available or permitted" in society. This tells us that you can be forced to begin a transformational journey or you can initiate the journey yourself. But that's just one of the factors that can spur the start of a transition journey. Take a moment to see how the changes you're experiencing came about:

- Did you initiate the change yourself, or was it forced upon you?
- Did you know the change was coming, or was it unexpected?
- Do you think the change you're going through is "good" or "bad?"
- Is this change timely and in sync with the "normal" pattern of your life, or is it untimely and out of sync?
- Are you making a decision or taking action?

To get some ideas about the kinds of events that might fall into each category, look at the following chart. Remember, how a change is categorized is in the eye of the beholder. For instance, depending on your circumstances, getting laid off may be the most devastating thing that's ever happened to you or the ticket to freedom you've been dreaming about for years.

Types of Changes

Self-initiated Changes			Forced Changes
	Breaking off a relationship Requesting a transfer Starting an exercise program	Losing your home in a hurricane Getting laid off from your job Losing a loved one in an accident	
Anticipated Changes			Unexpected Changes
	Child leaving for college Graduating from school Retiring	Having a heart attack Experiencing an earthquake Enduring an act of violence	
"Good" Changes			"Bad" Changes
	Getting married Having a child Being promoted	Losing a spouse Receving a difficult diagnosis Having a car stolen	
Timely changes			Untimely Changes
	Elderly person dying Young woman giving birth Young person leaving home	A young child dying An adult dying before parents A fifty-year-old getting laid off	
Making a Decision			Taking Action
	Deciding to leave your job Deciding to move Deciding to buy a pet	Leaving a lover Firing an employee Moving to a new state	

Although *all* transitions require us to take a journey of some sort, we tend, as a society, to place greater emphasis on some changes rather than others. Because we fear the dark, we're somewhat more likely to be sympathetic and supportive of those who are forced into a transition of an unexpected or untimely nature. As a result, even when we're fairly unversed in the ways of change, we generally offer these people more support, allow them more time to recover, and give them more space to be emotional than in other situations.

On the flip side, we tend to have less compassion, patience, and understanding for those who choose to walk into the dark, could have anticipated the change, or experienced a gain of some sort. We expect these people to glide through changes effortlessly without pain.

The most insidious part of this pattern is that you may carry out this bias even when *you* are the one in turmoil. As you go through a "bad" transition, for instance, you're likely to give yourself more latitude to grieve, to emote, and to take the time you need to adjust. Your patience with yourself wears thin, however, when you're launched into a "good" change, especially by choice. Then you feel you must cover up your tears of confusion, stop being silly, and hurry to get on with your life.

This double standard is unfortunate because no matter how you start your journey, it's a scary, lonely time. The last thing you need in times of transition is someone discounting your reasons or your methods for changing your life. Let's look at a few different situations where this might occur.

Take a moment to think about how your relationships have ended. If you were dumped (forced) unexpectedly just as you were heading to the altar (untimely), those around you probably supported you, consoled you, and gave you some space to grieve and recover. You probably felt justified in being emotional and distraught. If, on the other hand, you ended the relationship by choice because you were graduating and going to different states for graduate school (anticipated, timely), you may have gotten more static and little support from your friends and family as well as yourself. Regardless of how you left the relationship, however, you needed to grieve the loss of that partnership—the times you spent, the places you enjoyed, and the positive ways you interacted.

Our culture generally acknowledges that a loss will result in some kind of transition—the loss of a baby, a job, a home, a marriage, a fortune. But we tend to underestimate, or even completely ignore, the impact a positive change has on our lives—the birth of a baby, a marriage, winning the lottery, getting a promotion. From a Modern perspective, if positive changes are the key to success, how can they possibly result in sadness, confusion, and despair? Yet people embarking on these exciting new phases of life are also letting go of their old identities and lifestyles to fashion new ones. Under the surface, there are just as many adjustments to be made when you start a new life as when you let go of a part of your life that you've loved.

Another aspect of making a change that often gets overlooked is the decision-making phase. While you're deciding to initiate a change, your outer life often looks the same as it has. So it's likely that the people around you won't acknowledge the anguish you're experiencing as you decide to leave a marriage, relocate, or change jobs, because they may not even be aware that you're in the midst of a change. By the time you are ready to implement your plan and people know about it, you'll have probably already wrestled with many of the underlying issues, so the actual shift in your life may be less traumatic than the decision itself.

Remember that *every time* a change occurs in your life, you're called upon to embark on a transition journey, whether you know it or not. You have two choices—you can stand steadfast in your boots, refusing to answer the call, and end up living a static life in which you feel unfulfilled, frustrated, and depressed; or you can act on the invitation and embark on a journey toward expansion and growth. As we'll see, this journey takes time and has predictable phases that must be experienced. The more conscious you are about your own process, the less painful the journey is likely to be.

Now it's time to discover where you are in the transition journey. This information will help you appreciate not only where you are now, but also where you've been and where you're going.

Where Are You in Your Journey?

As you fill out the following questionnaire, think about your life as a whole. Read each statement and circle the ones that best describe what you're experiencing right now in your life. If you believe a statement only partially describes what you're feeling, make a note to yourself and/or use a half circle to select the item. There are no right answers. The most important thing you can do is be honest with yourself about how you're experiencing your transition right now.

Transition Questionnaire

1. I continue to live as if nothing is happening; I'm ignoring what lies ahead.

2. I'm afraid of what lies ahead.

3. I'm looking at my options and preparing for the future because I know a change is occurring.

4. I'm more tired than normal, and I don't feel like doing the social activities I used to do.

5. I just don't know—how I feel, what I want, where I'm headed. I use the phrase "I don't know" a lot.

6. I'm learning about myself and beginning to see my life from a new perspective.

7. I'm afraid to move out of the safety of the familiar elements of my current situation.

8. I know what I want to do next, but I'm hesitant to take action.

9. I'm energetic again, and I find it easy to take action to implement my plans.

10. I'm feeling insecure about the value of my accomplishments.

11. I've reached the milestone I've been working toward, but I'm already worrying about what will happen next.

12. I'm confident, happy, and enjoying life.

As you move through your transition, you may find it helpful to come back to this questionnaire periodically to see how your situation has changed. Once you become familiar with the questions and learn more about the change process itself, you'll be able to determine where you are in the transition journey by watching your life and recognizing the telltale signs of each phase as you progress.

Three

Where Are You in The Seasons of Change?

Imagine yourself in New England, taking a walk in a densely wooded area. As you enter the forest, your attention is drawn to the colorful mosaic of leaves surrounding you. Looking up, you're drawn into the canopy of rich reds, oranges, yellows, and burgundies with bits of clear blue sky poking through. As you look around you notice how these colors echo throughout the forest, on the trees, on the footpath, resting on top of the water, reflecting off the water, and falling from the tops of the trees to cover the forest floor. The kaleidoscope effect is awesome—perhaps even slightly overwhelming. As you become accustomed to the terrain and the display of colors, you're able to use your other senses to notice some of the more subtle signs of fall. Listen for the animals who are actively preparing for the colder months ahead. You might hear geese overhead, flying south in formation, and squirrels and other small animals rummaging all around gathering and storing their stash for the winter months. Smell the richness of the humus as the leaves littering the ground begin to decay to create the moist, rich soil the forest depends on. Sense the chill in the air, the shortened daylight hours, and how low the sun is as it illuminates the leaves from above.

Imagine you're staying in a cabin in the Rocky Mountains. Many days, as the storms rage and the winds buffet the cabin walls, you huddle under a blanket next to the fire to keep warm and feel safe. Whenever the weather permits, you bundle up and wan-

der around outside. You're stunned by the intense quiet that pervades the area during and after each snowstorm. Sometimes it feels as though you can almost touch the quiet, it's so thick. The air has a special quality to it because it's so cold outside. Although you occasionally see an animal foraging for food, you know most of them are hibernating, taking long naps in their nests, or are away for the winter in safer environs. The plant life around you is dormant, gray and lifeless, except for the pines and other evergreens. You marvel at how low the sun is in the sky and how short the days have become.

Imagine yourself on the coast of Northern California taking a walk through a meadow and onto a beach. It's easy to notice the essence of spring because everywhere you look there are signs of new growth: the tender, new shoots of spring-green grass, the smell of sweet grass in the air, and the pockets of wild iris blooming all over the meadow. After awhile you begin to spot even more magical signs of spring. Off the horizon, you see the spouts of gray whales migrating north with their young; across the meadow, you see a pregnant deer grazing warily with her adolescent young from last year; you witness the birth of a harbor seal in a tidepool; and nestled deep in the grass, you see tiny wild "belly-flowers" adding a splash of color to the meadow. The heightened energy and activity seem to emanate from everything as the sun warms the area and shines longer and longer each day.

Imagine you're in a small town in the Midwest, taking an evening walk through a quaint neighborhood. As you walk, your eyes are drawn to all the various plants and trees laden with ripening fruits and vegetables. You notice tomato, zucchini, and corn in backyard gardens, as well as a wide variety of fruit trees. Along a fence surrounding a field, you see that wild plants like the blackberry vines are also brimming with delectable morsels. You pick a few of these to savor on the rest of your walk. You hear cicada break into song as you walk by. You're glad the extra hours of daylight give you the opportunity to walk in the cooler part of the day.

The Seasons of Change

According to John Kotre and Elizabeth Hail, authors of *Seasons of Life*, the seasons have been used from at least as early as the time of the ancient Greeks to symbolize the phases of human life. This has become such a well-known metaphor that you'll sometimes hear adults acknowledge, for instance, that they are in the "fall" or "winter" of their lives.

As it turns out, it is also a very apt metaphor for the stages of the transition journey. As illustrated by the visualizations you've just read, the seasons offer a tremendously rich, multifaceted source of information about how change takes place. When you think of it, nature has been changing, quite gracefully and efficiently, with the seasons since the beginning of time. The various elements of the natural world, from the maple tree to the arctic hare, the Monarch butterfly to the tulips, have all evolved to survive in concert with the movement from one season to the next. Furthermore, the fact that each region and each species has a different experience of the seasons gives us a treasure-trove of ideas on ways to cope with and revel in change.

The beauty of this metaphor is that it is constantly available to us in the form of temperature changes, weather patterns, and duration of sunlight, as well as the flora and fauna of each geographic area. You'll find signs of the seasons no matter where you live. Furthermore, because it's right at our fingertips, the seasonal metaphor is well-known or can easily be learned.

As mentioned earlier, for cultures that live close to the land and retain their connection with the earth and her creatures, the seasons are an integral part of life. The peoples of these cultures would never dream of doing anything without integrating the seasons into their plans. This was especially true when they traveled. For certain tribes, such as the Oglala of the Lakota Nation, the season actually dictated their movement through their territory. Throughout the summer and into fall they stayed in areas that had the most abundant food sources, and used all their energies to gather and store food for the winter. Winter found them in sheltered camps in the part of their territory that experienced the mildest weather. Once springtime blossomed, the tribes moved about to locate fresh food sources and reconnect with family and friends from other areas. This pattern was such a part of their identity, it's hard to imagine the people and their culture separate from the seasons.

Although we can now travel safely without being fully in touch with the seasons, it's still useful to be somewhat aware of the weather at our destinations. If you've ever watched a planeload of people from San Diego or Florida disembarking in Chicago in late March, you'll know what I mean. There are always a few clad in shorts, T-shirts, and sandals who have no idea that it's still the middle of winter in the Windy City! By being disconnected from the seasons, these travelers run the risk of being cold, miserable, and isolated during their journey.

Because you've embarked on your journey, it's important to reconnect with the seasonal cycle of change so that you can navigate the transition safely. As you proceed, you'll pass through each season in turn. And, much like the Native American tribe described above, you'll have a particular focus and task during each phase of your trip. The familiar passage from Ecclesiastes tells us this: "There is a time for everything, and a season for every activity under heaven: a time to be born and a time to die, a time to plant and a time to uproot . . . a time to weep and a time to laugh, a time to mourn and a time to dance . . . a time to be silent and a time to speak . . . ." By understanding The Seasons of Change ahead of time, you'll know what actions to take (and not to take), and when to take them to make sure your transition goes as smoothly as possible. Here's a brief overview of how each season applies in transition situations.

- Summer represents a time when living is easy, and you have all the resources you need to flourish. Because there's not much to worry about, you can live fully and focus your attention on your harvest and results.

- Fall represents a time when shifts occur indicating that, in some way, life is changing—possibly even in ways you weren't anticipating or wanting. As a result, you begin to prepare for what's to come.

- Winter's a time when you're confused and emotional. Your best course of action is to take some time to just be with yourself to get new insights about your past and future. From this new perspective, you create a plan or vision for your future.

- Spring is the part of the journey you've been waiting for. Now you can begin to take action to implement your plan. Although it's a very exciting time, you may also feel a bit uncomfortable with all that's new.

- Summer comes around once again when you become comfortable with your new life and confident with your new role.

Figure C provides you with a road map of your journey. If you envision this to be an upward moving spiral, you'll see that it's consistent with the Cultural Creative view of success.

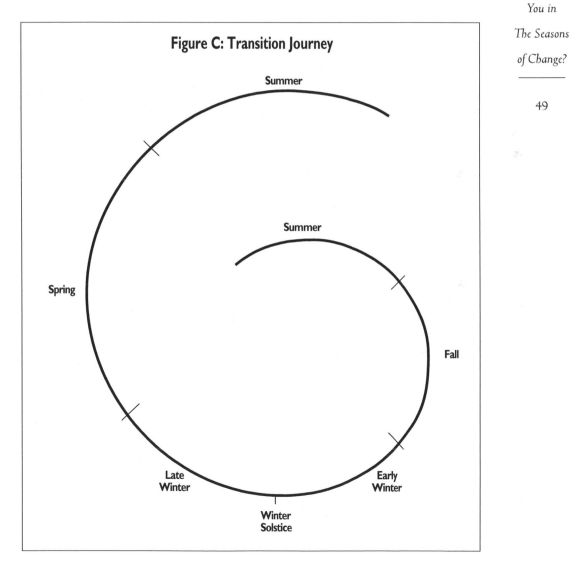

Figure C: Transition Journey

Summer

Summer

Spring

Fall

Late
Winter

Early
Winter

Winter
Solstice

A Journey Through the Seasons of Change

People in transition follow this same process no matter what kind of change they're going through. Here's a description of how The Seasons of Change applies in a career change situation:

Work's a breeze for you right now (Summer) because you know what you're doing and who to contact if you need any information. The best part is your work really matches your goals and interests.

But then, one day the rumors start flying (Fall). As the dust settles, you learn that the company's new strategic direction means that the entire management team is going to play musical chairs. There's even a possibility that your unit will be completely disbanded. Suddenly, within a week or two, everything looks different. Your network isn't holding up because so many people have changed positions or left the company. Furthermore, your job duties are changing. Although you're willing to sit tight for the time being, you're afraid you may have to make some significant changes before too long.

Now that a couple of weeks have passed, you realize how confused you really are (Winter). You're constantly obsessing about whether to stay or go. The worst part of it is there's no one left to talk to. One day, you put your finger on the problem: the company's new direction isn't in alignment with your values and goals. This thought frees you to start looking at options because you know you enjoy life much more when the work you do reflects what you believe in. Now that you know how to direct your focus, you start getting ideas about how to proceed.

As you talk with people in your network, you realize the idea you have is a viable one, so you invest as much time and effort as possible into making connections (Spring). You participate in job fairs, do lunch, and call old contacts you haven't spoken with in years. All of a sudden, leads start pouring in. You land a job that ends up being even better than your last position. Because you spent some time evaluating your talents during Winter, you're able to negotiate a package that's a perfect mix of tasks for you. Although there's a bit of a learning curve as you start your job, you're excited about the potential this job has.

You've reached a point in your career where you're at ease with your new job (Summer). Now that you've been through the entire cycle, you know to celebrate your accomplishments.

No matter what is happening with you, you're somewhere in this seasonal cycle. Knowing where you are in the cycle is the first step to becoming conscious of your journey.

What Season Are You In?

Because everyone's situation is so different, there are no hard-and-fast rules to define what season you're in. It's a matter of uncovering the trends and patterns in your responses to the Transition Questionnaire you completed in Chapter 2. Although the questions in the following sections will help you reach a conclusion, your first impressions are also important. Take a moment to think about how you responded when you read the descriptions of each season. Does it feel as though you're in Fall? Or Winter? Keep these feelings in mind as you proceed through the chapter.

The first step in discovering what season you're in is to look back at the questionnaire in Chapter 2 and fill in the dots on the spiral in Figure D that correspond to your answers. If you used any half-circles on the questionnaire, just fill in half the dot.

As you can see from the spiral, three questions correspond with each season. Begin by scanning the spiral to see if you marked all three items associated with any one of the seasons. If not, are there any seasons where you've marked two responses? If so, notice what season or seasons fit this pattern. For now, don't be concerned if you have a concentration of responses in more than one season; the additional questions in this section will help you sort it all out. Read the following brief descriptions to remind yourself what stage of the transition journey each season represents.

If your responses are concentrated in the Fall section, you're experiencing some kind of shift in your life that may impact your future. If the majority of your responses are in the Winter section, you're taking time to step back from your situation to reassess and reevaluate your life to create a plan for the future. If you have a series of responses in Spring, you're beginning to put your plan into action. If you circled a number of items in the Summer section, you're enjoying all that you've created for yourself.

Does this information match your first impression?

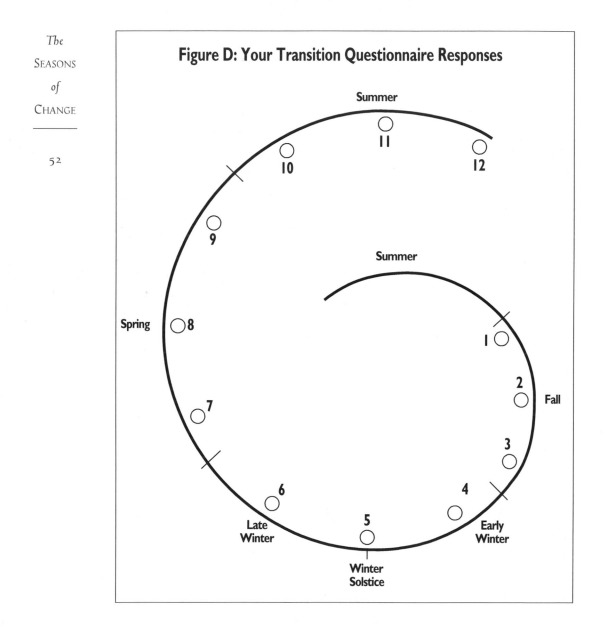

Figure D: Your Transition Questionnaire Responses

Are You Moving from One Season to the Next?

Notice if you marked statements at the end of one season and the beginning of the next. This usually means you're in the process of moving into the next phase of your journey.

For example, most of the clients I work with are coming to terms with a major change in their lives. When they complete the Transition Questionnaire, they usually begin by indicating that they're looking at their options (3). Then, they note that they're experiencing some or all of the Winter elements (4–6). Finally, they mark that they're either afraid to move out of their familiar situation or hesitant to move forward (7 and 8). When I see this pattern, I know that the person's completing Fall and moving into Winter. Their Spring responses tell me that they want to be in Spring, but just aren't ready yet.

You may notice that your responses indicate you're moving out of Winter and into Spring. If this is the case, you're most likely feeling as though you've been through the worst part of the journey and are now beginning to see the light.

If you've circled some responses in Fall and others in Summer, but nothing much in between, you're probably moving from Summer into Fall. Remember that the spiral is a continuous process. We never land in Summer and stay there indefinitely.

It's also important to check in with yourself. From what you know about The Seasons of Change journey at this point, what's your hunch about your movement from one season to the next?

Are You Going Through Two Transitions at Once?

Take a moment to remember what you were thinking about when you filled out the Transition Questionnaire. Were all of your answers about the same situation? Or were some based on your feelings about your career, while others were referring to your relationship or your health? If you switched your focus as you answered the questionnaire, there's a good possibility you're in two places on the Transition Spiral at once.

Let me illustrate this. One of my clients, John, selected all the items in Fall (1, 2, 3), a couple of items in Winter (5, 6), and all three statements in Spring (7, 8, 9). I immediately noticed that he was in the midst of a major transition, but the response that surprised me was Question 9. Usually, when people are in the midst of a transition journey, they don't indicate that they're feeling energetic or able to take action. Before I interpreted the pattern, I asked him to describe what was happening in his life. John's descriptions about his career confusion and the angst he was feeling about an ended relationship confirmed that he was indeed in Fall heading into Winter. When I asked why he circled Question 9, he said he was feeling better about himself and was taking action to make changes in his life. It was only after he told me he'd been sober for nearly two years that the overall pattern became clear.

As he explained, John had taken over two years to move through the process of acknowledging his need to make a change with his drinking (Fall), reassessing and reevaluating his life experiences vis-à-vis alcohol up to that point (Winter), and finally, taking steps to begin a new life of sobriety (Spring). The Fall and Winter he was experiencing now had more to do with the next level of his transition journey. Now that he was sober, it was becoming more clear to him that his career and his relationships weren't working. As a result, John was beginning the entire transition process again—this time with his career and relationships as the focus.

Where Are You in the Progression of Moving Through Each Season?

Take a moment to look back at the questionnaire again. For each season, the questions are organized to progress from the first question to the third. If you indicated the first question for any season, you're beginning to head into the next stage of your journey. Most likely, you haven't yet come to terms with all that's involved in the new season. You may be unaware or confused about what you need to do. If you chose the second question in any series, you're becoming aware of what's before you, but you're still working through fear or confusion. And, finally, the third question in each series indicates that you're fully conscious and actively addressing the issues at hand so you can progress to the next season.

If you have several responses in one season and then one (or even two) in the next season, chances are good that you're still working with issues in the first season; it would be premature to jump into the full expression of the next season. This frequently happens when people have circled two or three questions in the Winter section and Question 7 or 8 in the Spring section. I often see that people who have this pattern of responses are anxious to move into Spring, but haven't yet come to a level of clarity that would allow them to really move forward.

If you circled the last statement in Summer in addition to several statements throughout Fall and Winter, it's likely you've already been through a major transition of some sort. During *that* transition journey, you probably made a number of breakthroughs that enable you to be confident and happy even though you're now in the midst of another change. Overall, you'll most likely have an easier time than if you weren't feeling confident and happy.

Another pattern to be aware of is one in which you circle the third item in every season. I often see this with mature adults who've been through their fair share of transition journeys. The pattern either indicates you're very well-versed in transitions and are so at ease with all the seasons that you're constantly moving through them on a daily basis, or you're in denial and pretending you have it all together. The judgment call is yours to make.

Frequently Asked Questions

Now that you have a general sense of the transition journey and know what season or seasons you're in, you probably have some questions. Here are the ones I hear most frequently from my clients and workshop participants. For clarity, I'll capitalize the transition seasons (Fall) and leave nature's seasons lowercase (fall).

I'm in Winter, but it is summer outside. Did I get off course somewhere?

No. This approach treats the seasons as a metaphor for how change takes place. Your experience may or may not coincide with nature's seasons. When you're thinking about your transition process, focus on the season you're experiencing internally, not the season outside your window. In the upcoming chapters, you'll learn how to use metaphors from nature to help you understand even more of what you're experiencing and how to take action to move forward.

Having said that, you may find nature's seasons do actually impact your experience of a transition season. When your seasons are in sync with nature's, your experience of those seasons will tend to be fairly pure and intense. For instance, if you're in Winter during nature's winter, you may find it easier to hibernate and reflect because the weather and the short days support your desire to be home "nesting." On the other hand, the long, dark nights and stormy days may make your experience more emotionally intense because you don't have many sunny days to lighten and brighten your spirits.

Conversely, if you're in Winter when it's summer outside, you may find it difficult to hibernate because it's sunny and everyone around you is very active. The upside to this experience is that the sunny days may bring hope and brighten the roughest parts of your journey.

Being in Summer during nature's winter is no picnic either. Because my father died in December and we held his memorial service on the winter solstice, fall and winter were difficult for me for many years. I became accustomed to wanting to hibernate during those months and feeling very emotional at holiday gatherings. Then, several years later, after I'd started my business, I was feeling confident and celebrating my growth in December. Because I was in my Summer, I couldn't figure out why it was cold and dark and why everyone was talking about the holidays. Several times I had to pinch myself to remember that even though I was happy it really wasn't summer outside.

There's really no way to choreograph your journey to be in sync with nature's seasons. Each experience is valuable in its own way. Just

The
Seasons
of
Change

———

56

surrender to the process and learn what you can about yourself and your situation.

✤ How long will I be in each season?

I wish I could give you an exact answer to that question. Unfortunately (or fortunately), each person moving through every change embarks on a slightly different journey. When you think about it, even though the calendar gives us specific dates for the beginning and ending of each season, the weather and wildlife create our actual experience.

Many factors will influence the lengths of the seasons you experience. If you're in the midst of a powerful transition not of your choosing, your journey will most likely take longer than it would if you were initiating a minor change in your life. If you've avoided a number of changes because you saw them as a threat to your success, your transition process will be longer because you'll need to sort through some of your past transitions to clear the way for the future.

Although some seasons may last a week or several months, it's not unusual for some to last one or more years. After my father died, I was in the depths of Winter for three years. I know many people who say it took them four years to really get through the process of divorce. Typically, the time our culture allots for going through any transition is much shorter than people generally need to complete the process.

Your seasons will probably not all be equal in length either. I have a saying I use quite often: As with nature's seasons, Winter is always longer than we'd like and Summer is always shorter. You may find this to be true as well.

✤ When will I be out of Winter?

This is the most common question. Of course, it's a corollary to the previous question. What you really want to know is "When will I stop feeling so confused, emotional, sad . . . ?" Unfortunately, there's no way to force the ending of Winter. As in nature, Winter will end when the conditions are right for Spring to appear. Before Winter can truly end, you must entertain some brand-new thoughts about your life so you can create a new future for yourself. Usually new insights don't appear until we let go of old baggage and get quiet enough so we can sense our own new thoughts and feelings.

When you've been in Winter for an extended period of time, you may begin to get the feeling you'll never move forward. At that point, it's important to remember that Winter never lasts forever. Perhaps a trusted friend can reassure you that you really have made progress on your journey. It's also a good time to start training your eyes to see the signs of Spring. Be aware of any new ways of behaving, talking, thinking, or dreaming. At first these signs will be very subtle, so you'll have to keep your eyes open.

Typically, people who've been in Winter for an extremely long time are wrestling with a lot of unresolved transitions, perhaps even an entire lifetime of changes that they've never worked through. In some cases, in order to protect ourselves, we try to avoid the very issues we need to face to move onward. In other cases, we may have repressed all memory of a situation that's having the most impact on our lives. This is never an easy place to be.

If you've been laboring alone in Winter for a very long time, you're probably delaying your journey because, by now, your perceptions of your situation are locked in a rut. The key to moving beyond this space is investing in the right kind of support. Chapters 10 and 11 will help you understand and get the kind of support you need.

🦋 *I keep making changes in my life, but nothing ever seems to really change. What's happening?*

First, think about how you make these changes. I would guess that in most cases, you're not moving through all four seasons of the transition journey. If you're like many of my clients, the season you're most likely to short-circuit is Winter.

This pattern is usually easiest to see in other people. Did you ever know a person who was madly in love one week, and the next thing you knew he or she had started a new relationship before ending the first one? Or perhaps you've known people who've left one job in a huff and then started another job within a few days. These people are making changes, but usually all they're really changing are their circumstances, replacing one situation with another. They aren't making true changes in their lives because they haven't looked at the deeper reasons for the problems they had in their relationship or job in the first place.

If you've ended one situation (Fall) and jumped to something new (Spring) without taking any time in between, you're in what I call a Spin Cycle. This pattern is very common because we have such a difficult time with loss and grief that we usually aren't encouraged to spend much (or any) time in Winter. And yet, Winter is the key to unlocking the future. Unless and until we're willing to really feel our grief, sadness, and anger and get to the bottom of the part, if any, we play in our troubles, a true transformation will never occur. In the movie *Groundhog Day*, Bill Murray's character, Phil, was having the ultimate Spin Cycle experience. He woke up to the same circumstances day after day after day, until he started recognizing ways he could shift his behavior to change the events of February 2. The more caring and genuine he became, the better his day got until that fateful day when the clock radio alarm finally clicked on and it was February 3.

If you've been in a Spin Cycle for a long time, you probably passed over a series of Winters that were never really handled or resolved. Winter doesn't just disappear. All the emotions, fears, and confusion of the avoided Winters just wait for us to stop and reflect. Usually, a person will finally get the message to stop and listen after a major event such as the death of a loved one, a divorce, or a serious illness.

For example, all three of the main characters in the movie *City Slickers* had been given numerous wake-up calls before they headed out to the dude ranch. One had gotten a young grocery clerk pregnant and was pretending to fall asleep at parties to avoid all interaction with his abusive wife. Another had passed a milestone birthday and had recently had responsibilities and autonomy ripped away from him at work. And the third was always out to prove his manhood by suggesting high-adrenaline vacations and dating much younger women. Given the emotional state each was in, I've no doubt there were numerous other changes and difficulties that led to the moments we shared with them. It was only under Curly's direction and with the crisis of his later demise that each had the opportunity to stop and review their lives. It's not hard to see that each of these men was experiencing a midlife crisis. Thanks to Curly, the rigors of the trail, and Norman the calf, they each went home with a new understanding of themselves and a new vision for their future.

Although we've come to believe that a midlife crisis is a natural, required part of maturing, I believe it results from an extended period of spinning, years and years of stuffing down and glossing over numerous changes in an effort to stay on the ladder of success. By learning how to work through transitions consciously throughout our lives, we can avoid the huge dismantling process typically associated with midlife crisis. (Incidentally, I have clients in their twenties who are experiencing what we usually call a midlife crisis.)

If you want to make some long-lasting, significant changes in your life, you'll need to bite the bullet, fight your impulse to escape, fend off all the criticism from inside and out, and consciously begin your journey into Winter. Most likely you'll need a very strong, understanding support system to help you complete your journey. Believe me, it's possible to make it through to a whole new wonderful beginning.

Why is my transition so intense compared to what my friends are going through?

Just as the seasons are different each year, each individual's journey is very unique. In fact, transitions are so unique that the same person may have an easy time during one transition and a very intense time during another. Think back to how your relationships have ended. Although there may be some similarities, your experience in each case was, most likely, unique to that particular situation.

Many factors can impact the intensity you feel. If you're going through several transitions at once, or if this is your first transition process of adulthood or since you stepped off the Spin Cycle, your experience will probably be fairly intense.

Although it's common to want to compare your experiences to those of other people, I've found it to be very difficult to make any useful or comforting conclusions from these comparisons. About a year after my father died, while I was still very immersed in my grief process, a friend of mine called me to talk about an abusive relationship she was enduring. She kept apologizing because she felt that my transition was much "worse" than hers. She felt she should have been able to handle her situation on her own and that she shouldn't be bothering me with her "trivial" issues. Thank goodness I had the sense, even then, to encourage her to share her dilemma with me. We both needed support at that point in our lives; it wasn't relevant whose situation was "worse." All that mattered was that we were both in the process of healing. So, to the degree it's possible, try not to compare your situation to someone else's. Because each person's journey is unique, most comparisons just leave us feeling as though we're defective in some way. As long as you're participating in the transition process, you're on the right path.

If the people around you appear to be "doing better" than you are, there may be several reasons why. They might be ignoring the change they're going through and just forging ahead with life as usual. Although their life may seem easier than yours, this pattern will eventually catch up with them. You, however, may not be around when this happens because it may not occur for decades. Another possibility is that they're in the midst of a transition that isn't triggering deep issues for them. As a result, they're having a mild Winter rather than the stormy one you might be facing. Finally, the person you're comparing yourself to may have been through a horrendous transition experience before you even knew them. I've noticed that people who have gone through one major transition consciously and learned how to work with rather than against the process tend to have an easier journey the next time around, because they've acquired the skills required to work through the experience. In addition, they may remember the emotions and feelings associated with the journey and realize that Spring will come again! So they have a pattern they can follow to move forward.

❧ At one level I feel as though I'm in one season and at another I feel as though I'm in the opposite season. What's going on?

In certain circumstances, you may be able to track two spirals for the same situation. Usually this occurs when you're working through an issue within yourself even though your life situation is not yet changing.

I became familiar with this phenomenon when I was deciding to leave my corporate position. When I first acknowledged that my work wasn't fitting my needs (Inner Fall), I had just received a bonus for a big project I'd recently completed (Outer Summer). As I proceeded to wrestle with what I wanted and what would work for me (Inner Winter), my career continued to flourish (Outer Summer). For the most part, the people in my workplace weren't aware of the deep exploration I was going through. It wasn't until I began to take action to create my business (Inner Spring) that people began to notice a shift in my work life (Outer Fall). This intensified when I shifted most of my energy to my business (Inner Spring) and gave notice at my job (Outer Fall).

Although my colleagues picked up on my Spring energy, most of them assumed I'd fallen in love—they had no other explanation for why I was so happy. From there, I moved into Summer with my business by actually achieving my first milestones. Simultaneously, I was entering a Winter as I left the job I'd had for five years and began to reestablish a schedule that worked for me.

From this example, you can see that the spiral can be used in a variety of ways to help you understand various transition dynamics. As you read through the rest of the book, you'll become a bit more familiar with the transition process, and you will then be able to trace complex situations you may be facing.

✿ How do I know when I've moved into the next season?

On any given day, it may be difficult to figure out exactly what season you're in. This is true of nature's seasons as well as the transition seasons. In neither instance are there clear demarcations between the seasons. Usually, after you've been in the new season awhile, you realize with hindsight that you've made it to the next one. Have you ever been driving down the street and all of a sudden noticed that all the fruit trees are in bloom? Somehow you missed the moment when spring sprung, but now that it has, you can see it. The same thing is likely to happen to you internally. All of a sudden, you'll notice that you really *do* feel different.

✿ How can I handle several transitions at once?

Although I once read that it's best to go through only one transition at a time, the fact of the matter is that you're probably always going to be making your way through several changes at once. With some creative thinking and flexibility, it really is possible to find the flow that will work for you.

Say, for example, that you're trying to figure out how to handle a health issue (Winter) at the same time you're being promoted at work (Summer). As you experience different facets of these two aspects of your life, you'll probably move between the two seasons. You may carve out time to hibernate with your health concerns on the weekends and evenings while you bask in your new level of success during the work week. If your health situation doesn't require much attention, you may find that Summer helps you keep things in perspective and allows you to move more quickly through your decision-making and healing processes. If, on the other hand, your health situation is life-threatening, the energy you must put into Winter will probably diminish your experience of Summer. In fact, you may not even notice your achievement at all.

When my family attended my graduation from graduate school, it should have been one of the most exciting and proudest days of my life (Summer). Instead, all my energy was really going toward handling my father's rapidly deteriorating health (Winter). Even the photos we have of my graduation tell this story. To this day, it's difficult for me to enjoy the picture of myself in my graduation garb. My mother comments occasionally about how torn she was between wanting to celebrate my achievements and new life with me, and needing to take all the steps she could to complete her time with Dad.

When you're faced with several transitions at once, the best approach you can take is to pay attention to your intuition. Be compassionately aware of both spirals. See where your attention is drawn and where it's needed.

Part II

The Seasons of Change

Once upon a time, a man who had worked for years supplying his town with hand-ground flour was having a difficult time making ends meet. In an effort to improve his situation, he went into the nearby forest in search of deadwood that he could take back to the village to sell.

As he worked in the woods, a strange man approached him and offered to help him increase the output of his milling operations. He also promised to lessen the amount of effort it took at the same time. The Miller was ecstatic—finally, here was a way to lift his family out of financial despair!

The best part of the deal was that all the old man wanted was that which stood in back of the mill. As the Miller thought about this payment, he realized that he was more than happy to give the man the old, flowering apple tree in his backyard. So he made a deal with the old man.

The Miller and the old man began working together to turn the mill into a state-of-the-art operation, which began to produce more flour in less time at a lower cost. Suddenly, the Miller and his family had more time and money on their hands than ever before! The Miller was so happy to be living the good life that he forgot all about the payment due to the old man.

When his wife asked him to explain their newfound wealth, the Miller proudly explained he'd struck a deal with an old man he'd met in the forest. With a bit of trepidation, the wife asked what he owed in return. "That's the best part," the Miller said. "All he wanted is what's behind the mill. Surely we're willing to give up the apple tree in return for a life of wealth?"

In horror, the wife realized her husband was unaware of the fact that their daughter had been standing behind the mill, sweeping the yard, on the day he'd made the deal. Unbeknownst to the father, he'd sold his daughter to the old man—who, by now the mother knew, was the Devil—in return for prosperity . . . .

So begins the tale of "The Handless Maiden." A story of an innocent young woman's journey to the depths of the underworld and her return to a happy, fulfilling life. The rich metaphors within this tale provide a unique opportunity to learn firsthand what you can expect on your transition journey. Professional storyteller Susan Gordon tells this story whenever she's performing for people who've come together to reflect on their lives and their choices. She notes that the story "parallels and illustrates the process by which all actual change occurs."

Indeed, this tale told in more than a hundred different ways has provided guidance to people all over the world, from Russia, Italy, and Germany to Japan. The version told here is taken in large part from the literary version told by Clarissa Pinkola Estés in her book *Women Who Run with the Wolves*, which was given to her by her Aunt Magdalena, variations of which are found throughout Eastern and Middle Europe. Although her telling is the most thorough one I could locate, I did incorporate certain details from versions told by Susan Gordon, Marie-Louise von Franz, Robert Johnson, the Brothers Grimm, and Aleksandr Afanas'ev, when they helped explain the transition journey more fully.

Although this story is ostensibly about a maiden's journey, Susan Gordon says that "listeners of every age and both genders" resonate with the young woman's trials and recovery. Understanding a myth is much like interpreting a dream: each character of the story reflects an aspect of our psyche. Just looking at the story we know so far, it's easy for any of us to see ourselves in the father (the part of us that functions out in the world), who mistakenly agrees to participate in something that should make life easier, only to find in the process he's given away an incredibly precious part of himself (the daughter). Whether we've allowed time-saving technology to run our lives, bought into the notion that bigger is better, or agreed to sell our souls to multimillion-dollar companies for a minimal salary, we feel the father's self-directed anger and deeply felt loss.

As we follow the Handless Maiden on her journey, we'll explore each phase of the transition process, learning how to recognize the signs of each season, what actions we can take to move forward on our journey, and what detours might distract us or slow us down.

Four

Fall: Preparing for What's to Come

Signs:	Tasks:	Detours:
Getting News of Change	Acknowledge Change	Denial
Feeling Your Feelings	Get Support	Jumping at the First Option
Waiting and Worrying	Create Your Own Refuge	Being a Lone Ranger
	Review Your Options	

After the Mother tearfully explained to her husband that their daughter had been bargained away, they stumbled their way home, crying all the way. Once they told their daughter the terrible news, the waiting began, for they knew the Devil would return for his payment in three years. During the intervening years, the beautiful daughter didn't marry but continued doing her chores with "a temperament like the first sweet apples of Spring" (Estés).

On the appointed day, the Maiden bathed, dressed in white, and stood inside a chalk circle she'd drawn. When the Devil came, she was so well protected that he was literally thrown across the yard each time he tried to take her.

In disgust, the Devil screamed at the parents and forbade the Maiden to bathe. As the weeks passed, she began to look more and more like a beast until, by the time the Devil returned, she was filthy from head to toe. As the Devil approached the Maiden, she began to weep, and as she did so the dirt on her hands and arms washed away, revealing her white hands, the sight of which repelled him once again. By this time the Devil was so enraged he demanded that the Miller chop off his daughter's hands. When the Miller hesitated, the Devil threatened to kill the Miller and his wife and destroy all their fields if the Miller didn't carry out his order.

Not knowing what else to do, the Miller fulfilled the act, feeling great despair at both his actions and the outcome. The Maiden, believing that her father was only doing what he had to do, didn't resist.

When the Devil arrived the third time, the Maiden's tears flowed again, revealing the white of the skin of her stumps, which repelled the Devil once more. Realizing he'd lost his claim, the Devil ran into the forest and disappeared.

Though the daughter had been saved, she had lost her hands and her life was clearly never going to be the same. Her parents, who had aged greatly as a result of the trauma, tried to persuade their daughter to make the best of what they did have by living a life of leisure in a castle full of beautiful things. But the Handless Maiden decided it would be better if she left home and depended on the goodness of others for her food and shelter.

This part of the story illustrates Fall, the first phase of the Handless Maiden's journey, in which something has happened to take the heroine off the course of ordinary life. While it's true that the full extent and exact form of the change wasn't known for three years, the Handless Maiden's transition journey actually began the moment her father made his deal with the Devil. Notice that the Handless Maiden was forced into the change by events outside her control, while the Miller triggered his own transition by a decision he made himself. So regardless of whether you decided to make the change you're going through or it was thrust upon you, change is change and *always* requires a period of adjustment.

How Can I Tell I'm in Fall?

1. You Get News of a Change

The moment you receive news, whether it's extremely clear-cut or amazingly subtle and vague, that a change may be coming down the pike, you're taking your first steps on the transition journey. This information may come from sources outside yourself: a doctor asking you back to her office for more tests, a rumor surfacing at work about a possible layoff, a letter informing you that you're named in a distant relative's will. In each case, the results might be just what you want, or there's the chance your life could be irrevocably changed by the events that are about to take place.

Sometimes you'll receive notice of a change from deep within yourself: knowing it's time to leave a job, having a feeling that you're pregnant, realizing you've met the person you want to spend the rest of your life with. Be aware that we sometimes discount this kind of news because it comes from our own intuition, which we often don't trust.

2. Feeling Your Feelings

When we look closely at "The Handless Maiden," we see that everyone reacts differently to the upcoming changes. The Maiden's parents cry while she herself appears to be quite numb. Then, as the ramifications of the bargain become clearer, the Miller's emotions escalate as he's faced with the growing demands of the Devil.

Look at how you're responding to the change in your life. Moment by moment, you may be hit by waves of shock, anger, rage, fear, guilt, shame, dismay, distress, and grief. Add to this the fact that you feel dazed, numb, disoriented, and distracted as your world is turned upside down and you'll understand why, all of a sudden, you're clumsy, easily startled, forgetful, and without your usual sense of time.

The most important thing you can do is allow your emotions to be. Don't turn them off or hide from them—they need to be felt. Imagine yourself in the Handless Maiden's shoes as she watches her father chop off her hands. Would you say, "Do what you must, father. I trust your judgment?" Of course you wouldn't. But you do something like this every time you turn off your feelings and allow others to take actions that impact your life. Every time we put our emotions on hold because it's not proper to show them in public or with our families—even in the face of a trauma—we are, like the Handless Maiden, allowing our feeling selves to be stifled or cut off.

Although our culture believes tears are a sign of the weak and the young, they can be a very healing force. According to Jungian analyst Clarissa Pinkola Estés, they not only start the process of mending our wounds, but also allow our "process to continue instead of collapsing." We see this occur in the story when the Maiden's tears actually repelled the Devil. Dr. Estés also notes that tears have the power to "call spirits to one's side and repel those that muffle and bind the simple soul." Remember this and you'll never again feel the need to apologize for crying.

Learn to experience and honor the power that comes as you express and release your emotions. Later in this chapter, we'll look at how to create a space where you'll feel safe enough to allow yourself to do this.

3. *Waiting and Worrying*

Although the tale doesn't describe what the Miller's family did in the time between when the bargain was made and the Devil returned for his payment, we can imagine there was quite a bit of waiting and worrying going on. The only clue we have is that the Handless Maiden didn't take a husband during that time. From this we can conclude that events that normally would have taken place were halted and life was at a standstill. You may also feel as though you can't move, stay focused, make decisions, or even figure out what you want. The entire state of affairs is likely to leave you restless and frustratingly inactive.

The worst part is the waiting—for a lover to call, for test results to come back, for feedback about your recent job interview. While it may be uncomfortable, waiting is a natural part of Fall because there's absolutely no way you can have a full picture of your situation yet.

So here you are with your life hanging in the balance and too much time on your hands. Your mind starts filling the airspace with questions—what will happen next, what will happen in the long run, how will my life change, how will I handle what's to come, what's really happening, how will it all work out?

When Jeri found out her mother was having severe pain in her joints, she was worried. The worst part of it was that she lived so far away she couldn't drop everything to sit by her mother's side during the tests. Instead she had to wait, alone by the phone, for any word. As the tests proceeded, there always seemed to be a long delay between the time the appointment was supposed to end and the moment her family called with an update. As the weeks went by, the waiting became excruciatingly painful. She worried about everything—how her mother was really holding up, what the various diagnoses might mean, what extra care her mother might need, how the family was going to afford extra care, and what information she was missing by being so far away.

There's really no way of getting around the waiting and the worrying during this phase of the journey. Do what you can to make this time tolerable. One technique that might help is setting aside a specific time each day to worry. Then as you get caught up in your thoughts during the day, say to yourself, I'll worry about this at one o'clock. You might even want to jot your worries down so that you don't have to expend energy remembering what you need to worry about! Once you reach the appointed time, take fifteen minutes to focus on your concerns—write them out, tell a friend, talk into a tape recorder. Do whatever you can to clear your mind. By consciously moving your worry to a specific time of the day, you'll free yourself to attend to other needs.

As we proceed with the journey, we'll explore a number of ways to work with your worries and concerns. In the meantime, the books in the first section of the Tools for the Journey resource guide at the end of the book may be helpful to you.

Now What Should I Do?

Clearly, Fall is not a very comfortable place to be. Your best course of action is to prepare for what *might* come. If you begin looking at your options as soon as you know a change is in the air, you'll actually have more control than if you shy away out of fear. This is true whether your car starts to make strange noises, you discover a lump under your arm, or you start bouncing checks.

When I first read "The Handless Maiden," my biggest question was why did they just sit there for three years waiting for the Devil to return? Wasn't there something they could have done to avert the impending disaster?

In some situations, you may have an extended period of time to prepare for a shift. You may know in advance, for instance, that you must move an elderly parent or that your child will be heading off to college after graduation. As with the Miller's family, it's easy to get lulled into thinking you have plenty of time to do what you need to do, so you get involved with the everyday issues of living life and never get to the business of preparing for the change.

In other situations, the change may happen so quickly that you have no time to prepare for what's to come. This is especially true when it's an unexpected and far-reaching change—a car accident, a heart attack, a tornado. The hardest part of these scenarios is that you must "prepare" while you're in the midst of handling urgent circumstances. This scenario played out in "The Handless Maiden" when the father actually chopped off his daughter's hands. Due to the pressure the Devil put on the father, there was no good way to prepare the daughter or the family for how that event would change their lives.

Regardless of the timing of the transition you're experiencing, there are a number of constructive actions you can take to prepare for it, even if it's an instantaneous one. These actions won't necessarily provide the ultimate solution to your situation—you still have the rest of the transition journey to go through—but they will play an important part in getting you to a place where you'll have all the information you need to make appropriate decisions about your future.

1. Acknowledge the Change Is Occurring

Before you can do anything to prepare for your transition journey, you must face the fact that a shift really is happening in your life. For instance, you may decide the rumor about the layoffs really does have enough truth to it to warrant your attention; the preliminary results from your medical exam indicate that something's wrong even if the doctors can't yet confirm the exact diagnosis; the boredom you feel at work isn't going to subside until you make a change. This step may seem simple, but it's very profound.

Take a good hard look at how you're living your life. Are you being a good Modern by keeping up appearances, glossing over glitches, sleeping through wake-up calls, and dodging the proverbial two-by-fours being thrown your way? If you are, you're missing the boat. By avoiding change or failing to acknowledge that something in your life is changing or needs to change, you're delaying the start of your journey, which may, in the long run, make it a more difficult one. So be objective and acknowledge the truth of your situation. Only that will take you out of denial and set you on your journey.

2. Get the Support You Need to Weather the Storms

As children, one of the first things we learn about fall is that animals such as squirrels prepare for winter ahead of time by gathering and storing nuts and seeds. Then later, when it's cold and food is scarce, they have an easy source of nourishment to keep them healthy through the most difficult months.

Though nuts and seeds won't tide us over during our Winters, there are a number of ways we can prepare for what's to come. I learned just how critical this advice is when I spoke at a shelter for abused women. As the women shared their stories, I realized each of them was hoarding something—food, clothing for themselves and their children, money— to prepare for the possibility that her husband might, at any time, walk out of the house and never return. Due to the extremely abusive nature of their relationships, these women had absolutely no freedom—no access to the checking account, no driver's license, no job. They could rely on only their wits and what they'd stored for a rainy day.

Although your need to gather may not be quite so graphic, you may find you need one, two, or all three of the following crucial resources as you move forward on your journey.

Informational Support

If you're in the midst of a divorce or you've just received a difficult diagnosis, getting information about your situation is very important, whether you're facing the situation for the first time or you've been there before. Although information doesn't make the problem go away, it can help you make sense of what's happening now and what's likely to happen in the future.

Often when you're facing a new situation, you feel you're all alone. If you open your eyes and ears, however, you'll discover a world of resources on the topic that you never knew existed. Here are some suggestions:

- Find an association of people who've been through what you're facing.
- Talk to friends to see if they've experienced what you're going through.
- Check your local bookstore or library for a book on the topic.
- Search the World Wide Web using keywords that describe your situation.
- Listen to radio or television talk shows that address your problem.

You may actually discover so much information that you feel overwhelmed by it all. If that's the case, ask someone you trust to help you sort through it. Remember, your goal is just to become familiar enough with the situation to get a more realistic picture of what you're facing. For the time being, just collect the facts and begin to notice what applies to you.

Once you find you're getting the same tips from different sources, you can probably conclude that you have an adequate collection of information for now. Of course, as you learn more you can continue your search to elaborate on certain points or to explore new options that surface.

When Jenna's husband was dying, she felt very strongly that he should be given the opportunity to die at home with dignity. Although the hospital Fred was affiliated with provided excellent medical support through their hospice program, their coordinators didn't seem to understand what she wanted when she requested more emotional support. Even worse, they didn't seem to think it was even necessary! From their perspective, one cursory conversation about the emotions you might feel was sufficient. After making daily requests for several weeks, Jenna finally took matters into her own hands by taking a grief class, investigating other hospice programs, and making special arrangements to have one of them provide emotional support. Her research paid off. There was finally someone she and Fred could turn to in their time of need.

Emotional Support

Another invaluable resource during Fall is emotional support. One of the hardest parts of being in transition is the emotional roller-coaster you're on throughout the journey. You're in the dark, unable to sense the blind curves or anticipate the plunges that send your stomach into your throat. Getting support from people who've survived or are at least familiar with the roller-coaster ride helps tremendously.

Because adequate emotional support is so important I have devoted two chapters to this topic. In Chapter 10, you'll use the Supporter Questionnaire to assess your current support network and look at various ways to broaden it; and in Chapter 11, you'll find ways to ask your supporters for what you need during each season.

Financial Support

Getting the financial support you need during your transition is also important. When life changes, your income often changes with it. You might find your income has become severely limited, completely cut off, depleted by a series of unexpected expenditures, or even greatly increased. Or it may be difficult to predict just what your financial situation will be because it's in such flux.

Because the possibility of having insufficient funds is scary, it's common for people to look the other way when it comes to this area of preparation. Many just cross their fingers and hope they'll make it financially, but in the end, their lack of preparedness just adds to the stress they feel during Winter.

Do yourself a favor and sit down with your financial records. If you can, estimate what you'll need as your transition progresses. Figure out where the funds will come from to cover your expenses. Identify expenses you can cut back on to make your money last longer. Get creative about finding frugal solutions to your basic needs. If you have friends in similar situations, join together to find solutions. Identify what you need and put the word out in your social network. Amazing treasures can be uncovered in the most unlikely places. (Refer to Tools for the Journey for additional ideas about how to handle these hurdles.)

In some situations, you may find it necessary to line up financial support from other sources. If you decide to request money from people in your life, be sure to give them ample time to think about your request. By talking to them before you're in a full-blown crisis, you'll give them more latitude to make the decision that's right for them. If you're relying on financial institutions for a loan, you'll also need to allow them enough time to process your request.

Another option to cover financial peaks and valleys is to identify sources of interim income. For instance, taking a part-time or short-term job might ease your financial situation and give you some freedom of choice that you don't have at the moment. Just a little bit of extra income might decrease the worry and strain you feel as you watch your savings decrease.

3. Create Your Own Refuge

In addition to gathering food, animals also take special precautions to shelter themselves from harsh winter conditions. Squirrels and chipmunks build nests; bears and raccoons find natural hiding places like caves and hollows. Other animals, including birds, elk, and Monarch butterflies, migrate to places with better climates. Because we humans have lost touch with the natural cycle of change, we forget that we, too, will need a refuge for our Winter, a place where we're protected and sheltered from outside forces.

So, like animals in nature, take the time now to create your refuge before you enter Winter. Depending on your situation, your safe space may be a physical location or a place you design in your mind. Sometimes it's helpful to have both.

If you live alone or have significant periods of time when you're at home by yourself, you'll probably have a fairly easy time choosing a spot for your hibernation nest. You might choose your bedroom, a comfortable chair, the bathtub, a corner of a spare room, the couch, a sun room, or an alcove in the attic. Be creative, and think "comfort" and "quiet."

If you share your home with other people, this task may be a little more challenging. Think about the flow of movement through your house and identify areas that get the least amount of traffic. See if there's a way to create a little nesting space in one of those areas. You may also need to establish some ground rules with your family or housemates so they'll be able to tell when you need time by yourself.

Once you've identified a place for your nest, the next step is to choose a time when you'll have several hours alone to create a place that's so nourishing and inviting that you'll be drawn to visit it. Being mindful about this process will be healing in itself.

The Handless Maiden did just that as she prepared for the Devil's arrival. Using methods of protection from the Old Goddess religions, she was able to repel the Devil on three different occasions. According to Clarissa Pinkola Estés, the bath purified her for her journey, the white dress gave her the proper costume for her descent into the underworld, and the chalk circle created a protection of sacred thought around her.

You must listen, as the Maiden did, to the wise voice within you for instructions on what rituals and symbols will enhance your protection. Here are some ideas to trigger your own creative process: a source of music, pets to cuddle with, stuffed animals to hug, a soft blanket to curl up in, scented candles to set a reverent mood, beautiful pictures that hold special meaning, symbols that bring you hope. You'll also want to include a comfortable place to sit, whether it's a soft chair, a collection of pillows, a hammock, a couch, or a futon. When you're done, this place will allow you to be with and in your process without intrusions of the outer world. According to Clarissa Pinkola Estés, having this kind of retreat "enables our psychological descent to continue without swerving off course, without our vitality being extinguished by the devilish opposing force of the psyche," or by the forceful interruptions from those who share our lives.

If your home is where the shift is occurring—either you're moving or you're in the midst of a difficult relationship—you may need to find a place that feels safe enough. During some parts of the year, you may be able to use a quiet corner of your garden, a special tree at the park, or a spot next to some running water or crashing surf. As you check out various options, make sure you'll be able to relax, let your guard down, and feel comfortable expressing your emotions there. In many regions, outdoor locations probably won't be available throughout the entire year, so think about quiet indoor places you can go as well: a corner of your library, a certain café, a motel room, a beach hideaway, or a church sanctuary. If you have your own car, that can always work too. Remember that the best way to locate a space that will work for you is to think about where you want to be—what kind of environment are you *craving?* Please note, however, that if your home is particularly dangerous or toxic, it may be important for you to leave the situation entirely and take refuge in a friend's house, a motel, or a new apartment of your own.

In certain circumstances, the only reliable source of safety you'll have access to will be a quiet place you create in your mind. Take some time to visualize this space in as much detail as possible so you can go there anytime you need to feel comforted. It doesn't matter what form your internal refuge takes; it may be a place indoors or outdoors that you've known in reality or only in your fantasies. The main requirement is that you enjoy thinking of the space so much that you're drawn in and given a lifelike experience of safety.

If you can't spend as much time as you'd like in your haven, think about ways to carry it with you. Whether you have a physical space or one you've created in your mind, find a stone, greeting card, photograph, or other symbol that reminds you of your spot. The beauty of this is you can have this symbol anywhere—in your pocket, on your desk, on your dashboard, in a desk drawer, on your mirror—and no one will think anything of it.

This works extraordinarily well. Whenever Mary travels she carries a picture of her pets to remind her of her home and the unconditional love she receives there. During the last few years in my corporate position, I always had a desk calendar with exquisite pictures of nature. During meetings or on especially difficult days, I would find myself merging with the pictures. Just the other day, I happened to see one of these calendars and, even though I hadn't used this technique for over five years, the feeling of calm that settled over me as I looked at the pictures amazed me. Harriet carries a stone in her pocket so that in tense situations, she can reach in to touch the smooth surface and immediately remember to breathe.

If you can't have objects around you very easily, you can use color symbolism to invoke a sense of safety. Think about your refuge. What color comes to mind? Find a piece of paper of that color and cut it into one-inch squares. Then put those bits of paper in places you run across periodically throughout your day—your wallet, your dashboard, the silverware drawer, the medicine cabinet. Whenever you see the color, allow it to transport you to your refuge. No matter what your symbol, the idea is to use it to remember that you do have a place of safety even if you don't feel particularly safe in that moment.

One day, as you sit in your safe space, you may notice it has lost its draw; suddenly it feels stale and out of date somehow. This change signals that you're moving forward to the next step in your process, and it's time to rearrange, update, and enhance your space. Revitalizing the symbols and changing the surroundings will, in turn, revitalize you and your process.

4. Review Your Options

Now that you've done a few things to prepare for the changes taking place in your life, it's time to begin the process of figuring out what to do next. Although it's tempting to want to find the solution right now, you really don't yet know enough about yourself or your situation to make any good long-term decisions. This early in your transition you can only see your situation from the perspective of where you've been. If you really allow yourself to go through the process in the coming months, you'll experience a powerful transformation that will allow you to have an entirely new view of all that's happened and all that can happen. It's best to wait to make major life decisions until you've gone through the entire transformation from caterpillar to butterfly. Hang in there. For now, just list your options.

When you begin this review process, you may have difficulty listing potential next steps. All you can see is what you once had (which doesn't work or exist any longer) or an extreme opposite (which isn't likely to work, either). This is basically the situation the Miller faced. One option was to enrage the Devil by refusing to cut off his daughter's hands—probably not the wisest option, since the Devil had already demonstrated he was a very unsavory and powerful character. The second option, which he took out of fear, was to fulfill the Devil's request, maiming his daughter for life. The Miller no doubt felt a sense of doom and despair as he faced what he thought were his only two options.

You may be feeling similar frustration as you look at your limited choices. Perhaps, like Terry, you've finally acknowledged that you're in an abusive relationship, but you can see only two options: to stay or to leave immediately without packing or preparing. People in very toxic work situations often see similarly extreme options—stay in the job indefinitely, hating every minute of it, or quit tomorrow without any ideas or plans for future employment.

Although you may only see two options at the moment, there are always others. In Terry's case, we eventually generated a whole list of ideas that included getting out of town to clear her head; staying with a friend for a few weeks so she could get her bearings; packing a box or two each day so that when she knew where she was headed she could take her belongings with her; talking with her therapist about ways to protect herself; and looking into women's shelters in case she needed to leave in an emergency situation at some point.

Your challenge right now is to allow, perhaps with the help of a trusted friend or professional, some new options to surface. In time, as you move through the transition process, your perspective will shift enough so that seeing new avenues will become easier.

Although you're no doubt anxious to resolve your situation as soon as possible, I encourage you to just sit with your options for now until additional pieces of the puzzle surface to help you make the right decision. If your circumstances require you to make an immediate decision, talk your options through with several trusted supporters. First, determine if the immediacy you feel really does exist. It may be that you can ask for an extension of some kind to give you some time to think clearly. If a delay isn't possible, see if there's a way you can make a preliminary decision and then finalize it when you have more clarity.

Lucy was in a situation much like this when she settled her divorce. Because her ex-husband had just moved across country, Lucy was trying to come to terms with a visitation schedule she felt comfortable with. She was frustrated because she felt she had to see how her young child responded to the trip before she agreed to any kind of schedule. For instance, if her daughter had difficulty with a week-long visit, how could Lucy possibly agree to a six-week stay over the summer? To ease her mind, she made sure that her daughter would be accompanied on all plane flights, that there would be open lines of communication during the visits, and that some visits would occur locally when her ex-husband was in town staying with his family. Furthermore, Lucy included several checks and balances in the agreement so she could renegotiate the schedule when she had more experience with how the visits actually worked.

What Detours Should I Watch Out For?

1. Denial

From the little we know about what happened with the Handless Maiden in the three-year waiting period before the Devil returned, we get the sense that she and her family were in denial. No one seemed to acknowledge that the Maiden was going to be sacrificed for their prosperity. The only tidbit of information we have is that she had, as Clarissa Pinkola Estés describes it, "a temperament like the first sweet apples of spring." My guess is that while she put on a look of sweet innocence, deep within, under her beauty, lurked the bitterness of unripe fruit. Because the truth of their situation never bubbled to the surface, the Miller's family had no reason to find ways to protect themselves from the Devil. In fact, they avoided taking action altogether until the crisis was upon them.

If you fail to notice that shifts are happening or you choose to ignore them, you too are falling into a pattern of denial. You can expect three outcomes from this. First, your life will get more difficult because when you ignore changes, your problems continue to escalate, sometimes reaching crisis proportions, before you actually stop and take notice. Second, you'll delay the process of preparing for what's to come. As a result, you'll have a harder time in Winter because you won't have any resources to fall back on for support. Third, your journey will be longer than it needs to be because you've been ignoring the issues for so long they've become entrenched in your thinking.

If you find yourself in this situation, know that you aren't alone. Many of us have been taught to ignore bad news in the hope that we will wake up the next day and it will be gone (another form of magical thinking). We've been trained to put our noses to the grindstone, to hang in there. Your friends and coworkers, for instance, may be telling you to stick with your current job because "it's a good job, and it pays the bills." What they don't seem to take into account is that you're miserable. Unfortunately, one of the outcomes of this stance is that when we do finally get down to making the changes in our lives, we find that the path is long and full of debris from past situations we've never resolved.

2. *Jumping at the First Option*

As soon as many people see they have "a problem," whether it's the loss of a job, the ending of a relationship, or an internal spiritual crisis, they tend to jump into motion to fix it. Fast. Now. In so doing, they leap from the ending of one thing (Fall) into the beginning of something new (Spring). Granted, this action does allow them to escape the sense of loss and confusion inherent in all transitions, but in the process, they also bypass the self-assessment process (Winter) that's crucial to making true changes. This sets the stage for the "Spin Cycle" to begin.

In our tale, there are actually two instances in which the father jumps at the first option. In the very beginning of the story, we know the Miller is actively wrestling with how to improve his business because he's out in the woods cutting down deadwood (old ideas and beliefs). Before he has time to come to his own conclusion, though, the old man appears out of nowhere with a deal. Although the offer sounds too good to be true, the Miller leaps at the chance to make his mill profitable again. By jumping at the first offer, he seems to solve all his problems, but within a very short time he realizes this solution brought him much more devastating losses than a business on the brink of failure. So, within moments of reaching Spring and Summer, he found himself back in Fall—facing even deeper problems.

Later in the story, after the Miller has dismembered his daughter, he tries to entice her with the same kind of solution. Rather than dealing with the real issues the daughter is facing, the father tries to "fix it" by offering her a life of leisure. Luckily for the Handless Maiden, she knew she couldn't solve her problems so quickly and superficially. Instead, she gathered her inner strength and decided to work with what she'd been given.

The father in each of us is incredibly powerful and will do all he can to get us to fix our lives and get them back to normal. Although you may be tempted by a quick fix, I encourage you to come to terms with all the dynamics that created the situation in the first place—before you take action. Only then will you be able to make the new choices that will take you to the next Summer of your life.

3. Being a Lone Ranger

Some people, especially those who've been trained not to rock the boat, believe, very strongly, that they must tackle their transitions themselves. You may find yourself thinking that you don't want to burden other people with your problems and you certainly wouldn't dream of imposing on others for anything. Unfortunately, the premium we put on independence has its costs. By trying to do it alone, you make your journey even harder than it needs to be.

Have you ever had to find your way around an unfamiliar city in a foreign country all by yourself? It takes quite a bit of effort to look for signs, spot landmarks, keep track of where you are on your map, figure out the language, and drive safely all at the same time. The going gets even tougher if you don't have the right map or you won't ask for directions. When you do have to make snap decisions about which turns to take, you're so overloaded you often end up making the wrong choice.

By setting yourself apart from other people during your transition, you're likely to miss out on support—helpful information, emotional support, and new perspectives—that could ease an otherwise difficult journey.

Typically, Lone Rangers take this route because they don't have a ready-made support system they trust, and they don't know how to go about creating one. But when you think about it, even the Lone Ranger had the support of his trusted friend Tonto and his faithful horse Silver. So reach out and ask for help. You're going to need it during the long, cold Winter ahead.

Five

Early Winter:
Retreating and Reflecting

Signs:	Tasks:	Detours:
You Feel Tired	Renew at All Levels	Staying Busy
You Don't Want to Do the Usual	Create Time for Quiet	Starting Something New
You Don't Know	Reconnect with Essence	Forcing Yourself to Be Happy
	Practice Purposeful Reflection	
	Track Your Journey	
	Protect Yourself	

At daybreak the very next day, the Handless Maiden, her arms wrapped in white cloth, left the world she'd known all her life. She walked and walked the whole day long, becoming more disheveled and tired as she went.

Finally, at midnight, she came upon a moonlit pear orchard surrounded by a moat. When she couldn't enter, she collapsed to the ground, but her gnawing hunger kept her from sleep. In frustration she asked the forest, "How am I ever going to reach the pears?"

Soon after, a ghostly spirit dressed in white emptied the moat so she could move easily into the orchard.

Walking among the pear trees laden with ripe fruit, she still hesitated to eat because she knew that the pears, part of the royal gardens, were guarded and numbered. But suddenly, on its own accord, a branch bent itself low enough for the Maiden to eat a pear without even needing her nonexistent hands.

Now, the Gardener saw the muddy young woman eating the pear from his orchard, but because he recognized the spirit who assisted her, he didn't try to stop her. After satisfying her hunger, the Handless Maiden crossed back over the moat and spent the rest of the night sleeping in the forest.

When morning came, the King, inspecting his orchard, noticed a pear missing. After questioning the Gardener, he discovered that two spirits had come in the night and that a pear tree had actually offered its fruit to one of them.

That night, the King, the Gardener, and a Magician who knew the ways of spirits kept watch. At midnight the same thing happened. The Spirit in White drained the moat and entered the orchard with the Handless Maiden, whereupon one of the trees offered its fruit to the filthy Maiden.

At that point, the Magician approached them and asked the Handless Maiden, "Are you of this world or not of this world?" She answered calmly and clearly, "I was once of the world, and yet I am not of this world." When the Magician returned to the King, he asked if she was human or spirit. The Magician replied that she was both.

The King was ecstatic. He hurried toward the Maiden and promised to care for her always. Taking her directly to his castle, he immediately had his craftsman make a pair of silver hands for her. Soon thereafter they were married.

So begins the Handless Maiden's journey into the deep, dark forest. Just the fact that she's embarked on a journey is important, because it tells us she's leaving behind the world she has always known for the pathless world of the unknown. In fact, she doesn't know anything— where she'll go, how she'll eat, who will support her, or where she'll end up. Although the Maiden is scared, some part of her, deep within, assures her that even though her choices don't seem logical to her or those who love her, she is heading in the right direction.

Myths and fairy tales that speak of a young maiden entering the forest on her own ("Vasalisa the Wise" in Russia, "The Golden Tree" in India, to name just two) or the underworld where the dead reside (Persephone and Demeter in Greece; Inanna in Sumer) are told worldwide. Whatever the image, the heroine must navigate a dark, dense, mysterious place on her own, without so much as a path. Anyone who has ever embarked on a transition journey recognizes the trepidation the heroine must feel as she ventures into these unknown lands. As Jungian analyst Robert Johnson notes in *The Fisher King and the Handless Maiden*, however, every real myth provides information about how a healing can take place for the heroine who appears to be in such dire straits. By accompanying the Handless Maiden on her journey, we too will learn how to create our own healing.

In stories of this sort, the underground or forest represents the depths of our being—the place where our instincts, full knowing, and true nature live. By entering this space, we are, according to Jungian researcher Marie-Louise von Franz, "sinking into (our) innermost nature and finding out what it feels like" to live from that space. From there we can come to our problems from a different perspective, enabling us not only to resolve the issues at hand but also to reconnect with ourselves more fully.

Because this segment of the tale and the Winter phase of The Seasons of Change say so much about the healing process, we're going to divide Winter into three parts: Early Winter, Winter Solstice, and Late Winter. As Kisma Stepanich notes in *The Gaia Tradition*, the Celtic calendar mirrors this division.

On October 31 and November 1, the Celts celebrated Samhain, the third and final harvest of the year, as they slaughtered the livestock. The absence of flowers and the dormant trees also contributed to their calling this time the season of the dead. To the Celts, the time of the dead meant that the veils between the earth and the other realms were thin, making it easier, albeit a bit spooky, to get insights. It's no coincidence we celebrate this time of year with Halloween. I refer to the period between Samhain and the Winter Solstice as Early Winter.

The turning point of winter is the solstice, when the light begins to increase after the longest night of the year. As we'll see in Chapter 6, this is a very potent time for those on a transition journey, for it's at this turning point that we begin to see the glimmer and sparks of new life.

Late Winter occurs between the solstice and February 2, when the days begin to lengthen, bringing hope of Spring. Although it's not time for the new birth yet, it's clear that everything is moving in that direction. Our Groundhog Day and the Christian feast day Candlemas coincide with the Celtic celebration called Imbolg. We'll learn more about this phase of the journey in Chapter 7.

For now, let's return to the Handless Maiden and Early Winter.

How Can I Tell I'm in Early Winter?

In general, the best way to tell you've entered the forest is to recognize the signs telling you to focus inward. Just as animals conserve their energies in early winter to survive the long, cold winter ahead, you must do the same.

1. You Feel Incredibly Tired

Although the Handless Maiden had been wandering for a day by the time she reached the orchard, she had good reason to be tired. Just think of the stress and strain she'd experienced, waiting those three years for the Devil to arrive and then scrambling to avoid his clutches.

You, too, have good reason to be tired. Just facing the fact that your life is shifting takes great courage and requires tremendous amounts of energy. Add to this the effort it takes to adjust to changed circumstances and you'll understand why you're so worn out.

One of the pitfalls of our productivity-based culture is that our go-go-go schedule doesn't give us any space to be tired. Even when we struggle out of bed each morning or feel worn out just thinking about doing the dishes or paying the bills, we say we're fine and use whatever we can—coffee, sodas, sugar—to give us the extra punch we need to function. This scenario has become such a normal state of affairs, we don't even see it for what it is: exhaustion, pure and simple.

At first, the signs that you're getting worn down are fairly subtle: feeling sleepy, getting a headache, having a sore throat, body aches. If you take notice and provide your body with the attention it needs, you can move on. But if you mask or ignore these signs, your body has no choice but to escalate them. Then you might experience insomnia, ulcers, back pain, pneumonia, bronchitis, or strep throat. These signs will continue to escalate until you choose to stop or, in extreme cases, you're forced to stop by a heart attack, car accident, or fall.

One of my clients, Theresa, believed she had to work constantly to keep ahead of her bills; she rarely gave herself even one day off. Most often she was breathless, frantic, frazzled, and exhausted. Even when she started getting migraine headaches, she kept working because she felt she had to. Ironically, she pushed herself so hard and long that she ended up flat on her back with severe neck and back spasms that left her unable to work for the better part of six months. In her desperate need to make money, she had severely endangered her health, incurred numerous medical bills, and ended up being out of work for a much longer time than she would have if she'd taken a few days off here and there and tended to the warning signs.

Take heed. It's much better to stop *before* you've been flattened. Learn to recognize your body's signals of overload and stress. Then, when you feel this signal, make the choice to remedy the situation immediately. Sure, it may be inconvenient to miss a day of work or rearrange your schedule but, in the long run, attending to your needs now instead of later will lead to fewer long-term setbacks and more conscious handling of your transitions.

The main reason your journey is tiring you out is to get you to a point where you'll direct your energy inward instead of scattering it to the winds all the time. If you can heed the message early on, you'll avoid much of the struggle that comes from trying to force yourself onward in the face of exhaustion.

2. You Don't Want to Do What You Usually Do

This is a very strange time. As you cross from one world into another you find, for reasons you can't fully explain, that the people, activities, ideas, and passions that once defined and filled your life are seemingly meaningless. Even your most precious goals and dreams may hold little excitement.

The life-and-death nature of all transitions, big and small, gets us to pare down to the bare essentials. Frothy topics like sitcom plots, what movies are playing, and who won the championship game seem inconsequential as you wrestle with what cancer treatments to have, where to move your ailing parent, or how to meet your financial obligations now that your business has failed. You may also notice that keeping up appearances—through dress, social protocols, family traditions—holds little allure at this time.

At first you may feel troubled by your lack of interest in what was once your "real" life, but as you sink into your inner world and come to know its beauty, the conflict between the worlds will lessen. Eventually, when your healing is complete, you'll rejoin what Clarissa Pinkola Estés calls the "topside" life again. But, until then, be gentle and allow yourself to hibernate. Decline invitations to family dinners, parties, and gossip sessions with your friends if these events aren't in alignment with what you desire. Honor the part of you that's hungering for deep reflection and meaningful conversations.

3. You Feel Like You Don't Know Anything

By walking away from the life you've known, you've entered a place you've never been before. In this place, you have no idea what you're feeling, what you want, where you'll go next, or what will work for you. If you pay attention, you may even hear yourself using phrases like "I don't know" or "I'm confused."

Congratulations! You've entered the land of "I Don't Know"—a place with a landscape like no other. In fact, it's very difficult to describe because it's always shrouded with dense fog, so thick you can't see a step in any direction. On the rare occasion when the sun breaks through, you realize, very quickly, that you're still lost and confused.

When my father was young, he and his family would drive from San Francisco to Palo Alto along the ridge of a coastal mountain range. Periodically, they'd get to a stretch that was so foggy they couldn't even see the edge of the road. They couldn't stop on the narrow road, and yet they couldn't move forward very fast either. So one of the adults would get out, flashlight in hand, and walk the center line so the driver could be sure to stay on the road. Clearly, this was a slow process that took a fair amount of faith and patience, but eventually, they would reach an area where the fog had lifted, enabling them to see the road again.

Likewise, the fog *will* lift in your life. Although it doesn't feel like it, your entry into "I Don't Know" Land is actually a huge step in the right direction. Once you acknowledge your confusion, you release your grip on the old, outdated pictures and descriptions of your life and open the door to new understanding. Believe it or not, being in "I Don't Know" Land is one of the clearest signs that you're moving forward in your journey.

Chances are, however, that your uncertainty makes most everyone around you anxious. They may feel uncomfortable dealing with your feelings, which surface without much warning, they may be concerned that your confusion is a bottomless pit you'll never crawl out of alive, or they may be afraid that your bewilderment is contagious. To minimize their own discomfort, they'll probably offer countless suggestions about how to get your life back "on track."

Do your best to resist their suggestions, because they'll just put you into the Spin Cycle—changing your circumstances, but not your life. Remember: making small movements in the right direction is far more effective than taking bold actions when you have no sense of where you're going or need to go.

At this point, it helps to recall that the journey you're on is about growth, which every human being must go through to become wiser and more whole. If you can remember this, you'll know your descent is normal and as it should be. Even though you don't seem to know anything at the moment, the one thing you can sense, deep within your soul, is that you must heed the call, continue the journey, and ask for support from those who have gone before. Inherent in the "not knowing" is the promise that the journey will nurture you in ways you can't even imagine.

What Should I Do Now?

I'm willing to bet that right now you're more of a human doing than a human being—striving as hard as you can to achieve something—anything—tangible so you can at least pretend you're on top of things. However, counter to all you've known, the most productive thing you can do in Early Winter is to *do nothing* and learn to just be. To make this all-important shift, you must restructure your thinking, learn new skills, and change your priorities. So for now, instead of attempting to claim the golden sparks of insights, put your attention on training and setting the stage for the main event—the Winter Solstice. That is when, from a space of reflection, you'll turn a corner and be able to see a new future for yourself.

If you're still in the got-to-produce mind-set when you start your training, you're going to feel like you should be counting laps, increasing your repetitions, beating the stopwatch, or something! But that's not what you're here for. You're here to slow down and reconnect with the part of you that just *is*. Until you get the hang of this new way, you're going to feel very uneasy, unproductive, and like you're getting nowhere fast. But by the time you pass through Early Winter and enter the Winter Solstice phase, you'll be in a place of *being* where you'll actually welcome the unknowingness, your learnings, and the new realms you've discovered within yourself and the world. Enjoy the journey!

1. Renew, Renew, Renew

When the Handless Maiden arrived in the underworld forest, her first need was to replenish herself, but she couldn't enter the orchard because she was too exhausted to cross the moat of unfelt emotions.

Finally, with the help of the Spirit in White, she made it into the garden and a tree offered her a pear. Although nourishment alone can't solve the Maiden's problems, it does allow her to carry on with a new sense of fullness.

Before you can make any sense of your transition, you too must renew yourself, using your "hunger" as your guide. Begin by asking yourself, What have I been craving lately? and then take a good look at the answers. Our cravings—often messages from our soul—provide us with powerful information about what would be good for us. You have to be careful, though, because these messages often come in riddle form. For instance, suppose you're craving chocolate. If you take that message at face value, you might run out and eat a big bowl of chocolate ice cream. This might satisfy your immediate craving, but it also might make you sick—all in all, not a very renewing experience. If you look deeper, however, you may still find your craving for chocolate has an important message for you. Think about what feeling you get when you *imagine* eating chocolate. Is it a feeling of being loved because you used to drink hot chocolate with your mom when you were upset, or of getting a big hug, or of belonging? The trick is to make sure you fulfill the deeper craving in a way that's healthy and nurturing in the long run. Asking a friend to hold you while you cry, for example, may be more healing than finding yourself getting the touch you need through a one-night stand.

Remember that your renewal efforts must touch all levels of your being: physical, emotional, mental, spiritual. To rebuild your physical reserves, make an effort to take good care of yourself. No matter how tired or out of sorts, or how little appetite you have, find a way to eat healthy meals on a regular basis. Make sure you get the rest you need. If you feel tired in the middle of the day, take a nap or sit quietly for a short time. Sometimes just fifteen or thirty minutes will replenish you. Even if you don't have the energy for a full workout, find some way to move your body—stretching, doing yoga, walking—because getting oxygen throughout your system really will help you feel better.

Take the time to tune into your own needs to determine the activities that will calm your inner restlessness and soothe your emotions. You might want to get a relaxing massage, take a bubble bath, go to a quiet spot in nature, sit with your pet, listen to your favorite music, go for a run, take a long drive, or talk to a close friend. Consider what will work best for you on a daily basis.

Your mind is likely to need some clearing as well. If you're like many of my clients, your inner critic (the negative voice or voices that have so much to say about how and what you're doing) will be very active in draining your energy through constant criticism. This is the last thing you need right now. The first step in clearing your mind of this excess noise is to begin to notice it when it happens. Once you catch the commentary as it occurs, you have the power to stop it. Create a standard phrase you can use to shut off the critical voice whenever you hear it: "Thank you for sharing, but I can handle this" or "Cancel, cancel." After a while, you may find that you don't think the same self-defeating thoughts anymore.

Early Winter is also a very good time to reconnect with spirit in some way. If the religion you were raised with is comforting and healing, tap into that source. If your original tradition is no longer working for you or you haven't had much contact with religious or spiritual ideas, take this opportunity to explore new realms. Give yourself permission to discover a faith that fits your current needs. This kind of connection doesn't necessarily have to occur in a traditional house of worship—it can happen in nature, in your safe space, or in your heart.

The Handless Maiden entered the forest for her healing and was gifted a pear by the tree. This tells us that going into nature is a powerful source of renewal. Consciously connecting with the ever-present cycles of life in nature will help bring you back to yourself. Trust that nature will respond to your need for sustenance.

2. Create Time for Quiet in Your Life

Since your life is unlikely to stop and you can't continue barreling along at breakneck speeds, you *must* find the time to slow down to renew yourself. Given your responsibilities at both work and home, this is sure to be no small feat. And yet, if you want to move through your transition, you must find a way to create space to discover your truths and receive new information from your wise inner self. So, as you read these ideas, be open to finding new options for yourself.

First, I recommend that you devise a way to spend quiet time by yourself each day. Now, don't panic! I'm not saying you must devote two hours to this endeavor. What I am suggesting is that you carve out a time oasis—whether it's for five, fifteen, or thirty minutes—in your refuge. For now, just start with an amount of time that feels remotely workable. Think of this as an intention, but don't become obsessed with the goal. If you miss a day here or there, that's okay.

How do you find these blocks of time? The trick is to look at your life as it is right now and think about ways you can capitalize on the uninterrupted solitary moments you already do have. You may be able to find some time as you get ready for your day in the morning, when the kids are down for their naps, or as you prepare for bed. Perhaps you can escape from your busy workday schedule during your lunch break. If your weekdays are jammed, think about your weekends—what opportunities do you see then? Once you've identified several options, begin to experiment. Keep tweaking and refining your system until you find something that works for you.

To make it easier on yourself, consider starting a new ritual in your home—quiet time—a period when everyone has the opportunity to do activities alone in silence. Because television has such a prominent place in most homes, extended periods of peace and quiet are very rare. Yet it's crucial for children and teenagers to learn how to be alone. Their comfort level with silence will serve them well as they face changes throughout their lives.

Begin by helping your children choose appropriate quiet-time activities—coloring, reading, drawing, thinking, writing. Then set a timer for fifteen minutes. You may find that as everyone gets accustomed to how it feels to be quiet, they enjoy themselves so much they actually go beyond the original time limit.

When you first start this practice, focus on getting used to how it feels to be by yourself in the quiet. The items you put in your safe space will come in handy now. Turn on some soothing music, light a candle, read your favorite book, or just stare out the window at the stars. Remember, there is no one right way to do this.

One of the fastest ways to move into a calm frame of mind is to become fully present in the moment. To do this, sit quietly with your feet on the floor and take a few deep breaths, releasing each one with an audible sigh. Then imagine a root or a cord stretching from your tailbone to the center of the earth and devise a way to attach it by tying it or hooking it to something. Continue taking deep breaths as you pull the earth energy—a rich brown or deep green color—up through the cord to fill every cell of your body. Then envision the top of your head opening to allow light from the heavens to mingle with the earth energy. When you complete the process, just sit with the feeling of calm that envelopes you. A regular daily practice of this exercise will help you feel calmer and more grounded.

I also encourage you to find ways to spend one or more days (and nights) alone, away from your normal surroundings. From where you sit, as you look at your pocketbook, your family, and your work, the idea of going on a retreat by yourself may seem rather extravagant. But if your goal is to see your life from a new perspective, there's no better way to achieve that goal than to get away. Taking time in a new environment, without responsibilities, will give you a wonderful opportunity to remember who you are and what you feel like when you're relaxed, at ease, and away from everyday drudgery. When you return home after such a retreat, you'll get a second layer of insights as you overlay the "true" you with the "day-to-day" you.

When I was suffering from fatigue and burnout, I treated myself to a five-day retreat at the beach. The day after I returned home, I had a dream that gave me the idea to start my business. Juli, a client, attended a week-long retreat at a healing center in the Southwest. As a result of her stay, she realized she wasn't living up to her potential; by delving into herself she began to see how she might incorporate her gifts more fully into her work. Paula had the luxurious opportunity to stay in a remote cabin for several months to sort through her past and reweave it in a way that enabled her to look forward instead of backward all the time.

So, keep your eyes open for possible opportunities to get away. If you hold your intention, the right situation will pop up when you need it most. Have the strength and courage to seize it when it comes!

For now, begin playing with this idea by studying a map. Figure out where you might go to experience a change of scenery without having to travel a long distance. Then check out the book called *Sanctuaries* (listed in Tools for the Journey) and find a retreat center in or near that area which provides the mix of structured activities, contact with others, and quiet time alone that you're looking for. Or, create your own retreat by renting a cabin, camping, going to a hotel, or house-sitting.

Remember, the main purpose of your retreat is to have an opportunity to live in the moment for as long as possible with as few distractions as possible. Even if you're tempted to take your partner or a friend for company, you'll have many more opportunities to see your life in a new way if you venture out alone.

3. *Reconnect with Your Essence*

Now it's time to begin *using* your quiet and away time to be and reconnect with what it means to be you. This notion may be rather foreign to most of us. In the hustle and bustle of everyday life, as we try to meet others' expectations of who we should be—whether from parents, adult children, or employers—we can lose track of what is most important to us. One day, usually in the midst of a crisis, we wake up and realize we've lost touch with who we are. As a result, we can't make decisions that are in alignment with what we value and desire because we don't even know what we hold dear anymore. Any change—good or bad—is a wake-up call to refashion our lives, no matter how long or short they will be, into something that more closely fits our essence.

Before you can redesign your life to fit you fully, you need to discover or reconnect with your natural way of being. Just think about nature for a minute. Each plant has evolved to thrive in a particular environment with specific characteristics: temperature, soil, sunlight, and water. When plants live in the areas to which they are well-suited, they're called natives. Native species are naturally hardy, easy to grow, and withstand the local pests with ease. If these plants are taken to an entirely different environment, they're called exotics. Because the conditions aren't right for them, exotics tend to need a lot of attention, have a low resistance to pests and diseases, and very often grow only with difficulty.

Are you a native or an exotic in your workplace, your relationship, your church? Do you thrive naturally without effort in these environments, or do you require a high degree of maintenance to exist in them? Linda, a creative artist, is a native in her studio, but an exotic in the windowless cubicle of her corporate job. Mary, born and raised in New York City, never thrived during her thirty years there. In fact, she suffered at all levels—physically, emotionally, mentally, spiritually—because she wasn't suited to the constant noise and chaos of the city. When she moved to rural California, she discovered she's a native there. If you often get sick or find you must struggle to succeed, you probably aren't in your native environment.

Reconnecting with your essence is a crucial step in the transition journey, whether you're making a career change, changing your relationship, or reestablishing your life after a death in the family or a serious illness. The more you know about yourself and your natural way of approaching life and those around you, the more you'll understand why certain situations work for you and why others don't.

When you're in touch with your unique passions, style, rhythms, and needs, they'll provide you with all you need to succeed, make a difference in the world, and be happy and fulfilled. When you allow yourself to live and work in ways that support your essence, you'll be amazed at how much easier life is. Here are the methods I use to help my clients discover their natural way of being.

Play Detective

Look for clues that show you how and where you've become disconnected from your essence. Here are some questions to help you focus your investigation:

- Are you forcing yourself to do something you're not comfortable doing, not capable of doing, or do not want to do because you believe you "should" be doing it?
- Are you doing something to please a boss, spouse, friend, or family member to uphold appearances or to meet your own or others' expectations?
- Are you forcing yourself to reach a goal you no longer believe in?
- What do you do that takes more effort or energy than you'd like it to?
- What do you worry about?
- Where do you procrastinate?
- What areas of your life lack color, excitement, and passion?
- What areas are overwhelming and chaotic?
- Are there situations where you "disappear" or hesitate to voice your opinions or thoughts?

As you answer the questions, stay vigilant. First appearances can be deceiving. You may have been doing certain things for so long that they seem to be part of your essence, when really they aren't.

As you discover places you've been selling yourself out, see if there are any trends. Are there certain situations in which your essence is more likely to get lost? Use the purposeful reflection methods described later in this chapter to see what else you can learn from these insights.

You can also use your investigative skills to explore various sources—psychological, esoteric—to enhance your understanding of your essence. Although it may feel disconcerting at first to pinpoint your personal style using a questionnaire or specifics about your birth, the trick is to remember that the information is not a restrictive label or category, but input to a larger picture you're constructing of yourself. If you keep this in mind, any time you can obtain information about yourself—whether at work, from a magazine, in a therapy session, in a career assessment process, or in a workshop—it's worthwhile.

One of the most popular assessment methods is called the Myers-Briggs Type Indicator. Because this instrument must be administered by a psychologist and scored by the company that publishes the questionnaire, you may have some difficulty completing this particular questionnaire on your own. For ideas about systems that are more readily available, consult Tools for the Journey.

Become an Idealist

Pretend you have the opportunity to create a life that expresses your essence in a balanced, whole way. If, as Clarissa Pinkola Estés puts it, you felt "entirely in and of yourself," how would you live your life? Giving yourself full permission to look beyond the world you live in today, will open up your creativity. So, in an ideal situation:

- How would you make decisions? Would you weigh the pros and cons, act on your intuition, or dawdle until you were forced to decide?

- How would you take in information? Would you be more apt to understand information if you read it, heard it, or experienced it?

- How would you organize information? Would you make sense of information in your head, in a diagram, or in random notes? Would you use files or would you prefer piles?

- How would you like to use your time? Would you prefer to be active from sunup to sundown or do you like some downtime during the day? Would you do better if you started your day gradually or jumped right into action?

- What would your natural rhythm be? When would your body like to wake up, exercise, eat, work, sleep?

- When would your mind think most clearly, creatively, productively?

- How would you interact with others? Would you prefer to interact with large, social groups or small, intimate groups? Would you like to talk in person, on the phone, or via the Internet?

- What would life success look and feel like?

If you find your answers vary by situation or period of your life, step back to see if you can find what Mary Catherine Bateson, in *Composing a Life*, calls "the more abstract underlying convictions that have held steady" over time.

When you first enter Early Winter, you may not be able to answer these questions because you really don't know who you are anymore. That's okay. Ask the questions anyway, and sort through what used to work for you and what might work for you now. As you connect with your essence, you'll become more confident in discerning what you'd like in your ideal world.

As the top salesperson in her company several years running, Jan lived the high life. She had impeccable clothes, a big expense account, an impressive office, and a great income. Recently, she left her job, got married, and started coming to terms with a painful childhood—effectively dismantling the life she'd built and known. As I asked her about her ideal work environment, she became very flustered and didn't know how to answer me because the responses she would have given me just a year prior no longer made sense to her. As we sorted through her responses, she realized she no longer wanted the lifestyle she once thought she loved, but she couldn't yet define what she did want, either. As Jan continues to heal, her new preferences are becoming more and more clear.

4. *Practice Purposeful Reflection*

By now you're feeling more renewed, you've created quiet time in your life, and you've begun the process of discovering who you are. Now it's time to discover tools and techniques that will allow you to use your quiet time to reflect and make sense of all the changes in your life. Make a list of what works for you so you'll have it the next time you're wrestling with an issue.

Although you're probably hoping "the answer" will appear in neon lights, your focus in Early Winter is to set the stage for insights rather than obtaining the answer. The revelation you desire can appear only when the conditions are right—and not before. Just take the steps to reflect and ideas will begin to flow while you're in reflection or while you're driving, drifting off to sleep, walking your dog, or gardening. Be patient with the process and allow it to work for you.

Reading

Books and books on tape can bring you a wealth of insight and new ideas, whether you read them cover to cover or allow your intuition to take you straight to the gems of information you're searching for. But how do you decide what to read? Begin by browsing in your favorite bookstore or library and notice what you're drawn to. Sometimes the books you need to read will literally fall into your hands! Seeing or hearing references to the same book repeatedly is another sign that it would be worth your while to check it out. You might also want to ask someone who's traveled a path similar to the one you're on now what books they found to be helpful and inspiring.

Taking a Walk Without a Destination

When the Handless Maiden leaves home and enters the forest, she has no idea where her steps will take her. Yet, by putting one foot in front of the other, she finds just what she needs—the Spirit in White who connects her with the people and places that transform her life. So it's important to remember that even though you don't have a particular destination in mind at this stage of your journey, there are people and places your intuition will guide you to as long as you take the first steps.

Taking an *actual* walk without a destination will help you become more familiar with how it feels to proceed without a goal or direction. It really doesn't matter where you walk as long as it's safe, fairly unfamiliar, and seems like a fun place to explore. It could be in a park, a different neighborhood, or a commercial area with cute shops.

Let your senses guide your steps. At each crossroads, sense which direction you want to go. What signals guide your actions? Do you make your decisions on visual cues, an inner feeling, how it sounds, or an inner voice? Where do you feel or sense these signals in your body?

As you repeat this exercise, you'll begin to hone your ability to use your intuition.

Notice how it feels to navigate the unknown. How comfortable are you with this adventure? What would make you feel more at ease? How can you use this information to help you handle your current transition? How does it feel to stay in the moment as you explore an area? Is it uncomfortable, or do you like to anticipate how things will unfold?

Although Kate was motivated to expand her business, she was so afraid she'd make the wrong choices that she couldn't make any. I gave her an assignment to take a destinationless walk. But before she'd even left my office, she told me she was petrified because she'd never done anything without having a goal attached. To simplify her homework, I told her all she had to do was walk out of her house, decide whether to go left or right, and then walk until she felt like turning around. In doing the exercise, she recognized just how much she allowed fear to influence her life and how much her need for control was actually limiting her success. Since working on this issue, she's made great strides in growing her business.

On your walks, you'll also learn more about your personal style and passions. After you complete each trip, think back to what you were drawn to explore, what captured your attention, and what repelled you. Add this information to your growing understanding of your own essence.

Once you get a sense of what guides you, use it in other situations, such as choosing from a menu, picking a movie, or deciding on a book. Over time, you'll become so sensitive to these signals that you'll trust and value implicitly the intuitive information you receive.

Asking Open-Ended Questions

Asking yourself open-ended questions is an incredibly easy way to access your intuition. The more questions you ask, the more insights you'll see, feel, and sense. Often the question that opens the door to your future is so incredibly obvious that, like a detective, you must get past your preconceived notions to even see it. Remember, the way to get new answers is to ask new questions.

When you're faced with a situation or pattern of behavior you want to understand, start exploring where you are right now:

- Where am I with _____?
- Where's my energy regarding _____?
- How am I feeling about _____?
- What does my higher self have to say about this situation?

Your next goal is to understand the deeper purpose of what you're facing:

- What am I gaining from this experience?
- What's the challenge of this situation?
- What is the gift of this?

Then look at what's getting in your way:

- What's blocking me?
- What do I need right now?
- What could I do differently next time?

Depending on the situation, it's sometimes helpful to look at the big picture to sort out what role you're playing and what roles others are playing:

- What part do I play in this situation?
- What part is _____ playing?
- When have I played this role before?

Once you have a better understanding of what's been happening, ask yourself questions about the next step in the process:

- What's my next step?
- What wants to happen next?
- How can I approach this situation?
- What should I keep in mind as I move forward?

As I mentioned earlier, one of the most effective ways to spark your creativity is to think about the ideal solution.

- What do I *want* to have happen here?
- What's the ideal outcome for me?
- What's my ideal picture of this situation?

If your transition has shaken your foundation, you may also be questioning your philosophy of life. If this is the case, questions from *The Little Book of Big Questions*, listed in Tools for the Journey, may help stimulate your process.

After sitting with these questions, you may discover that just thinking about them isn't working because you keep going around in circles. If this is happening, experiment with the techniques described below to bring a new slant to these open-ended questions.

Randomly Access New Information

Tapping into resources randomly is one of my favorite ways to stretch my views about a situation or pattern I'm wrestling with. The first step is always to state your intention as concisely as possible, so you'll be able to interpret the information you receive. So, what do you want to think about more clearly? The previous list of questions may guide you to a good starting point.

To use this technique, you need to have a source of information you can access somewhat randomly: a dictionary, Bible, poetry book, inspirational self-help book, or daily meditation guide. After stating your intention, open the book at random, point to a word, passage, or verse, and read it. What comes to mind? Free-associate for a moment. Then look for connections between the information you came up with and your intention. If the message is incredibly obvious, you may laugh out loud; if it's not, you may need to sit with the information for a few days before you see the link. Recording these insights may bring even more connections to light.

Intuitive card decks, runes, or the *I Ching* can also be used in much the same way. There are a number of intuitive tools on the market. If you find the seasons to be a helpful way of making sense of your transitions, you may want to look at my *Nature's Wisdom Deck.* I created this deck so people can access nature's guidance any time—day or night. Each card uses a different aspect of nature as a metaphor for where you are in your transition. (See Tools for the Journey for more information about the deck and how to obtain a copy.)

You can also use objects as a catalyst to shift your thinking. Any object will do—a safety pin, a pine cone, a bird soaring in the sky, a candle. There are several ways you can choose an object—pick an item that appeals to you in the moment, or choose a color and then use the first object you see of that color. You can also create a collection of objects ahead of time and number them. Then, whenever you want to think about something creatively, pick a number and use the corresponding object as your focus.

Once you have the object, look at it and jot down its characteristics. For instance, if you chose an abalone shell, as many of my clients have, you might say that it's rough on the outside, holey, shiny, smooth, colorful on the inside, and a home for a creature.

Then select the one characteristic that intrigues you the most. One person might pick the contrast between the inside and outside, while another might focus on its iridescent colors. There are no right answers here; the element that triggers the strongest response in your mind is the one you want to play with.

Your next step is to free-associate with the characteristic you highlighted. You might think of situations that have the same elements, or list how you feel when you think of that element. Just let your thoughts flow.

Then make connections between your brainstorming and your original question. The person who focused on the contrasts might realize that while on the outside he's rough and unrefined, within he has the potential to be polished and unexpectedly smooth. Iridescent colors might lead a person to conclude she needs to bring more pleasing colors into her life—literally and figuratively.

5. *Track Your Journey*

One of the most curious details in "The Handless Maiden" is the fact that every pear in the orchard is numbered and tracked by the Gardener and the King of the underworld. As Clarissa Pinkola Estés explains, this inventory process is not for material reasons, but to announce that a new initiate entering the forest requires assistance. Because this transition is so important, nothing is left to chance—not even the Maiden's first steps in the forest.

In a similar way, it's important for you to track your transition process. Because so many subtle changes are taking place, it'll be helpful for you to have a record to review periodically to see patterns you can't see any other way. This doesn't necessarily mean that you have to write down every single thing that happens in your life. Here are several ways you can follow your process.

Journaling

Whether you write in a beautiful bound book, a simple binder, or on the computer, you may find it helpful to record what you remember about the past, what you can do to resolve a situation at hand, and what you're grateful for. You may even want to describe the insights you receive when you ask open-ended questions or access information randomly. Remember, you're not writing an essay to be graded. Long rambling pages, lists, single words, and symbols can all work. Do what feels best in the moment.

You may think that the only way to journal effectively is to discipline yourself to do it every day at a particular time. In truth, the only way it's beneficial is journaling when and if it helps you. If you're connected to your essence, you'll know when it's the right thing to do—such as when an event pushes your buttons, you're in a dark place, or you want to acknowledge an achievement.

Creative Arts

Expressing yourself through creative arts is another illuminating way to record your journey. Because this method is nonverbal, it is especially good if you have a difficult time expressing yourself in writing. You can explore your unconscious directly without translating concepts into words. Begin by giving yourself the opportunity to experience as many different media as possible—clay, dancing, making music, taking pictures, finger-painting, drawing, making collages—to see which ones give you the most satisfaction and release.

Many people cringe at these suggestions, and protest that they're not artists. I'm not asking you to be an artist—I'm only asking that you express yourself. No special talent, technique, or skill is required, only a willingness to enter into the creative process. In fact, no one need see the final piece unless you choose to share it. If you feel hesitant to express yourself in this way, take heart. As you reclaim your essence, you'll reconnect with your inborn creativity as well.

One of the self-expressive methods I've used for years, which many of my clients have enjoyed, is drawing your emotions. Begin by sitting quietly with your eyes closed. Take a moment to just feel the emotion in your body. What color or colors do you associate with it? What shape comes to mind? What texture does it evoke? Try not to control it; just allow it to evolve. If your mind is busy trying to interpret the colors and the drawing, just listen and continue your process.

When you feel complete, date your picture and then sit back to notice what draws your attention. If certain colors have special meaning, jot that down on the picture. If you heard words or phrases as you worked, write those down so later you'll remember their significance.

In the depths of my grief, this was one of the few ways I could access my emotions safely. By the end of those years, I'd filled three drawing journals with pictures that still elicit powerful emotions in me and keep key insights at my fingertips—in fact, my safe space is still decorated with my favorites.

If you draw a picture that evokes so much emotion you have a hard time looking at it, use the same colors to create a pleasing mandala—a design that's round and symmetrical—to begin shifting your pain. Then keep the mandala version where you can see it so the healing process will continue.

Although I speak of drawing, any creative medium will allow you to explore your emotions and come to new understandings of them. Experiment and find the methods that work for you. Several books in

Tools for the Journey provide information about specific creative expression activities.

Dream Work

Understanding your dreams can also help you track your progress. The first step is recording as many dreams and dream fragments as you can in a dream journal or on a tape recorder. When you become more familiar with how to read dreams, you may find that by the time you wake up only the interpretation you've done in your sleep is still intact. Other times, the dream may be so involved and meaningful that it jolts you awake. Write those dreams down! Your soul is definitely trying to get a message across.

You may notice your dream life picks up speed when you enter Early Winter. This is because your unconscious is working overtime to integrate all the new information you've been discovering. You can also stimulate your dream life by rereading your last dream before you go to sleep. You may also find it helpful to reread your dreams over a period of time to see how you've grown and what key themes you've been working on lately.

If you're interested in learning how to interpret your dreams, check out the dream books included in Tools for the Journey.

6. Protect Yourself

In winter, the most important task an animal undertakes is staying safe—from the cold, storms, and predators. A study of grizzly bears conducted in Yellowstone Park by the Environmental Research Institute in the 60s, reported in *Our Amazing World of Nature*, illustrates this. The bears were observed, tracked, and tagged during the fall and winter over seven years to discover what triggered their hibernation. One year, even though two intense storms hit the park in early fall, none of the grizzlies entered their dens. When the researchers observed the bears in November, they noticed the bears were so tired they could hardly keep their eyes open and yet still they wouldn't pack it in. Finally, on November 11, a storm hit and the final piece of the puzzle fell into place.

The bears were waiting for enough snow to fall so the drifts would erase both their prints and their scent. Somehow the bears could sense which storm would protect them.

As you continue your descent into Winter, exploring the landscape within, it's important to protect yourself and conserve your energy. It might be tempting to release your hold on the topside world completely at this point, but it's important, as Clarissa Pinkola Estés points out, to keep one foot in the mundane world at all times so we have a way to return to our lives after our journey. The task of keeping your everyday life going while you're wrestling with the darkness of "I Don't Know" Land is challenging at best and requires setting limits and making wise choices.

The key test in any circumstance is to ask yourself whether you feel safe. If you feel threatened or uncomfortable with the prospect of participating in an event, graciously decline the invitation. Although some folks may not understand you, it's your prerogative to focus your energies inward.

In work situations, it may be a little more difficult to set limits because you have certain responsibilities you must fulfill. Get creative in devising win-win solutions that enable you to fulfill your duties while maintaining your sense of safety. Recruit others to help you brainstorm and then ask them to help you implement your solutions. If the people around you won't work with you, you'll need to look beyond them for help.

If you do negotiate special terms, be diligent in keeping to the agreement. Don't take advantage of the situation by abusing the flexibility that's been granted. When it becomes possible, resume your normal duties and thank those who have helped you during your time of need.

Carlos, who suffered from chronic fatigue syndrome, found he had a difficult time being productive all day unless he took a nap during lunch. By taking longer lunches whenever he needed to, with his manager's approval, he missed only four full days of work, while other staff members, who pushed themselves continuously, ended up missing several weeks.

When I spoke with Marlo, she was having a difficult time adjusting after her miscarriage and feeling guilty for being short-tempered with her children and "pouncing" on them for their youthful exuberance. As we talked, she realized what she needed most was some time alone with her husband to reestablish her equilibrium. She saw that the best solution for all involved was for the kids to spend a few nights with their grandparents so that she and her husband could mourn their loss and reconnect with each other.

The most difficult threats to your feelings of safety will occur if you work or live in a toxic environment. If you're constantly on guard against nasty, uncalled-for comments, or if you feel your privacy may be invaded at any moment, chances are good that your environment is toxic. Because people in these situations won't be supportive, it will probably be necessary to migrate out of the situation before you can heal. If you've been in the toxic environment for a long time, you'll most likely need some outside support to help you detach from the situation.

What Detours Should I Look Out For?

1. Staying Busy

The most common detour in Early Winter is staying busy—so busy that you have no time to renew yourself or reflect on your life. Many people, whether consciously or unconsciously, choose to stay busy in order to avoid the feelings of turmoil rising within them. They hope that by staying active they'll be able to get through the change without feeling anything. However, frenetic activity, whether self-imposed or created by circumstances, doesn't eliminate the need to go within—it just postpones it until a later time.

Examine your commitments, such as relationships, committee meetings, and family events, to find the ones that aren't fulfilling you but causing you to delay your real work—your journey.

2. Starting Something New

You may also be tempted to start something new to escape the inner chaos you're feeling. By marrying the King of the underworld so soon after entering the forest, the Maiden avoids the emotions that are bound to surface as she attempts to live on her own without hands.

You may feel the urge to start a new job, a new relationship, a new exercise program, or a new diet just to get yourself to feel better. Unfortunately, lurching forward at any point during Early Winter means you skip over the Winter Solstice. Without this turning point, you'll continue to create the same sorts of difficulties you've been facing over and over again.

Nearly all of my clients get the urge to jump forward at some point during Winter. Although Jack had been through a hard year, he was making tremendous progress in developing his career plan. Unfortunately, a big part of him just couldn't see his growth because his internal changes hadn't yet manifested in his "real" life—he still lived in his parents' house and did manual labor to make ends meet. I knew that if he'd just hang in there a bit longer, he'd finalize his plans, but right then he fell in love. By starting something new, he has, for the time being anyway, jumped out of his confusion. But Jack has also distracted himself from putting the finishing touches on his plan, which could have given him a clarity and solid direction in short order.

3. Forcing Yourself to Be Happy

We know very little about how the Handless Maiden feels about losing her hands or her upcoming marriage; we just know she agreed to the King's obviously enthusiastic proposal. But when people hide their true emotions or are completely unaware of them, they're skirting the real, deeper issues that must be resolved in order to move on and complete the journey.

Eva came to my office because she'd just gotten notice that she'd be laid off in several months. As we discussed her situation, she laughed, smiled, and joked with me. She told me she was consciously looking at her options and planning ahead. It wasn't until the end of the second session, as she described other transitions she'd been through in the last several years, that her true emotions surfaced—she was hurt, but trying desperately not to show it.

In our first conversation, she'd been trying to stay strong, to see the change as an opportunity, and to gloss over the painful feelings of this and other difficult transitions that she'd never completed. If Eva had continued along that path, she would have done herself a great disservice. Old transitions don't just go away—healing only occurs when true resolution is found. So it's okay not to feel happy right now. You don't have to pretend—in fact, it's far better if you don't!

Six

Winter Solstice: Catching Sparks of Hope in the Darkness

You are seated with the other members of your tribe around a fire. A storm rages outside and darkness prevails. On this special night, the tribe has come together to bring back the sun. Over the past few months, the sun has moved lower and lower in the sky. So low, in fact, that the hours of sunlight have decreased significantly. All those around the fire have come to offer their strength to the prayer for the sun's return, for each one is worried that this time, the sun's strength may not return. They know that if this were to happen, all humans, animals, and plants would die. As the tribe prays, the shaman performs a series of rituals at the boundary between the mundane world and the spirit world to ensure that the balance between the earth and the sun is maintained. Although no one knows for sure whether the process has worked, the people continue their celebration with faith and hope—seeing in their minds' eyes the abundant harvest that will grace their existence within months, if the sun returns.

The Winter Solstice is the turning point in your transition journey, the time in the process when you let go of the old—patterns, goals, explanations, thoughts, ideas, ways of perceiving—and usher in the new. Until you experience this shift in your thinking, you can't possibly create a new vision of your future, let alone implement it in the world.

It's no coincidence that these new sparks of light come to you in the darkest time of your life. Numerous philosophers, poets, and theologians wax eloquent about the magic of darkness. For instance, in his conversations with Bill Moyers in *The Power of Myth*, Joseph Campbell related that one of the clearest messages from myths "is that at the bottom of the abyss comes the voice of salvation." Matthew Fox emphasizes the important role darkness plays in the process of creativity when he writes in *Original Blessing*, "Darkness is the origin of everything that is born." Jungian researcher Marie-Louise von Franz mirrors this concept in her interpretation of "The Handless Maiden" when she notes that it is in the "extreme moment of loneliness and sadness" that the Handless Maiden's deep healing begins. And St. John of the Cross refers to this time in a person's life as "the dark night of the soul."

In nature, darkness is the rich, fertile soil that enables seeds to sprout and grow into the plants that will ultimately provide a harvest. The same is true for you. Although you're wanting a harvest, it's far too cold and stormy for new growth in the outer world. Inner growth is the only thing you can nurture now. The insights you're searching for mirror the moment of conception, the moment a seed casing breaks open to allow the first root to sink into the earth.

At this point, when all the conditions are right, nature's magic takes place. Clarissa Pinkola Estés uses alchemy to explain the powerful processes that occur within us when all parts of our psyches—male/female, positive/negative, light/dark—join together in union. It's through this *conjunctio*, the "union of unlike substances . . . inhabiting the same psychic space that soulful energy, insight, and knowing are made." One day this union will occur for you in a way you can't predict and the result will be an idea, a simple solution, or a creation that will eventually take you to a new place.

You may not have known it, but by traveling through Early Winter, you've been setting the stage for your Winter Solstice. Before I give you some tips on how to allow Winter Solstice insights to happen, let me share some examples of this turning point.

Although it had been six years since my father's death, I always seemed to be more emotional during the winter months. In January 1992, I remember being mad at my father for a whole list of things—for dying so young, for leaving me before he could teach me important things about taking care of my car, managing my money, and speaking up for myself, and for missing the conversations we could have had about our shared professional interests. For a time, I ranted inside my head about all these injustices. A few days later, I was taking stock of my new business and really enjoying all the ideas I had. In a flash of insight, I realized that my father and I were really business partners—his passing and its effects on me are the cornerstone of my work. As I looked for his influence on my business, I saw it everywhere—in the books he'd given me, in the seasonal photographs he'd taken throughout his life, in my memories of the grief process. In that instant I realized that without him I wouldn't be doing the work I love. My anger turned to gratitude and awe. Within two weeks, after a bit of urging from a friend, I sat down and wrote the first version of the natural approach to change that you're reading.

Bob had a Winter Solstice shift when he first heard about Attention Deficit Disorder (ADD). After years of thinking he was lazy and stupid because he couldn't keep a steady job or stick with school, he learned that much of this behavior was due to the chemistry of his brain. Just knowing that ADD existed was enough to give Bob a new way to look at his past, which led to new explanations for many of his past difficulties. He began to understand how he was different from "normal" people and how he could capitalize on his differences to excel. The new insights he came to served as a catalyst to create a new life for himself.

When Denise and I began our work together, every question I asked led to some discussion about how her marriage and recent divorce had restricted her life. The impact of this lengthy and difficult marriage was evident in Denise's beliefs about herself, her lack of paid work experience, and her limited picture of what was possible in her life. During the first three months of our work together, I challenged her to expand her view of herself and of what was possible. We focused on distilling the essence of her entire life experience, both paid and volunteer work, but

Winter Solstice:
Catching
Sparks of Hope
in the
Darkness

119

Denise was still wrapped up in the pain of her former marriage.

Then, nearly ten months after we started our work, I suddenly noticed a significant shift in her. When I pointed it out to her, she explained that when she met people now, she had a new way to talk about her past. In fact, she'd been able to reduce the entire saga into a single sentence: "Although I had a hard marriage, my experience has given me compassion and strength to help others through difficult times." Her new understanding of her situation enabled her to let go of the past and move into the future with a new excitement. That turning point was her Winter Solstice.

How to Catch a Solstice Insight

Unfortunately, there is no way to request or demand a Winter Solstice. All you can do is to create the right set of conditions, and then allow the insights to happen. As Marie-Louise von Franz points out, for a person who is used to our culture's ways, "to wait, let things come, is sometimes the most difficult." The ancient Chinese philosophy described in the *I Ching* gives us another insight into the Solstice moment in its description of the hexagram *Fu*, "The Return" or "The Turning Point": "There is movement, but it is not brought about by force." Here are several suggestions on how to set the stage.

1. Be in the Dark

Now that you're comfortable with the underworld and its ways, you'll find you actually enjoy your moments in solitude and quiet. You're more at ease than you've ever been finding your way through the dark forest. It no longer frightens you to lift the lid off patterns to see what lessons are lurking there.

Whenever a fairy tale incorporates a night scene, it tells us the characters have descended into the dark of the unconscious. You can even see this in the myth we've been following—recall that the Handless Maiden found the pear orchard at night. As Clarissa Pinkola Estés points out, "Nothing makes the light, the wonder, the treasure to stand out so well as darkness." When we sink into the darkness and surrender to its emptiness, we become more aware of subtle sounds, sensations, movements, and thoughts. In fact, our sensitivity allows us to see more. So it's the very darkness you may be trying to avoid that will allow you to see the sparks of transformation.

Usually at this point in the process, you notice that the veil between the topside world and the underworld is very permeable. As you move between the two worlds, just remember to keep a part of yourself centered and connected to the darkness so that even when you're out in the world you can still see your insights. Although you might be tempted to release the topside world completely and delve deeply into the darkness, it's important to keep some balance by maintaining a foothold in the work-a-day world.

Winter Solstice:
Catching
Sparks of Hope
in the
Darkness

121

2. *Know the Feeling That Heralds Your Insights*

Clients often ask me how they'll know when the Winter Solstice is near. Although I'm good friends with this feeling now and I've learned, over the years, to attend to its call, I've never before attempted to put words to these sensations. The best I can do is share how it is I sense that something—a poem, plan, idea, piece of art, theory—is about to be born.

Usually I feel a combination of things: an unnameable fullness, a sense of anticipation, a feeling that there's something I want to say, a premonition that something is about to happen, a desire to just sit and hold the space for magic to happen, a craving to draw/write/think/dance, a deep-down quickening or stirring, a powerful dream about being pregnant or having a baby, an unstoppable drive for new clarity, a bundle of energy in my throat that begs to be released, fragments of ideas flitting around in my mind that I catch and weave together into a picture.

The next time you're in the fertile land of the Winter Solstice, notice what you felt just prior to your big breakthrough. Over time, you too will know the subtle sensations that foretell your turning point.

3. Allow the Process to Take You

The *Fu* hexagram offers more wisdom about the turning point when it says, "The movement is natural, arising spontaneously. For this reason the transformation of the old becomes easy." The unfolding of your insights will happen quite naturally if you follow your intuition. If you find you have a sudden urge to sit in the park in the sun, as one of my clients once did—do it. If you have a desire to put pen to paper, do that. If you need to visit a friend, look at a book, find a poem, hug a tree, or skip down the street, do it. Then keep following your inner guidance. One clue often leads to the next piece of the puzzle.

For now, don't worry if the message you receive doesn't make any sense. In my experience, there is *nothing* logical about the way Winter Solstice events occur; your soul and spirit don't work from logic.

4. Keep a Soft Eye

Looking for solstice insights is a lot like looking for shooting stars or migrating whales. When they are happening, you just need to be in the right place at the right time to notice them. Furthermore, to spot them you must scan, using a very soft focus, a vast area of the sky or sea, in order to catch any movement in your field of vision.

Recently, this same soft-eye strategy paid off as I was viewing the Hale-Bopp comet. Although I'd seen the comet from my yard in the Bay Area, I also had the opportunity to see it from a beach house in a community where all but the dimmest outdoor lights are forbidden. When I first compared the two views, I wasn't all that impressed. But then, as I turned my head to look at the other stars, I saw the comet out of the corner of my eye. It was amazing—I could see the comet's tail stretched out five times longer than I could make out from home! So, when you begin to see insights, remember to use a soft eye and take an oblique view every now and then. You may be able to see layers of understanding that aren't apparent when you search straight on.

Part of the difficulty in spotting insights is that you really have no idea what you're looking for or what packaging it will arrive in when it comes to you. It might be one vision that lays out your new plan in one fell swoop, or it might be a series of tiny feelings which, when pieced together, provide the emotional resolution you need. Don't worry so much about the form at this point. Any insight, idea, dream, vision, or explanation will be a blessing. Just try to notice it as it flies by.

Sometimes your Winter Solstice insights will come to you through different channels. For instance, philosopher Albert Camus, quoted in *A Gift of Hope*, said, "Great ideas come into the world as gently as doves. Perhaps then, if we listen attentively, we shall hear, amid the uproar of empires and nations, a faint flutter of wings, the gentle stirrings of life and hope." This reminds you that it's important to listen to the whispers around and within you that are just barely audible in the everyday world. Being in the darkness will also help heighten your sensitivity to sound so that you can better hear these calls.

Triggers That May Open the Door

Sometimes, if conditions are right, you can ignite the sparks. This is a tricky business, however, because you must be more motivated to open yourself up to the process than to "get" an answer.

1. Turn Things Upside Down

Each year at the winter solstice, the Romans held a week-long festival called Saturnalia to celebrate world renewal. For its duration, all elements of social order were abolished. Describing this tradition in her book *The Winter Solstice*, Ellen Jackson explained that servants ate and acted like their masters without any sort of punishment, while masters took on their servants' duties and provided for their needs.

The Winter Solstice is also a great time for you to turn the tables on yourself. Instead of thinking about how miserable you are and all the terrible things that have happened to you, shift your focus a bit. Ask yourself what you've learned and gained from the traumas you've survived. What are you thankful for? How have these situations strengthened you and allowed you to shine? This shift in perspective might just open you to a whole new future. For additional ideas about how to find blessings in all that's going wrong in your life, refer to the book *No Enemies Within* described in Tools for the Journey.

By discovering gratitude in the darkness, joy in the sadness, and life in the ruins, we're given the gift of a new perspective. The moment this happens is the heart of the Winter Solstice. Paul Veninga, author of *A Gift of Hope*, quotes Marcel Proust describing it this way: "The real voyage of discovery consists not in seeking new landscapes, but in having new eyes." Create opportunities for yourself to see your life from a new perspective.

2. *Draw a Line in the Sand*

Although you can't claim completion of an experience prematurely, there often comes a time when you have to just let go of all the wrongs and hurts you've suffered in a situation. By consciously saying "Enough is enough!", you're giving notice to the universe that you're ready for a new reality—a new way to define your existence. In the process of laying down your claim, you consciously divorce yourself from all the baggage that's been weighing you down and keeping you stuck. As you make this shift internally, it's important to realize that your circumstances in the outer world may not change one iota. Over time, however, you'll see the ramifications of this shift throughout your life.

Be conscious about the way you complete your old role and situation, however. As Richard Heinburg, author of *Celebrate the Solstice,* writes, "the health of a nascent cycle is largely conditioned by the way in which the previous cycle was released: whether gently or violently; with compassion or animosity; with courage or with fear." If you're really ready to complete the cycle or pattern that has been running your life for months or even years, do what you can to establish closure and release the situation with grace in your heart. That sense of grace will be the energy that blesses the conception of your next situation.

There are many ways to mark the completion of a relationship, situation, or time in your life. You can:

- Cleanse your space using sage and prayers.
- Write a letter of gratitude and completion to the person who is leaving your life.
- Take a bath in Epson salts.
- Write a list of all the attitudes, behaviors, ideas, and relationships you're ready to release, and then burn it.
- Change to a new journal.
- Draw a line in the sand or dirt, say an intentional prayer, and step over the line.

Winter Solstice:
Catching
Sparks of Hope
in the
Darkness

125

As theologian and mystic Meister Eckhart wrote, "Only those who dare to let go, dare to reenter."

3. Tell a New Story

Passionist priest Thomas Berry says, "It's all a question of story. We are in trouble just now because we don't have a good story. We are in between stories. The old story, the account of how the world came to be and how we fit into it, is no longer effective. Yet we have not learned a new story." Though Berry is talking about how a culture revitalizes itself, these words have great relevance to individual revitalization, too.

As we've seen, one of the fastest ways to create a new understanding of your future is to repicture your past. Seeing your past from a new perspective allows you to discover doors to your future you didn't even know existed.

As you prepare to tell your story, don't just hit the play button and repeat the same litany you've been spouting since the change took place. Now is the moment to stretch beyond that picture. Think about all you've learned on your journey. In her book *Mythmaking*, Patricia Montgomery outlines a series of exercises you can complete to create a myth which tells the essence of your life and your healing. (If you'd like to explore this method, see Tools for the Journey.)

If you listen, you may catch threads of your new story as you meet people who don't know your history. If you're still giving the blow-by-blow account of your divorce, a loved one's death, or your car accident, you aren't yet ready to let go of your story; it still defines you. When you forget to tell your same old story or tell it in a sentence or two, that is a great sign that your story is changing. In the act of stepping away from defining yourself by your change, you are creating a new foundation from which to define yourself as you are now.

When you're ready, give yourself the opportunity to tell your new story. Write it down, make a tape recording of it, invite a circle of friends to listen to you tell it. It really doesn't matter what the forum is as long as you speak your truth—your new truth.

What If Nothing's Happening?

We might think that after the King married the Handless Maiden, they lived happily ever after. But in the tale, that is not to be just yet.

> *In time, the King was called to war, so he asked his mother to care for the Handless Maiden, who was now his cherished Queen. His parting comment was, "If she gives birth to a child, send me a message right away." Soon after, the young Queen did give birth to a beautiful baby, and the Queen Mother sent the news to the King.*
>
> *On his way to see the King, the messenger felt terribly tired so he sat down by the river's edge and fell fast asleep. Coming out from behind a tree, the Devil quietly approached him, reached into the messenger's pouch, and replaced the original note with one telling the King that the Queen had given birth to a creature that was part child and part dog.*
>
> *Of course, the King was distraught on receiving this news and sent a return message asking the Queen Mother to love the Queen and care for her during this trying time. Again, just as the messenger reached the river, he found he was tired again and sat down for a quick nap. This time, the Devil changed the message to read, "Kill the Queen and her child."*
>
> *The Queen Mother was very upset with the request so she sent another message to the King to confirm his instructions. Each time the Devil switched the messages, they became more and more disgusting. The last message the Queen Mother received asked her to keep the tongue and eyes of the Queen to prove she'd been killed.*

The Queen Mother couldn't bring herself to carry out the order, so she sacrificed a doe, keeping the eyes and tongue to show the King upon his return. Then she did what she felt she had to. She helped the young Queen prepare for yet another journey by binding her baby to her breast and veiling her. They both knew without speaking of it that the Queen had to flee for her life. As the Handless Maiden set out once again, both women wept their good-byes.

Since the moment the Handless Maiden left her father's house and entered the forest, there have been a number of signs to suggest that a Winter Solstice insight might be just around the corner: the Handless Maiden's connection with the Spirit in White, her eating of the pear from the Tree of Life, her meeting with the Gardener, King, and Magician, who represent all the aspects of her psyche, and the birth of a child who represents new perspectives and new life. But in this part of the story all hell breaks loose, thanks to the Devil and his conniving ways.

Let's take a deeper look at this chaos to see why the conditions aren't leading to the Winter Solstice event we expected. When we look back at the King's proposal and marriage to the Handless Maiden, we first notice that she didn't have any response whatsoever. Furthermore, the union occurred so soon after she started her journey that she hadn't had a chance to complete her transition journey and come to a new place within herself. In essence, the Maiden exchanged the palace and life her father offered with the castle and life promised by the King—a clear indication that she'd jumped on the Spin Cycle and avoided the process of Winter.

According to Robert Moor and Douglass Gillette, authors of *King, Warrior, Magician, and Lover*, the King of the underworld represents the part of us that takes our inner knowing back out into the world. All well and good—but before the King can do his part, some inner knowing must occur within the Handless Maiden. From all of this, we can conclude that their union occurred a bit prematurely. Lo and behold, the King departs for war in the very next scene. So, once again, the Queen is given the opportunity to rely on herself and the wise one within her (the Queen Mother) to nurture her new insights (the child).

In general, pregnancy and birth are wonderful signs of new growth, perspective, and hope. But in this case, we know something is wrong because the birth of the baby brings the Devil back into the picture. Once again, the Queen is in a vulnerable place and the Devil, an unresolved past issue, raises its ugly head, causing as much confusion and upset this time as the last. This tells us the Queen has unfinished business that is keeping her from living a happy, healthy life in her changed circumstances. If we see the Devil as an aspect of the Queen, we realize that a part of her doesn't want to change and experience new life.

Another clue that something's amiss is the fact that the messenger who relays information from the Queen Mother in the underworld to the King in the real world keeps falling asleep. Sometimes after we get our first new idea (baby), we let down our defenses, thinking we've got it made. Actually, this is the worst time to fall asleep on the job because you're bound to miss key insights and opportunities to move forward.

The Queen Mother is the saving grace in this passage. Unlike the Handless Maiden's father, she finds a way to get around the Devil's demands. By refusing to buy into the torture, she enables the Queen to get back to the business at hand—her journey through the underworld.

As you look at your own situation, you may realize that the "Devil" is wreaking havoc again in your life as well. You may notice, for instance, that no matter how much processing, reflecting, and thinking you do, you keep ending up face-to-face with the same old issues. This is a hard time. There is nothing more frustrating than finding yourself swirling in circles in the depths of Winter. Several things can contribute to this scenario. Take a look at whether any of these are true for you:

- You haven't been able to devote much time to quiet reflection. Perhaps you need to find a way to cut back your schedule and take some time off—preferably before you have to take a stress leave or find yourself in the hospital. Or perhaps you do have the time, but are avoiding the reflection process because you're afraid of what you'll find.

- You're in a toxic environment and have to spend most of your time poised to defend yourself. As a result, you have little or no time or energy to devote to healing.

Every single time Tanya walked into her home, she was attacked—verbally, and occasionally physically by her unemployed, alcoholic mother. When she got to work, her boss harped on her constantly for her attitude and tardiness. To protect herself from the toxicity of her life, Tanya had developed a very strong defense system that was nearly always engaged. Her sarcasm, sour humor, and resigned helplessness told me she was stuck. Nothing could really change until Tanya found a way to create an oasis where she felt safe enough to be with herself. By making some changes at home, creating a relationship with a therapist, and taking time away, she's beginning to create a new life for herself.

- You're afraid of what will happen if you change. Perhaps you feel that your new life will replace the one you have and you're just not ready to give up everything yet. Perhaps the piece you're trying to let go of provides you with the only bit of identity you have left. Or perhaps you fear that if you begin to unravel one situation, your entire life will fall apart. For right now, staying where you are feels safer than any other option.

- You're so entrenched in one way of looking at your situation that you can't surrender to the fact that the answers may come from an entirely different angle. I call this "the chicken or the egg" problem. Typically, the goal people in this place think they must achieve is actually an inevitable outcome of the process of healing. What they have a difficult time believing is that they need to let go of the outcome they've been striving for and find new ways to handle what is actually standing between them and what they want.

Let me give you a few examples so you can see the dynamics of this situation. When Matthew came to work with me, he was certain the right career would turn his life around and resolve the intense anxiety he was feeling. After working together a few weeks, it became clear to me that his anxiety was so pervasive it would continue to run his life no matter what job he had. To improve his life, Matthew needed to uncover the core cause of his anxiety and learn specific ways to handle it. Only then would we be able to find a career that would suit him.

Kara believed the only way to enhance her life was to have a job that brought in enough money so that she could move out of her parents' house. Unfortunately, her home life was so draining, she didn't have any energy to take the steps necessary to get a new job. She needed to find a way to create a better living environment at home or somewhere else before she could value herself enough to land a higher-paying job.

Joanne had been working very diligently to complete her college degree. Over the years, despite all her hard work, she kept losing her focus. Although she received several suggestions to investigate Attention Deficit Disorder, she felt she couldn't divert her attention to look into it until she graduated. In reality, however, learning more about her personal style may have saved her time in the long run.

If you find yourself beating your head against the same wall over and over again, it's time to acknowledge that the door to your future lies somewhere else. There's a common saying to keep in mind in these situations: "If you keep doing what you've been doing, you'll keep getting what you've been getting." If you're stalled in Winter, you probably won't be able to make significant progress until you look outside yourself for help. I strongly encourage you to find healing professionals who can assist you in identifying and unlocking long-standing patterns that are keeping you stuck.

If, however, you're beginning to experience the insights of the Solstice, congratulations—you're on your way up and out of the depths of Winter!

Seven

Late Winter:
Defining Your Vision

Signs:	Tasks:	Detours:
Catch New Insights	Follow Your Insights	Ignoring Insights
Open to New Ideas	Clear Out the Old	Doing What You Have Always Done
See Glimmers of Spring	Create a Plan	Charging Ahead

After leaving the castle, the still handless Queen wandered with her baby bound to her breast until she came upon the densest forest she'd ever seen. Although she couldn't find the path others had used before her, she knew she needed to enter the forest. Since she remembered what it was like to be in the forest, she proceeded with-out fear, putting one foot in front of the other, completing the jour-ney she'd started when she left her father's house.

Near nightfall, the Spirit in White appeared again and showed her the way to a humble inn. A shield hung above its door that read, "Here all dwell free." Another maiden, also in white, called the Queen by name and showed her to her room. After getting her child settled, the Queen asked the Maiden in White, "How did you know my name?" The maiden replied, "We who are of the forest follow these matters, my Queen. Rest now."

Just like the Queen, you're continuing your journey through the last part of Winter. Although it's tempting to think your new insights mean you've moved out of Winter and into Spring, it's important to remember that the time between the winter solstice and Imbolg (February 2) is still cold, stormy, and desolate. Yes, the sparks you experienced mean something is brewing. But, as the conditions are still too harsh for you and your dreams to flourish out in the world, your best plan is to focus on exploring your insights. As the *Fu* hexagram indicates: "In the Winter the life energy . . . is still underground. Movement is just at its beginning." Give yourself time in the forest to allow your ideas to grow so that by the time Spring arrives, you *will* be ready to blossom.

How Can I Tell I'm in Late Winter?

1. You Continue to Catch New Insights

Although you've passed the Winter Solstice point on the transition spiral, each day continues to bring the promise of more insights about your past and more clarity regarding your future. At this point, there's no such thing as too many new ideas. Just keep 'em coming. Let yourself be open to as many new angles as possible. Because your intuition and reflective skills have been honed, you'll find yourself catching subtle insights you would have missed just a short time ago. Suddenly everything around you is rich with meaning and symbolism.

2. You Are Open to New Ideas

Because you've shifted your view of your situation, you're now open to exploring ideas you probably would have ignored or avoided before. When I first started working with Matthew on his extreme anxiety, I asked him questions about how his childhood had affected him. Although he'd spent most of his early life in and out of hospitals for a series of life-threatening illnesses, he told me his experiences were normal to him, so they hadn't impacted him in any way. It was quite clear he didn't see any reason to discuss it further.

About two months later, I read a newspaper article that made me pursue my original line of questioning. This time Matthew had experienced enough shifts to see that his extensive hospitalization had, in fact, caused him a tremendous amount of trauma and distress. Through our conversations, we were able to pinpoint the source of the anxiety that had haunted him for years.

3. You See Glimmers of Spring

As you proceed through Late Winter, you also begin to see signs of the future. As with nature's seasons, these signs of Spring will at first be so subtle you may not notice them at all. Begin by training yourself to spot what's different in your thoughts, behaviors, dreams, and conversations. You may notice, for instance, that you're handling difficult situations in new ways, saying things you've never said before, craving new adventures, or wearing an entirely new style of clothing. These encouraging signs of progress will brighten your life as you move through the last stages of Winter.

From the little we know about the Queen and her journey, we can see several signs that tell us something's new: she's not as afraid to enter the unknown as she was in the past. This time she's guided to an old inn run by women of the forest with a sign above it that says "Here all dwell free." From these descriptions, we immediately sense the Queen is going to be nurtured this time as she connects with the wisdom of the earth—a far cry from being ensconced in a castle filled with servants or wandering hungry and alone in the forest. The Queen's actions are different here, as well. Instead of allowing herself to be whisked off to start something new, the Queen listens as the Maiden in White encourages her to rest for a while. This is a good sign because it tells us the Queen is ready to stop her Spin Cycle and be in Winter.

My client Jill, who was in recovery, began noticing signs of Spring after just a few sessions, when she uncharacteristically spoke up for herself in meetings, initiated conversations to clear up misunderstandings with her boyfriend, and negotiated win-win solutions with her roommate. Each time she caught sight of her new behaviors, she was reassured that Spring really was on its way. These successes gave her hope as she continued to handle the more difficult issues brought to the forefront by her recovery.

What Should I Do Now?

1. Follow Your Insights

Just before I started writing this section, I closed my eyes for a short nap, wondering how I was going to explain the concept of following your insights. Almost immediately, an image of a birthday party I gave my younger brother when he was seven and I was ten popped into my mind. When I woke up, I couldn't figure out how that party, which I hadn't thought about in years, had anything to do with my book. Still, I decided to take my own advice and follow my insight. Please join me on this journey.

My friend Laura and I spent hours designing, creating, and placing the props for this party. The main attraction was a maze of thread we'd strung so that each partygoer could follow his own colored thread to reach a prize chosen especially for him. These threads crisscrossed the backyard between tree branches, around patio furniture, and under bushes to create an enormous spider web. Looking at the game for the first time, the kids were both overwhelmed by the complexity and excited by the opportunity to discover their prize. Ah, that was it! The web was a metaphor for following insights!

The next time you get an insight, imagine there's a thread attached to it. If you follow the thread as it moves around and through your life, you'll eventually find yourself looking at the answer. If you set it down or break it by moving too fast, however, you'll lose an opportunity to reach a key destination. Take your time. Notice who you might meet as you unravel your maze and others unravel theirs. Remember, you'll be making progress as long as you're following through on your insights and taking the actions indicated to you.

Sometimes we hesitate to follow our insights because they seem strange or off the mark. Imagine what must have been going through the Queen's mind as she entered the forest once more—this time with a baby strapped to her chest and silver hands that looked nice but weren't very functional. What was she doing scrambling through the under-brush again? What would have happened if she'd been frightened by the forest or the lack of a trail? Although it was no doubt a bit unsettling not to find a path, she somehow knew that she needed to enter the for-est. As is true with so many insights, her idea to wander in the forest was not the final answer, but by taking those steps on faith, she met the Spirit in White who showed her to ultimate destination. Just like the Queen, your job is to take that next step and trust that the rest will unfold as a result.

One of the best ways to follow your insights is to use the reflection methods you learned in Early Winter. Think of yourself as a treasure hunter pulling together clues to lead you to your future. When Lilly was beginning to look for a sales job in a new industry, she decided to start by visiting several stores that sold products she enjoyed. When she made the first stop on her tour, she thought she was just going to look at products. Imagine how happy she was when she left the store with con-tact names, the inside scoop about several companies, and a couple of job leads. As you begin exploring the right path, the next steps will gen-erally reveal themselves with very little effort on your part.

Once you have new leads, your next step is to explore the ones that strike a chord in you. Depending on your situation, taking action might mean talking to contacts, reading up on the topic, or visiting a place of relevance. Remember that your focus during this phase is just to gather enough information to pull together a cohesive picture of your direc-tion. This is not the time to plow ahead and implement your plan com-pletely—there will be plenty of time for that later.

Here are four more reflective methods you can use to deepen your experience of Late Winter.

The World as a Messenger

By now you're probably noticing you get flashes of insight just by observing your interactions, what you say, how you think, and what you do. In addition, seemingly unrelated events are beginning to speak to you as well. Congratulations, you've graduated to the next level of reflection. Now, instead of needing to be alone in the quiet to make connections, you're able to see the links in the midst of your daily activities. As with most skills, the more you use this ability, the more powerful it will become.

Let me give you some guidelines on how to see the world as a messenger rather than just a series of random events. As you walk in your neighborhood or in a park, observe the natural world. Notice what scenes or elements attract your attention—either the same images appear repeatedly or something is so striking to you that it won't leave your thoughts. Trust your mind to take you to the images that have something to teach you.

I know you may think this silly. How can nature give us an insight? In a workshop I led some time ago, I took all the participants on a walk near my office. There was nothing special about the neighborhood, really; it was just houses with gardens. At my instruction, everyone walked in silence, focusing on their surroundings for twenty minutes. When we regrouped, I was amazed to find that each person remembered something completely different. One woman who'd been through a tremendous number of abrupt and drastic changes throughout her life saw only winter images: bare trees, broken limbs, dead patches of grass. The person who walked right next to her saw daffodils and new grass shoots coming up through the soil. This exercise was a dramatic example of how our minds filter what we see to give us images that are consistent with our perspective.

Once you identify an image, go through the same four-step process you follow when you're using an object as a catalyst for creativity. Describe the characteristics of the image, choose the element that speaks to you the most, free associate with that element, and apply what you come up with to your life. If you want, you can also look at all the images to see what themes appear.

Another way your world can send you messages is through unusual, unexplained events. Native people all over the globe take such events to heart by meditating on them in order to understand their meaning. To some of us, such events might look like pure coincidence—and they may be—but they can also hold a tremendous amount of meaning for the conscious observer.

An event that sticks in my mind occurred one May afternoon. I'd just returned from a long dentist appointment. All of a sudden the phone rang, and at the same time I heard a very loud thump and saw white feathers flying just outside the sliding door. It took me a long moment to realize that a bird had hit my window. Finally I saw it, a mourning dove huddled on the ground, breathing rather hard. Then something else caught my eye. Sitting on a telephone pole at the back of my lot was a hawk! I was stunned. I'd never seen a hawk in my suburban neighborhood before. About ten minutes later, the hawk flew away, and I went out to sit with the dove, which was no longer breathing but was still warm to the touch. As I cleaned up, I tried to reconstruct what had happened. I guessed that the hawk had been in pursuit and the dove, hoping to escape, mistakenly flew into the reflection of the sky in my window at full speed.

For weeks, I was haunted by the images and sounds of this event, so I spent some time trying to decipher its message for me. By thinking about the circumstances, reading about hawks, their capabilities, and metaphysical meaning, thinking about the characteristics of the mourning dove, and talking with various friends, I ended up with four possible messages:

- It was time to release the part of me that was mourning (the dove's death), to stop rehashing old issues, and to begin to go after "live" opportunities (hawk).
- It was time to take action and pursue my goals with focus (the hawk's pursuit).
- It was time to take a step back from my goals and look more strategically at the big picture of my life and business (the hawk's keen eyesight).
- It was time for my "masculine" nature (the hawk) to become stronger than my "feminine" nature (the dove).

As you can see, I looked to see how each element in the scenario represented a part of *me*. It took strength to be present with myself during the interpretation process because I saw some things I didn't want to see and was asked to step into several new roles that weren't, at that time, all that comfortable for me.

My friends offered their own interpretations when they heard the story. After hearing them out, I took the pieces I resonated with and let the rest go. As you interpret events, ask for insight from others, but always trust your own knowing for your ultimate explanation.

Unexpected events can occur in any form, not just in nature. For instance:

- A chance meeting with someone you haven't seen in a long time or with someone you've never met before;
- An accident or near-miss;
- A mystical experience in which you see, hear, or feel something you've never known before;
- A vivid dream;
- A pain or illness;
- An emerging opportunity that is in alignment with your new insights.

No matter how the messages appear, your responsibility is to be awake enough to catch them, to ponder the meaning of each event, and to decide how to apply what you've learned. If something difficult has occurred, such as an accident or an illness, look for possible points of significance and learn from it, but don't take 100 percent of the responsibility for the event. That degree of blame and guilt is unjustified and will consume you in the long run.

Once you begin to experience the world this way, there's no going back. In fact, when you do look back, you may wonder how you survived without it. Being able to read the world in this way brings a richness to life that's inspiring and hopeful. There are several books in Tools for the Journey that can show you how to use your body, your home, and your life experience as messengers.

Other People as Mirrors

Gaining clues from our interactions with the people around us is another valuable tool for insight, once you get used to the concept. Let me start by giving you an example.

As Janet told me about several interactions she'd already had with her new boss, she became very upset, sarcastic, and hurt. As I listened to her rant and rave, I realized that she was overreacting; the circumstances were just not extreme enough to be eliciting that degree of response. I asked Janet what got on her nerves most when she was with the manager. She immediately said, "She's so critical and hard on me. I can't do anything right." I then asked her, purposely using the same words, "Are you critical or hard on anyone in your life?" She denied this immediately, so I asked, "Are you critical or hard on yourself?" Of course! By looking at the elements of the situation that had so much emotional pull, Janet was able to see that she was overreacting because she was recognizing in someone else what she needed to work on within herself.

How can you learn to recognize when people are serving as mirrors of your own life? The first step is to notice when your reactions are way out of proportion to the original incident. Whenever you think of the situation, do you raise your voice, feel your heart pound, obsess over every little detail, or cry uncontrollably? These are usually overreactions. When you realize you're being overly emotional, take a deep breath and ask yourself:

- What is it that's really bugging me about this person?" Perhaps it's a tone of voice, an attitude, or a behavior. Distill it until you identify your main grievance.

- What issues does this person need to deal with?" Of course, any time we get overly invested in how someone else is or isn't dealing with an issue, we owe it to ourselves and them to look at why we're so hooked in. Usually, our interpretation is a projection of our own issues. For instance, if you think your spouse isn't taking responsibility, look at how you're handling responsibility in your life. If your friend is dealing with issues of trust and you're emotionally invested in her process, look within to see how these issues are playing out for you.

- How might I be doing that to other people?" Just explore this idea. You may do it in a slightly different way, in a different setting, or not at all. You may also want to see if you're doing the flip side of the issue. If you think someone else is taking too little responsibility, are you taking too much? If you really can't see any connections, you might ask a trusted friend what he or she sees.

- How do I do this to myself?" Sometimes what we hate the most in others is exactly what we do to ourselves. The other person is just acting as a mirror so we can see our own tendencies. As you learn to be with yourself differently, you'll begin to attract fewer people who trigger that outdated response in you.

Sometimes a person we're drawn to, startled by, or envious of can mirror a part of us that we're capable of but haven't yet fully developed. For instance, when the Queen was startled when the Maiden in White knew who she was, we get the impression that the Maiden in White actually knew even more than she was letting on. If we look at this as a mirroring of the Queen, we understand that the Queen has the potential to know herself much more deeply than she ever has. In fact, she may know more right now than she's even aware of.

Although it takes a while to learn how to see the ways others are mirroring us, it's a powerful way to understand the dynamics of any heated interaction whether in the workplace, a relationship, on the freeway, or in the checkout line at the grocery store.

Seeing Old Patterns

Identifying old patterns is another second-level reflection skill. In this case, your goal is to notice how your current situation is similar to other events that have occurred in your life. Certainly the Queen in our tale has a few old patterns she's wrestling with: the Devil who surfaces at the least opportune times; the men who attempt to rescue and protect her, thereby delaying her true healing; her family's tendency to jump into solutions without thinking them through. The Queen is still wrestling with these issues because she hasn't yet come to terms with the patterns that have been such a defining part of her life.

As you look at your life you may see, as Janet did, that the issues you're dealing with as an adult are the ramifications of unaddressed and unhealed wounds from your past. Janet quickly realized that part of her response to her manager was due to the fact that her new boss was intimidating and giving her mixed signals. This was very similar to how her mother and a former boss interacted with her. By working with this boss, Janet's getting a chance to try out new attitudes and behaviors that will eventually allow her to create healthier relationships with her mother and other authority figures. Although it's scary to be in this situation, as Janet heals these wounds from her childhood, she'll be able to move forward with her life.

As you wrestle with your current situation, notice what you're feeling. When have you felt this way before? What were the circumstances in that instance? Try to recall as much as you can. If several situations come to mind, it's time to acknowledge that the situation may represent a long-running pattern. Ask yourself these questions:

- What role do I play?
- How do I act?
- What was I thinking about then?
- Why do I do what I did?
- Who do the other people in this situation remind me of?
- Has anyone else treated me in this way or made me feel like this?

As you think over your answers, notice if there are any similarities between then and now. Is the current situation essentially a replay of the past? Usually the events that stick in your mind and cause you to feel angry or sad carry significance for your healing. The key to moving forward will be to go back to the initial instance, possibly with the help of a hypnotherapist or therapist, and heal that wound.

If your memory isn't bringing anything to the surface, you might ask family members or childhood friends what they remember. Sometimes we repress painful memories because we aren't yet ready to handle them. As you develop your intuitive skills, your ability to work with your emotions, and your support system, memories you've been suppressing may bubble to the surface to be healed. At first, you may feel as though you're going backward—all of a sudden you're having flashbacks and experiencing tremendous emotional swings. You may fear that this disintegration process will continue until there's absolutely nothing left of you. In actuality, you must temporarily "fall apart" in order to reintegrate in a whole, healthy way—the seed must crack open so that the plant can sprout.

Even though you may not consciously remember the events that have created a long-standing pattern in your life, they have been affecting you by clouding and distorting your beliefs about yourself, your philosophy about how the world works, your fears, your actions, and your emotions.

Let me give you an analogy. For many years, you seemed like a mountain—very strong and capable of living your life in a straightforward, "normal" way. Then one day, you and those around you began to notice steam rising from the mountaintop. Although it was somewhat startling, the steam seemed to disappear before you could investigate it further, and you continued living life as before. Sooner or later though, the steam reappeared and lingered. By the time the steam started coming out in puffs, it became clear to those around you that something was definitely brewing. They became worried and started asking, "What's she holding inside?" Then one day, lava shot up. Not a lot, but enough to emit a warning that *this* mountain was not an ordinary mountain. It was a volcano that could blow, without warning, at any time, with devastating results.

People often wish they could cap the volcano and keep everything the way it's always been. They find ingenious ways to rationalize why their outbursts and periods of acting out aren't really that bad. In fact, these incidents seem much easier to handle than the possibility of having the whole thing blow open.

Let's pretend for a moment that it is possible to cap the volcano. In the short term, life would indeed continue on as it has. But, all the while, the steam would be building up inside until there was so much pressure the volcano could only violently erupt.

With this in mind, it's clear that capping the volcano is really not a viable option. The only long-term solution is one that allows you to let off steam by releasing internal pressures and cooling off. To do this, you need support in healing and releasing the past memories which have fed the internal fires for so long.

If you're just beginning your healing process, you're bound to have some kind of volcanic activity brewing within you. Whether it's the result of abuse, other serious traumas, or a series of fairly mundane childhood experiences that set you up in a particular pattern, your volcano deserves attention. Allow the inner fires to fade and the solid rock of your own essence to strengthen, and you'll be amazed at the feeling of lightness and joy that fills you.

Watching Your Words

Other clues to the state of your unconscious are the language, metaphors, and exclamations that you use. Because your unconscious is so literal, it takes all that you say, even jokes, casual complaints, sarcasm, and empty threats, as its reality. As Leo Buscaglia, author of *Love*, writes, "For the words you use will tell you what you are, what you have seen, what you have learned, and how you have learned it. For you are your words." Think about how each of these statements, which I've actually heard in my practice, have influenced my clients:

- "My job is such a pain in the neck."
- "I need a break."
- "When I come up for air, I'll do that."
- "I won't leave this job. They'll have to put me in a body bag first."
- "We're on a death march. I've got to keep going."
- "I'm so sick and tired of _____."

As you become more sensitive to the subtleties of your surroundings, you'll become more attuned to what the words you say mean to your well-being. Really listen to what you say. When you catch yourself saying something you don't want your unconscious to get hold of, say "Cancel." Create new sayings to replace the phrases you commonly use.

Clearing up your language will help you become more optimistic and hopeful.

Just for the record, I'll give you a little background on the people who said the phrases above:

- This person spends a great deal of time with a chiropractor.
- This woman broke her ankle and couldn't work for months. What she really wanted was a vacation!
- After months of using this phrase to explain why he had to work all the time, this man contracted a case of pneumonia that worsened with various lung-related complications.
- Although this woman loved her job, it was keeping her stuck. So stuck, in fact, that it took a life-threatening allergic reaction to the material she worked with on a daily basis to get her to release her hold.
- This Silicon Valley employee was on call twenty-four hours a day for months during the final countdown for the rollout of a new product. Unfortunately, the "death march" was taking its toll: signs of burnout were overwhelmingly evident.
- I finally caught myself saying this phrase after I'd been sick for months. You can bet I quickly eradicated it from my repertoire of complaints!

2. Clear Out the Old

Now that you're clearer about your new direction, items and ideas that are inconsistent with your future may become unbearable to you. Clothing, furniture, and decorations that don't fit your newfound style may begin to feel so oppressive that you'll have to clear out your nest. To do this well, ask yourself "Do I need this?" "Will I ever use this again?" and "Does this fit me anymore?" I'll bet you'll end up getting rid of things you've had for years. Although cleaning may feel a bit off-track at first, you'll find that the details of your new life can't and won't fall into place until you clear out the old and open up space for new, more relevant elements to enter your life.

This clearing-out process is very common during the latter stages of Winter. After starting the detoxification part of her health program, June found herself not only cleansing her body, but also, unexpectedly, clearing out her home. She rearranged one room, discarded old, heavy furniture that had ties to her past, purchased new furniture that was consistent with her emerging style, and started painting the interior of her home.

A key to working with clutter is to notice where it accumulates. According to *feng shui,* the ancient Chinese art of spatial harmony, each area of your home represents a different area of your life—career, family / past, wealth, fame, relationships, health, children / future, and the like. By noting where stuff seems to pile up, you can gain information about what part of your life is congested. I've been truly amazed at how useful this method is in highlighting issues that are up for me. When I find myself unexpectedly reorganizing or redecorating a certain area of my home, often in the early-morning hours, I laugh when I realize that the area I'm obsessing over points directly to the area of my life that needs my attention. According to this system, making adjustments in your home will actually begin to shift the energy in the corresponding area of your life. Even if you don't want to become an expert in this elaborate system, you might be interested in the books listed in Tools for the Journey that describe various ways you can use your home as a mirror of your life.

During this phase of Winter, you may also find yourself letting go of relationships that are no longer fulfilling, professional affiliations that aren't in alignment with who you are anymore, volunteer roles that aren't a good use of your time and talents, and family traditions that feel stale and outdated. Although this may feel like one more round of losses, think of it as clearing the decks so there is more room in your life for new friends, organizations, and traditions that will bring you energy and joy.

3. Create a Plan

Now that you've begun the healing process and have discovered new ideas and interests, it's time to pull everything together into a plan that will define your new destination. It's here that we begin to ask ourselves how we can take a profoundly personal idea and allow it to blossom into a form that will nurture us and those around us.

Your first step in creating your future is to think about or write down everything you now know about your situation. Even if you've done this before, try it again—your Winter Solstice experiences may have changed your outlook. Although the exact method you use to create your plan will depend on your unique situation, let me offer some questions to stimulate your thinking:

- What do I know for sure?
- What more do I need to find out before I can proceed?
- What are my options?
- What are the pros and cons associated with each option I'm considering?
- What option best matches my personal style?
- If the best option will not work, what tradeoffs am I willing to make?
- What steps can I take to move from where I am to where I want to be?
- Do I need any help in carrying out my plan?

Ask yourself these questions several times in different ways to make sure you're looking at your situation from more than one perspective. Then sit with your plan for a day or so. When you return to it, ask yourself:

- Is there any piece of the plan that pulls at me or causes me to worry?
- What's the basis of my worry?
- Is my worry realistic?

Careful here. Sometimes our worries seem realistic because we've lived with fear and scarcity for so long.

Worries generally have two sources. Something in your plan may, in fact, be off the mark in some way and needs adjustment. Think about what you might modify to ease your concerns. You may have forgotten to factor in a key variable, or you may not have had all the information you needed when you put the plan together. After you make the changes, these worries will disappear. Other concerns may have been reasonable in a different time and place in your life, but they're now out of sync. It takes some careful discernment and comments from trusted friends to be able to categorize your concerns correctly.

Let me give you an example that illustrates both kinds of worries. When I first heard about a three-week tour of the sacred sites of Egypt, I sat on the fence for a good long month, battling all sorts of fanciful demons. When I finally decided to go, I realized I had to work through a whole laundry list of worries before I could really feel excited about the trip.

As I looked at my fears, it became clear that part of the problem was that I knew nothing about Egypt. By watching a travel video, reading several books, and talking with a few people who'd been to Egypt, I was able to put some of my concerns to rest. I learned, for instance, more about what I needed to take with me to handle the possible effects of jet lag, extreme heat, "Pharaoh's revenge," and hunger between meals.

By easing those practical concerns, I came face-to-face with another source of anxiety, which was two-pronged: I was afraid to leave my home and dog for an extended period of time, for fear something would happen to them while I was away; and I had some trepidation about my physical safety. As I explored these fears with several trusted friends, it became clear that this venture into the unknown was awakening feelings that had lurked under the surface all of my life. As I continued to look into them, I began to see that these fears weren't based so much on my own experiences but had become part of my conditioning, passed along from generation to generation through my father's family.

By working through my fears before I left, I was able to travel through Egypt without worrying about my home, my pet, or my personal safety. This was a huge accomplishment, given the magnitude of fear I'd lived in and around all my life.

If your fears are interfering with your ability to plan your future, imagine how they can sabotage your progress when you begin implementing your plans. Make the effort to take care of your fears now, so that when you're ready to put your plan into action, you'll be free to spring ahead!

Now that you've reviewed your ideas and cleared away your concerns, it's time to pull your plan together in a more organized way. You
can write a complete plan, spell it out in an outline, or use a treasure
map or collage to illustrate your plan in colorful pictures and words. I
have three treasure maps, and it's amazing how many positive things I
can trace back to those collages.

Treasure-mapping can help you in two ways. At a very practical
level, the process allows you to define your goals, focus your energies,
and remind you of your vision on a regular basis. It also has a more esoteric impact, as well. Because your unconscious takes everything literally, seeing a vivid display of what you want helps your unconscious
believe that it's already part of your reality. As this shift takes place,
you'll become more and more aware of new opportunities to achieve
your goals.

Sometimes treasure map success stories are incredible. In one treasure-mapping class I attended, the instructor related what happened
when she put a picture of Tom Selleck on her treasure map. She was
living in Hawaii at the time and within a short time of completing her
map, Tom Selleck had a casting call for several youngsters to be part of
the cast for a *Magnum, P.I.* show. Believably, her daughters got the
parts!

In the years Serena had owned her own business, she'd had a difficult time reaching her financial goal. Her financial treasure map con-
sisted of several sections, including enhancing her knowledge about
the financial world, investing in socially responsible companies, marketing her business, increasing net profits, and aligning her spending
habits with her values. In the area relating to her income, she put the
following phrase: "Make $1,000 or more a week, $4,000 to $10,000 per
month." She had no idea how she was going to reach her goal—in fact,
she didn't even know if it was possible—but she decided to trust the
process. The month after she completed the treasure map, she grossed
$4,500—more that she'd ever made in a month.

Before you begin your map, define its scope. Is it about a particular
aspect of your life, such as your career, health, relationship, or
finances? Or do you want to focus on something you'd like to manifest

or create, such as a new home, a vacation, more balance in your life, or an enhanced sense of self-esteem or body image? Be clear about your focus, whether it's fairly broad or very defined. If your goal seems "way out there," you might want to focus your treasure map on an interim step. For instance, say you want to get married, but you aren't presently dating and you have little or no social life. Focus your first treasure map on a feasible next step—expanding your social circle and dating. Once you've built that part of your life, then you can create a map to highlight a committed relationship.

With your goal in mind, look through old magazines, newspapers, and calendars to gather brightly colored pictures and bold, easy-to-read words. These should capture the essence of your idea in a way that is so pleasing to your eye that your attention is naturally drawn to it. Just the process of choosing some words and eliminating others will help strengthen your vision. As you begin to see clusters and patterns, you may want to set your collection out on a cardboard backing to get a sense of the overall collage and what you're missing.

If you use images of people on your treasure map, be sure to choose pictures that emanate the feelings and essence you want in your life. Remember, the unconscious is very literal, so if you don't want to smoke, don't include a person smoking cigarettes in your map. Furthermore, if you don't want to manifest the models you've got on your board, cover the faces of the models with snapshots of you (seeing your own face in the picture will help your unconscious get the idea that you're living your success) or cover the eyes of the models with words that add to the overall scenario you want to create in your life. I know this sounds strange, but it really does work.

Once you have your collage laid out, make sure everything is stated in the present tense, even if you don't yet have that element in your life yet. Look carefully; a friend of mine once put on her map that she desired a relationship. For the next year that's exactly what she had— the desire for one, but no relationship. I once put that I wanted to develop business opportunities. Until I changed that phrase, I had a lot of opportunities that never turned into money-making contracts. Not quite what I had in mind.

Once you glue everything down, put your treasure map where you'll see it every day: above your computer, next to your bed, on the ceiling above your bed, or on the wall. You don't have to read it consciously—just look at it.

What Detours Should I Watch Out For?

1. Ignoring Insights

If you deny the significance of the insights you're having or avoid them altogether because they seem too odd or scary, you limit your progress. Remember that at this point you don't have to have a full understanding of your idea or see how it will eventually unfold in your life. In fact, it may help you to realize that you can't have it all figured out yet, because these insights are just the first few clues to point you in the right direction for the rest of your journey.

2. Doing What You Have Always Done

Suppose that in her wanderings the Queen had come across another castle owned by a man who wanted to rescue her and give her a good life. She would have been doing what she'd always done, and the cycle would have repeated itself.

If you fall back into old habits, you also limit your movement because you aren't yet taking full advantage of all your insights. Living your life as though you had never been through your Winter Solstice means that for some reason you're retreating from new possibilities in your life. Is it fear of the unknown? Discomfort with some aspect of your plan? Look at your hesitation to discover what's holding you back.

3. Charging Ahead

Another detour occurs when you charge ahead with only a half-formed idea. The Queen did this when she got pregnant before she was healed. I know you're ready for Spring, but jumping ahead too fast will just backfire on you. If you don't have all the information you need or a clear picture, you won't make it to Summer. Instead, you'll jump onto the Spin Cycle and head back into Winter again. Hang in there. You're almost ready to enter a true Spring. Give yourself what you need to make a significant change that will last.

Eight

Spring:
Bursting into Bloom

Signs:	Tasks:	Detours:
Bursting with Energy	Trust Your Own Timing	Making No Movement
Experience Spring Storms	Prepare the Soil and Water the Dirt	Ignoring Your Own Wisdom
Struggle with Reentry	Birth the New	
	Stretch and Grow	
	Come of Age	
	Blossom Fully	

At the inn the Handless Maiden rested. She found she enjoyed life there so much that she and her child stayed for seven years. During that time, she regained her strength and her hands began to grow back—gradually. At first, they were like the hands of a baby, then those of a little girl, and finally a woman's hands.

While this was going on, the King and the Queen Mother reunited. Understandably, the Queen Mother was quite upset with him and asked, as she showed him the eyes and tongue, "Why would you have me kill two innocents?" The King was deeply shocked and started weeping with grief. Realizing that he hadn't sent the messages after all, the Queen Mother told him that the eyes and tongue were really from a deer, and that she'd sent the Queen and child into the forest in hopes they'd be saved.

The King immediately set off to find them, vowing not to eat or drink until he reunited with his family. Somehow, with the help of a force greater than himself, he kept moving for seven long years.

At last he came to the inn. There, after a Maiden in White invited him to lie down, he entered the deepest sleep he'd ever known. As he awakened, a lovely woman with a child at her side said calmly, "I am your wife, and this is our child." The King wanted to believe her, but he protested when he saw her hands. She quickly explained, "Through my travails and my good care, my hands have grown back." As evidence, the Maiden in White brought the carefully packed silver hands out of storage to show him. At that, the King embraced his wife and child. Everyone in the forest rejoiced with them.

Ahhhh! It's finally Spring. Can you feel it? The anticipation, excitement, and activity of new beginnings. Imagine the wonder the Queen felt as her hands grew back and her joy when she reunited with her husband. The rewards are certainly plentiful for those who have made it through the darkness of Winter.

After all this preparation, it's time to put your plans into action! What area of your life will blossom as you journey through the fields of Spring? Perhaps you have a new work project or ideas about how to enliven your relationship or your social life. You may even be your own project—you may want to develop a new relationship to your body, or learn to skydive!

Right about now, you're probably coming face-to-face with our culture's typical John Wayne attitude, which says the best way to start something new is to take any risks necessary to *make* the change happen as quickly as possible. Unfortunately, this "ready, fire, aim" mentality often backfires when people jump forward before they're fully prepared to be on the road again after the long Winter.

Other folks are petrified to move forward. They've learned through past experience that taking risks is scary and leads to unexpected, sometimes devastating, outcomes. As a result, they're paralyzed by a Catch 22: they can't move forward because the risk is too big, yet they can't avoid movement because something needs to happen.

By observing Mother Nature and her continuous expansion during Spring, we can see that there is another way. In fact, if you think about it, each of us, and nearly everything around us, is a product of this beautiful birthing process. By working with rather than against this process, we can manifest our dreams and watch them grow, quite naturally, to maturity.

How Can I Tell I'm in Spring?

1. You're Bursting with Energy

The first sign of Spring is newfound energy. This is readily apparent in nature, as wildlife scurries about eating, romping, mating, preparing nests, and feeding and tending their young. Plants burst forth with new growth and showy colors. Suddenly, with the longer days, it seems nearly impossible to stay inside. All we can think about is being out and about.

It's important to realize that this new energy is not the frenetic busyness you might have felt in Winter when you were trying to avoid your confusion. Rather, it is a force that comes through you, quite naturally, without any prodding or forcing. One day, you wake up and know, for the first time in a long while, that you can easily convert your energy into action. Isn't it exhilarating to finally feel as though nothing can hold you back?

2. You Experience Spring Storms

One day big, dark, heavy clouds appear on your horizon. You're shocked at first. Then, as the rain begins to fall and you slide down into a pit of depression, you're devastated. You were so sure that this time you'd made it into Spring. So sure, in fact, that you'd already put away your tissue boxes, your comfy blanket, and your comfort foods!

Take heart. This is just a Spring storm, and the sun will be shining and brightening your world again in a day or two. Take a moment to think about how winter turns to spring in your area. Perhaps you recall beautiful, warm, sunny days suddenly being replaced by the winds, snow, and rain of an intense spring storm—yet it passes fairly quickly. If you think back over the past few years, you'll probably notice that these seemingly unanticipated bumps between winter and spring really are common.

When you feel as though you're headed into Winter again, reaffirm the progress you've made since Fall, with the help of a trusted supporter. Reassure yourself that you haven't really returned to the depths of Winter. And remember—just like weather in spring, your emotions will soon turn around.

3. You Struggle with Reentry into the World

Inherent in Spring is a paradox—part of you is thrilled to be venturing into a new period of your life, while another part is afraid to leave the comforts of your nest, the precious solitude of Winter, and the connection you've made with spirit and with yourself. This paradox often surprises people who don't expect to be afraid of something they've been wanting for so long. However, when you realize that the new "you" has never been out in the world before, I think you'll agree that it's natural to feel a bit anxious and apprehensive. As you take steps to reenter the "real" world, you may find that even the simple act of interacting with people again is overwhelming. What you're experiencing is much like the reentry on returning from a vacation or conference in which you were transported to a different reality. Give yourself a little time to adjust to the noise, the ways, and the people you've been away from.

The fact that the King and Queen don't reunite until the end of Spring gives us some additional insight as to why the reentry process is difficult. When we remember that all the characters in the story represent an aspect of ourselves, we see that just as our feeling side (the Handless Maiden) heals and is ready to move forward, our outer-world side—the part that's responsible for taking our inner knowing into the world (the King)—begins its own descent to grow strong enough to match the knowing we have within us.

Sometimes this reentry process is complicated by the fact that the change we started internally in Fall must now happen in the outer world. Becky went through this process in her marriage. During her Inner Fall, she realized her relationship was no longer fulfilling nor supporting her. As she delved into the dynamic of the relationship (Inner Early Winter), she came to the conclusion that she needed to raise the issue with her husband (Inner Late Winter). As she brought more and more of herself to her relationship by sharing her concerns (Inner Spring and Summer), both began the transition spiral again. Together they wrestled with their options (Outer Fall) and looked at their patterns and roles within the relationship (Outer Winter). Then as they took their first steps into Spring, they began to implement what they'd learned in workshops and therapy sessions. In this case, their relationship not only survived but grew as both participated in the full transition journey.

As you reenter, notice your hesitation and honor the paradox within you. You'll discover there's nothing that says you must bolt forward before you're ready. Be gentle with yourself as you proceed.

What Should I Do Now?

1. Trust Your Own Timing

In Spring, timing is everything. A flock of birds migrating north before the last winter storm may have to put up quite a struggle just to survive; seedlings coming up before the last frost have to be very hardy in order to withstand the harsh conditions. Most animals and plants have an internal sense that tells them when it's safe to venture forth and pursue spring activities. A rancher once told me that an alpaca she had imported from Peru held off birthing her baby until they'd passed through the mandatory quarantine in a concrete paddock in Florida. The alpaca only gave birth after being transported 3,000 miles to its new, grassy home in the coastal hills of California.

In many cases, we've learned to honor this ability in animals. For instance, we know it isn't wise to wake up hibernating bears prematurely; they tend to have nasty attitudes when their winter's sleep is cut short. Furthermore, we recognize that if animals miscalculate their timing or we purposefully push their process, it creates a tremendous amount of pain and struggle.

The importance of timing is so clear when we're talking about nature. Yet I'm willing to bet that you've been ignoring your own sense of timing by pushing yourself out of the safety of Winter before you're ready to reenter the world at large. Be honest with yourself. Have you been pushing yourself to make more visible progress or are you frustrated because you can't move as fast as you want to? If you answered "yes," you're not trusting your own timing.

Believe me, I understand how anxious you are to move forward, and no doubt the people around you are beginning to champ at the bit as well. I'll share a secret with you, although I suspect you'll end up having to learn this on your own. In the ten years I've been observing my own transitions, I've come to learn that I always end up making more progress when I trust my own sense of timing than when I try to push things along.

Every part of Spring depends on an acute sense of timing. The best indicator of when and how to move forward is within you—not the part of you that's anxious to get going, but the part, deep in your core, that senses what is best. Because our society tends to see logic as more reliable than intuition and values the Moderns' way of "hurry up, solve the problem, and get on with life," many of us have never been encouraged to follow the small, still voice within us. Certainly, there are situations where logic is incredibly important, but I suspect your ability to take action based on logic is well-developed from frequent use. Therefore, I want to describe how to develop a good internal sense of timing by listening to your environment and yourself.

Imagine for a moment a group of fox kits playing outside their den. They're fully engaged in their chasing and tumbling games when something, a loud noise or an unexpected movement, spooks them and they scurry back to the safety of their den. There they stay hidden until they sense it's safe enough to leave the den to play again. If you observed them over a series of weeks, you'd notice that the fox kits gradually begin to move farther away from the den. Through each cycle, the fox kits learn a little bit more about their circumstances: what to fear, what to investigate, what to ignore, how to handle a variety of events. They also develop a finely tuned sense of when it's safe to go back to their normal activities and when it's critical to stay put. This natural ebb and flow process is a crucial part of development in all mammals—including humans!

To develop your plans naturally, it's important for you to learn to sense this ebb and flow in your own life. Having this skill will enable you to identify safe opportunities to continue your journey, as well as conditions that warrant stepping back to protect yourself.

Usually the signs that indicate it's time for you to move forward are situations that serve as a catalyst to jump-start you into action. Suddenly, circumstances in your life make it easier to move than to sit still. You may notice an increase in seemingly amazing coincidences—you end up meeting a person who gives you the information you need, finding research that confirms your idea, seeing an ad for just the product you've been searching for. Opportunities you've dismissed as highly unlikely begin to appear. Progress without struggle is a key indicator that you are indeed on the right track. When circumstances support your movement forward, go for it! It's a tremendous feeling when conditions encourage your success.

A friend of mine, Gary, has been working toward launching a performance photography business since I met him several years ago. His route has been rather bumpy, with a number of unexpected detours and delays. But after months of taking hundreds of rolls of film at open mic nights and at local radio promotion concerts, he's finally hitting pay dirt. By being present at these events, he has met, "by chance," a number of contacts who have since helped him gain access to event promoters and set up a cooperative studio. The best news of all is that he just got his first paying job from one of the open mic musicians! All these synchronistic connections indicate that Gary is moving in the right direction at the right time.

Just as there are times to move forward, there are also times when it's natural to step back and review your situation. Although this pulling back may feel frustrating and nonproductive at first, you'll soon learn, if you follow your intuition, that stepping back will allow you to spring forward even farther the next time around.

What are the signs that it's time to hold back? Any time you procrastinate, hesitate, or struggle, pay attention. This often means you're missing a key piece of information or that your surroundings aren't yet ready for you to take action. If you feel anxious or afraid, there may be something in your plan that needs further attention. If you're having to "push the river" or doors keep slamming in your face, it may indicate you aren't meant to go down that road right now. Listen and take note so you don't have to keep hitting your head against the wall!

When you're ready to look at your situation again, identify the source of the procrastination, hesitation, struggle, or fear. What seems to be the glitch? Use your reflective skills to get insights about what's getting in your way. Apply your detective skills to determine whether your plan needs to shift, you need to grow in some way before you can move forward, or your idea is good but the time isn't right for it just yet. Work through your frustration; you'll be amazed at how much your adjustments improve the ultimate outcome.

Several years ago, I completed the research to trademark my company name and started filling out the paperwork. But there was one section I just couldn't figure out. I must have picked up the form twenty or thirty times before I realized that, for some reason, it wasn't the right time to finish the process. Every six months or so, it would flash into my mind and I'd make another attempt. This went on for nearly two years. I just couldn't understand what the problem was, until finally I realized through a strategic planning process that my logo no longer reflected my business. Once I finalized my new logo, that same paperwork fell together in a snap. Finally, it was time to submit it. As further confirmation of right timing, I received the official designation on my birthday, six months earlier than expected! Timing is everything.

At first, it may feel rather odd to trust your sense of timing because your intuition may be telling you to do the exact opposite of what you'd do if you were acting on logic. This is where trust comes in. As you become more attuned, you'll know better when to sit with ideas and when to act.

Even "The Handless Maiden" illustrates the importance of timing. Rather than rushing into the King's arms when he first shows up at the inn, the Handless Maiden chooses to wait until the King has completed his part of the transformational journey. This conscious delay in revealing herself isn't the passive, helpless, codependent waiting that princesses do in the youth tales. Instead, it's a sign that she's not only sure of who she is, but is willing to wait for the King to know himself before reuniting with him. Now that you're clearer about who you are and what you want, you too can pace yourself when it comes to taking action in the world.

2. *Prepare the Soil and Water the Dirt*

As you begin to implement your plans, one of your first tasks is to prepare the soil, refreshen your nest, and open space in your life for something new. Although you did a fair amount of clearing in Late Winter, now's the time to do the final sweep in preparation for the imminent rebirth in your life. Remove anything and everything from your space and from your life that no longer supports your goals. Look around: is there space in your life for this new "baby?" Do you need to rearrange anything in your home, your schedule, or your relationships to make room for it?

Over the years, I've watched many people go through this preparation for starting something new. When Jean came to me, it was clear that she was having trouble getting her home business off the ground because the room she'd designated as her office was still being used by members of her household for storage, paperwork, and overnight guests. She realized rather quickly that before she would see any movement in her business, she needed to set up new ground rules with her family, create other places for all the stuff, and delegate the responsibility for handling these matters back to the family.

When Carly, another client, decided to become a vegetarian, she was completely overwhelmed until we talked about how she could prepare for this change. Her first goal was to understand how to get the nourishment she needed. Then, she rearranged her kitchen and purchased some staple ingredients to make her food preparation easier. Finally, after gathering recipes from other vegetarians, she felt more comfortable with the lifestyle she'd chosen.

Although you're anxious to see evidence of Spring in your life, your next task after you plant your seeds is to "water the dirt," trusting, all the while, that the seeds will indeed sprout. If you're marketing, networking, or dating, just imagine that each person you meet is a seed waiting for the right time to sprout—you might get a call tomorrow or a referral two years from now. If you're in therapy, know each insight contains the seed of a breakthrough. Even when it feels like nothing is happening, keep up the process—you may notice a new sprout as early as tomorrow. Above all else, withstand the understandable urge to poke under the soil to check on the seeds, for that would surely disturb or kill them. Have faith and keep watering!

3. Birth the New

The time has finally come for the seed to break through to the light, the young to be born, your project to take form, or a new you to blossom. Whether the birth is a clear-cut event or a subtle process over a period of time, the important thing is to allow it to just be what it is. Your main objective, at this point, is to guide the natural birthing process so that it's as smooth and gentle as possible. Don't rush or force it; work in concert with it.

As you give birth, experience all your emotions—from exhilaration and excitement as you witness the miracle, to nervousness, fear, and anxiety as you enter a vast new territory. Stay in touch with yourself and use the skills you developed in Winter to help you understand how to proceed. The birth itself may go fast or slow. You just never know.

For several months, Lynne has been aware of her connection with a man she met at a social gathering. Although most of her previous relationships blossomed rather quickly, she knew from the start that the tim-

The

SEASONS

of

CHANGE

___

162

ing on this one was going to be different. Instead of pushing it to go faster, she's been focusing her attention on trusting the natural unfolding that has been occurring steadily over time. Because she feels content within herself, she's comfortable allowing this birth to occur in its own time.

In other situations, the birth process happens so quickly it can make your head spin. When Louise started looking for a new house after her old one burned down, she went through the steps of narrowing her target neighborhoods, determining her financial parameters, and putting together her wish list. During her first appointment with her realtor, they went to five open houses just to explore the possibilities. As it happened, the first house they toured turned out to be the one. Within two months, she owned the home she's lived in for nearly ten years.

Even different versions of "The Handless Maiden" illustrate these two kinds of Spring births. In the version told here, the Queen's hands grow gradually, while in the Russian story, her hands reappear spontaneously when she's forced to save her child from drowning in a well.

Try not to judge the form the birth takes. Just be present and celebrate the miracle of new life.

4. Stretch and Grow

As soon as the birth occurs, your role will shift considerably. You move from focusing all your energy inward—defining and refining your vision—to guiding the growth of this new aspect of your life as a parent or guardian, so it can eventually stand on its own without so much support from you.

As you take on these new responsibilities, you'll need to learn or refresh your "parenting" skills. Take yourself back to a time when you were parenting a toddler or training a young animal. When you worked with these youngsters, you allowed and even expected them to make mistakes, to wobble and stumble. This time in the transition journey is symbolized by the baby hands the Queen has when she begins to heal. Patience, support, and love are called for as you enter this stage of your own journey.

In a world where we've come to believe instantaneous perfection is not only possible but preferable, the toddler stage is a bit disconcerting. We want so much to be sure of ourselves again that we forget that confidence builds layer by layer as we experience new things in our lives. Gradually, as you give yourself space to practice and explore, you'll be able to figure out more and more things on your own. Of course, it always helps to have the wise, confident part of you present and available when you need to make course corrections. Know that there will come a time when you'll be sure of yourself and independent once again.

The only way to reach that point, however, is to take the time to learn new skills the way a child does. The fact that the Queen's hands pass through a stage where they're like a young girl's tells us she spent some time learning practical skills before she completed her process. When professional storyteller Susan Gordon tells her version of the tale, the Queen uses her time in the forest to teach her son how to find edible plants and snare game. Both stories demonstrate the importance of gaining new skills. Be patient and tolerant as you venture into this new territory.

Whenever you learn a new behavior, whether it's learning to drive, express your emotions, or set boundaries, your results may be a bit erratic at first because you don't yet have the knowledge or the finesse to match the intensity of your actions to the situation. In one situation, you might step on the gas pedal a bit too much; in another, you might put on the brakes a little too hard. The pendulum swing between these two extremes can be a valuable learning tool, if you stay conscious of what does and doesn't work in each situation.

Although Sally was very shy and reserved, her work with several professionals convinced her it was time to learn to express her anger. Her first attempts scared her, however; she lashed out indiscriminately without having the skills to discern what was appropriate in each setting. To counteract her bold moves, she began holding back again, but that wasn't satisfying either because people didn't respond to her needs at all. As she vacillated between the two extremes, she gradually learned to judge how to share her emotions in ways that freed her and led others to understand and fulfill her requests. Now she very rarely finds herself missing the mark.

As you continue your journey, you're probably coming upon situations that feel a bit awkward. Rather than avoiding these situations or forcing yourself to participate, I encourage you to break them into more manageable steps.

When I first started my business, I had my idea and was ready to move forward, but I'd been in hibernation for several years and dreaded networking events, especially Chamber of Commerce mixers. Yet to be successful, I had to overcome this intense discomfort. I began setting a series of safe goals for myself. My first target was just to show up at the events. I made it safe by assuring myself that I didn't have to talk with anyone or stay if I felt too distraught. Sometimes I stayed and sometimes I didn't. After several meetings, I found I could stay without too much trouble, so my next goal was to talk with people I knew. Then, over time, I got so that I felt comfortable enough to introduce myself to people I didn't know. Through this process, I learned how to network in a variety of settings.

You might try this process if you want to become more comfortable with dating, socializing, going to parties, networking for a new job, or taking a trip by yourself. The possibilities are endless. Just remember that the entire purpose is to take small, safe steps to become more at ease with new situations.

If you'd like to explore whether a new idea is worth pursuing, follow the guidelines used by scientists when they do an experiment. After establishing a clear focus for the study, scientists isolate and change one variable at a time to determine the effect that change has on their results. Once you're clear on your direction, to the extent that you can, begin to implement your plan one element at a time.

Scientists also review their research and choose the variables that have the greatest potential to perform. Look at your plan: which aspects are most likely to help you reach your goals? Begin by trying out the elements that will require a low investment of time, money, or resources. Later, as you get confirmation you're headed in the right direction, you can take on other aspects that require greater investment.

Scientists know from the start that some experiments will succeed and others will fail. They actually learn as much, if not more, from failed experiments as they do from successful ones. As you put your plan into action, know from the beginning that some things won't work out as expected. When this happens, don't throw the whole idea away. Look instead for what worked and what didn't to see what adjustments you might make the next time.

Unless you're tremendously well off financially, it's unlikely you'd buy a home just to figure out whether or not it works for you. Instead, you'd test out your ideas before you make an offer. One very low-cost experiment is to drive around neighborhoods you can afford to identify the ones you feel most comfortable in. Once you know the kind of neighborhood you want, then begin looking at individual houses. At this stage of the experiment, ask yourself a series of "What would it be like . . . ?" questions. For instance, what would it be like to wake up in this house? Raise your kids here? Come home from work? Entertain your family and friends? Ask as many detailed questions as you can. From your answers, you'll be able to confirm whether a particular home meets your needs or not. If, and only if, the home suits you, do you begin the process of formalizing your purchase by making an offer.

Whenever you try something new, it's important to pay attention to your inner cues. Are you excited about what you're discovering? Are you feeling anxious or uncomfortable in the setting? Use your responses to help you determine what pieces to pursue and what pieces to drop.

When you start paying attention to your inner responses, it may take a couple of hours or even several days to evaluate how you're feeling about a situation. Then, as you become more familiar and comfortable with this process, you'll be able to assess situations more accurately in the moment.

As you grow, be sure to celebrate each milestone along the way. Learn from your setbacks and be encouraged by your successes. With time, the new element in your life will mature and your role as guardian will shift again.

5. Come of Age

Spring culminates with the implementation of your plans. If your plans are multifaceted, you may feel confused about where to begin—

what to learn first, what leads to follow up on, how to prioritize all the steps you see out in front of you. First, take a deep breath and recall how far you've come. The fact that you, like the Queen, have made your way through the pathless, underground forest and have regrown your adult hands reassures you that you have the skills to make sense of this chaos. The scariest part of where you are now is that the confusion is above ground, in the real world, where you still feel a bit tentative about how to proceed. Consciously reconnect with your essence so you'll have access to all the intuitive navigation skills you've honed throughout your journey. Only then will you feel ready to proceed.

As you think about your plan, notice which aspects draw your attention. If you have trouble sensing this, think back to your destinationless walk. How did you sense which way to turn or which shop to enter? That internal mechanism is the same one that will help you out here.

Practice using this strategy as you move through your daily life. Look at your to-do list. What feels easy to do, given the amount of time you have, what you're wearing, and your mood? After you've completed that task, come back and ask the same questions to decide on your next action.

At first, you may feel as though you're shirking your responsibilities by focusing on all the "fun stuff," but you're actually honoring yourself by doing what is most consistent with where you are in the moment. Remember, there's absolutely nothing wrong with taking the actions you're in the mood to take. In fact, in the long run, you may find you actually get more done! I use this method in all areas of my life—when I run errands, do yardwork, tackle my to-do list, write. As a result, I spend far less time struggling and a lot more time producing. Of course, there are times when you must attend to one thing when you'd prefer to be doing something else. This is when your logical side plays an important role and helps you meet your overall objectives.

In the early stages of Spring, one of the hardest decisions is what to do first. Usually, you're teeming with ideas and feel so excited you can't prioritize any of them because they all relate to each other. When Linda, an artist, came to me she had so many ideas she was scattered all over the map! She had three different business ideas and wasn't making progress with any of them. As I probed her feelings about each business, it became abundantly clear to both of us that the business she saw as an instant source of money wasn't producing results and was actually taking her away from the business that held her interest. The business she was so passionate about was really more of a hobby, from society's perspective, so she worried that it wouldn't be viable. The third business, she decided, was a long-term goal she could put aside for now. By paying attention to how she actually felt about each idea, she was able to focus her attention on making a solid attempt at growing her favorite business idea. Since that conversation, several key opportunities have opened up for her that may, in fact, enable her to make a living with her art.

Sometimes when you're enacting long-term plans, your initial hit about something can provide you with valuable information. When I was first thinking about finding a publisher for this book, I went to a book festival at the urging of my publicist and literary agent. As I walked through the throngs of people and browsed in various booths, I came across one booth that felt like home. I was attracted to their displays, their books, and the people tending the booth. Throughout the day, I kept finding myself back in that booth over and over again. Eight months later, I'd signed a contract for this book with that same publishing company.

You can also use this method when you make big decisions about your career, relationships, and where you live. One of my clients, Laurie, learned this lesson the hard way when she needed to get a job after being a stay-at-home parent for eight years. She felt so much pressure to make the right decision for her children's sake that she put her own needs on the back burner and took a job that seemed to have a more stable and reliable schedule than the one she was more inherently interested in. After four very stressful days on the job, it became abundantly clear that she'd made a mistake sacrificing her personal style for her children, so she quit that job and started searching again. Although it took some time, she found a job that's a great fit and both she and her children are thriving.

As you implement your plans, be attuned to subtle indications that your priorities are changing. If you're running into dead ends or having difficulty getting a piece of information or a required element to proceed, you need to shift your focus for the time being and implement another facet of your plan that feels easier to put into place. In time, you'll see the right opportunity to return and finish what you started.

6. *Blossom Fully*

Now that the Queen and King are reuniting within you, it's time to become an activist. Take positive, direct actions to implement all you've learned as a detective and idealist during your inner journey. As Clarissa Pinkola Estés says, speaking of women who have been through a transformative journey, "that which a woman has learned will be reflected not only in her inner soul but will also be written upon her and acted upon outwardly as well." So now it's time to take all your new-found knowledge about yourself—your preferences, desires, style, visions—and begin to weave them into your life, so that all you do reflects all that you are. As you make these adjustments, you'll begin to experience the inner joy that comes from being within your own skin.

Part of this process may involve accepting parts of yourself you've been fighting for years. Perhaps you'll discover, as I have, that you're very visual and must see all the projects you're working on. This knowing will enhance your acceptance of "filing in piles" on and around your desk. In fact, you may be able to capitalize on this new awareness by purchasing desktop organizers that enhance your natural style. Perhaps you can even create more space in your office by getting rid of the file cabinets you never used effectively in the first place. When you stop fighting your habits and natural preferences, you'll have a lot more time to devote to your work and personal life.

Of course, there may be certain discoveries you won't be able to implement immediately. Perhaps you discovered in Early Winter that your body prefers to wake up between 7:30 and 8:00 in the morning, but in the job you have right now you have to be at work by then. Although at first glance it may seem impossible to think you could ever sleep in every morning, remember there are always options. The trick is in recognizing them and taking action. Perhaps your company has flex-time or is willing to consider it. Perhaps you can change your morning routine, so you can have at least a few more minutes in bed. Perhaps your spouse can get the kids ready several days a week so that you can get the sleep you need more often. Perhaps the next job you take will allow you to choose your own start time. Perhaps you'll start your own business and have the flexibility to plan your day in a way that works for you. The possibilities are endless. The key is to remember your ideal and keep your eye out for practical ways to implement your vision—next month or next year.

Sometimes you may be shocked at how fast a clear, strongly held vision can manifest itself. When I asked a client if she'd like animals in her work space, she answered yes, but rolled her eyes with a look that said "fat chance." In fact, she was so sure it was a pie-in-the-sky idea that she suggested I not even include it on her ideal work environment list. The very next day, a recruiter called with an unexpected job interview. I wish you could have heard the sound of surprise and disbelief in her voice when she told me that several of the people who interviewed her had their pets in their offices with them! A month later, she signed on to work with that company full-time. This just goes to show how important it is to be clear about your ideal.

Although this process may feel awkward at first, trust your new sense of knowing as you make changes in your home, clothing, schedule, and style of interaction. The more you can incorporate your personal style into your life, the easier it will be for you to move forward.

Of course, converting your life into one that's a natural extension of who you are will take time. I've been an activist for the past six years. Although there's still room for improvement, I can truly say, without an ounce of hesitation, that my life has gotten better and more fulfilling with each passing year. As you claim who you really are, you will become more and more like the native plant that thrives without undue effort because it's in its natural environment.

What Detours Should I Watch Out For?

1. Making No Movement

When, in the Russian version of our tale, the Queen's child fell into the well, she panicked. She couldn't move because she was stuck in her belief that she had no hands and in the logic that with no hands she had no way to save her child. In this scene, there's the threat that the Queen's growth (the child) will be lost to the unconscious (the water) and all her travels and trials will have been for naught.

If you find you're unable to move forward, even though you've taken the steps described so far, you haven't yet addressed all that you must before you'll be free to create something new in your life. These blocks can be any number of things, but until you discover and work through them, you won't be able to move beyond Spring, no matter how hard you try.

Once, after I had given a presentation to a group of real estate professionals, a realtor told me about a man and woman she worked with for a year who were so clear about what they wanted in a home that they'd made a very detailed list of all their requirements. Although the agent had shown them dozens of homes that matched these requirements, they always found some small element that made each house unworkable. Even though the couple said they were ready to begin a new chapter in their lives, their actions indicated just the opposite. Some issue was getting in their way—perhaps they were afraid of the responsibilities of owning a home; perhaps one of them was uneasy about formalizing their relationship to this degree; perhaps they really didn't want to live in the area but were staying to please their parents. Whatever the reason, nothing will shift for this couple until they look at why they're passing up homes that match their requirements.

If you're in a similar situation, it's very important for you to pull in professional support to help you break through whatever blocks are in your way. When the Queen called out for help at the well, the Spirit in White appeared and asked her why she didn't rescue the child. When the Queen replied that she had no hands, the spirit said, "Try." It was at that point the Queen reached under the water for her child and her hands regenerated instantly. Reach out for help so that you can rescue the new life you've been tending.

2. Ignoring Your Own Wisdom

So much of Spring depends on sensing when and how to move forward in your life. If you ignore your own inner wisdom due to pressure from people around you or your own fears, you'll be relegated to the no-man's-land between the confusion of Winter and the excitement of Spring.

Imagine what might have happened in the story if the King had stayed in his castle grieving, or the Queen Mother had discouraged him from doing what he needed to do. The King and Queen would have been unable to reunite. So do what you can to find out why you're afraid to listen to and act on your own wisdom.

You're also limiting your progress if you're ignoring your own personal style. The time and energy you spend keeping up with society's expectations means you can't devote that energy to creating your own success. Look at why your needs don't count in your own mind and come back to yourself.

Nine

Summer:
Celebrating Your Harvest

Signs:	Tasks:	Detours:
Feel Confident	Allow for Ripening	Raising the Bar
Have Clarity	Savor Your Success	Backing Down—Too Hot to Handle
Life Is Abundant	Celebrate!	Waiting for the Shoe to Drop
	Play!	Being a Worry Wart

When they heard the news that the King and Queen were reunited, the dwellers of the inn celebrated with a fine meal. Then the King, Queen, and their child returned to the King's castle and rejoined the Queen Mother. There they had a second wedding to renew their vows. Over the years they had many more children who all shared their story, which is how we know of it today.

We made it. We reached the part of the story where the King and Queen "live happily ever after." But, except for the feast, the renewal of their vows, and the fact that they had many more children, we really don't get much information on what to do next. Somehow, we're just supposed to know how to handle our dreams coming true. Sounds like it should be easy, right? Wrong!

It's at this point in the journey that our Modern view of success clashes with life's realities. Although we've invested much time in dreaming, scheming, and praying to "live happily ever after" with a good (well-paying) job, the right partner, a loving family, and the perfect house, we know from living life that things happen—bills pile up, relationships end, people get sick, the roof needs repairs. How can we reconcile the dream we hold (whether consciously or unconsciously) with what we know from our day-to-day lives? The part of the fairy tale ending that gets us into trouble is the "ever after" part. That's the part that promises that once you've made it, life's a breeze—no more worries, no more upsets.

Even if we toss the "ever after" part out the castle window, though, we're still left with "live happily." That's not such a bad goal, is it? The problem is, we've spent so many years defining success as having the full picture—the royal partner, the castle, the riches—that we feel we can't be happy until and unless we have it all. Our fairy tales confirm this because we know the Prince and the Princess are never happy until all the pieces of their lives are in place. We've become so dependent on the pretty picture as a guarantee of happiness, we haven't a clue how to just "live happily" with what we have.

These conundrums are what makes Summer hard. When you have a patch of life when you really are happy, your mind jumps straight to the punch line. Okay, if this isn't going to last forever, exactly how long will it last? Can I count on being happy till the end of the week? The month? The year? Then you start to wonder, if it's not going to last, is it really worth being happy at all? Do I really want to risk being that vulnerable? Do I want to open up to life and experience it fully if there's a possibility it might all disappear? Right about now, you start backpedaling because you don't want to experience the hurt and loss you know will follow if you let go and have fun now.

The bottom line is that we're taught life should be a perpetual

Summer and along the way we pick up the message that something's wrong with us if we can't manifest this all the time. Yet, because we have a few years under our belts, we know the good times always end—and we have the emotional and physical scars to prove it. As protection, whenever Summer does arrive we hold back and keep ourselves from "living happily."

What kind of life is that? What if trees were afraid that one day somebody would take their fruit, so they held back the nutrients and their fruit never quite ripened? What if the sun held itself back, and the days were more equal in length so humans wouldn't have to experience the disappointment and loss each year as the days shortened in fall? What if the birds withheld food from their young, so they'd never leave the nest? Seeing this kind of philosophy played out in nature shows us just how preposterous it is to hold back from living life fully. You've made it this far, so open up to experiencing your sweet success. You deserve it!

How Can I Tell I'm in Summer?

1. You Feel Confident

One sure way to know you're in Summer is that you finally feel confident again. Clarissa Pinkola Estés has a wonderful description of a woman who has entered Summer after her underworld journey: "with eyes on straight, palms outward, with the hearing of the instinctual self intact, the woman goes into life in this new powerful manner . . . with a deep sense of her own destiny . . . she is truly 'within herSelf.' " In the movie *City Slickers*, Billy Crystal's character, Mitch, shows this same kind of confidence when he greets his family at the airport after successfully completing the cattle drive with his buddies. His smile, his sense of comfort within himself, and his ability to bring Norman the calf home with him show us that he is, once again, sure of himself and what he's about.

By now, your sense of confidence emanates from deep within you in a way that others notice and comment on. You may find that you receive more compliments than you have in a while. With your enhanced sense of self-esteem, the feelings of vulnerability, which have been such a part of your life throughout the other seasons, diminish.

2. *You Have Clarity*

After experiencing so many months of swirling confusion, your newfound clarity feels absolutely exquisite. Just as the King and Queen knew they wanted to be together and return to the castle, you now *know* what you want and where you're going.

The clarity you feel may show up in various parts of your life—your goals for the future, how you present yourself, the activities you immerse yourself in, your priorities, your relationships. For the first time in a long while, you no longer dread the questions: "So, what do you do?" and "What are you up to these days?" Because you know where you're headed, you find it easy to talk about yourself, answer questions, and share your goals.

3. *Your Life Is Full of Abundance*

Everywhere you look you see evidence of abundance. All the time and effort you've put into your transition process is coming to fruition in a bountiful harvest. Because you're confident and clear about yourself and your situation, you're attracting opportunities galore.

All that you've been striving for is coming your way—love, well wishes, resources, contacts. Even if it's not in the exact form you envisioned, know that you have everything you need to live happily today—right now!

What Can I Do Now?

These are the steps the fairy tales gloss over at the end of each story.

1. Allow for the Ripening

It's close now. You can see it. You can touch it. You can even imagine what it's going to taste like when you pluck it from your life. But, for now, hold off your harvest for just a few more days. Remember that the fruits of your journey are more likely to reach their peak of perfection if you allow them to ripen naturally in their own time. Have patience and trust the ripening process. Don't push, pull, or yank too early, or your fruit will have an edge of bitterness to it.

When are you going to know it's time to harvest? What milestone will tell you you've made it? For some transitions, there's a traditional event that serves as the culmination of the journey—a graduation, a wedding, a baby shower. In other situations, it's not that clear-cut, so you need to take it upon yourself to choose a specific, observable goal to aim for—a specific sales figure, a running distance, the first anniversary of your completing chemotherapy. The clearer you are in defining these goals, the more likely you'll be to harvest your rewards at the peak of their flavor.

2. Savor Your Success

In *Original Blessing*, Matthew Fox says, "Anyone who has taken time to savor the blessings of life knows that they are profoundly, deliciously, deeply sweet. And naturally so."

As you wait for the perfect moment for harvesting your success, savor the anticipation of what's to come. Feel the sweetness building within you as the day gets closer. Dwell on your delight as you harvest your dream—whether it's a promotion, landing your first client, putting the finishing touches on a home, or celebrating a new level of intimacy in your relationship. Relish the glow you feel in the days that follow.

Use all your senses to appreciate how powerful each Summer moment is.

- Take in all the visual elements of your new level of success. Perhaps you have a new home, a new office, a new person in your life, or a new look. Enjoy the thrill you feel when you look around and realize that all these elements really are a part of your life now.

- Notice how your body feels when you're confident and clear about your direction. You may notice that you're more comfortable with yourself than you've been in a long time.

- Listen to your surroundings to hear what others are saying about your successes. Compliments are part of this season's harvest, so be sure to receive them with an open, sincere "thank you." Avoid the temptation to downplay your efforts or deflect these comments out of modesty. Given the hard work you've put in to get here, you certainly deserve the praise you're hearing.

If you're having a difficult time embracing your achievements, create a success altar for yourself with physical symbols of your present success and all the other ones that preceded it. Observe yourself as you do this. How do you feel? Proud, embarrassed, hurt, nervous? What memories surface? What beliefs about success and your worthiness bubble up? Work with your insights so you can release them once and for all.

3. Celebrate!

Wow! You've done it. What was once just a spark of insight is now yours. It's time to celebrate this feat. To grasp the full extent of your achievement, take a moment to think about how far you've come. Treat yourself to a review of your journal, recorded insights, or drawings to immerse yourself in all the fears and dreams that have occupied you over the past few weeks, months, or years.

Now, think about where you are today. What milestones have you just passed? Even if your life isn't "picture perfect," acknowledge just how much has changed in your life. Start a list so you can actually see your progress. Pat yourself on the back. Give yourself a hug. Truly honor yourself for lifting your life to this new place.

Ironically, as author Richard Heinberg points out, the season that naturally deserves a celebration—the time of harvest and abundance—lacks a formal holiday in our calendar. Whereas there are still numerous celebrations in the dark of winter, the traditional summer solstice and Celtic Lammas (August 1) ceremonies have been forgotten. In many ways this reflects how cut off we are from the natural bounty of the earth.

To celebrate your harvest, I encourage you to create a private ritual or special event to acknowledge your movement forward. Take some time to think through how you'd like to mark your arrival at this new level of success. There may be a special place you'd like to visit, a certain event you'd like to participate in, or some other memorable experience to honor what you've accomplished. If you'd like, invite one or two special friends to share the experience with you. Allow your desires and situation to guide how and when this ceremony takes place. If you listen to your intuition, you'll know when you've found the plan that will match your innermost needs.

Jeremy and Ann contemplated their celebration each month when they wrote the checks to pay off their credit cards. After months of testing out various ideas, they finally decided to treat themselves to a concert series—a luxury they'd foregone over the last few years while they were paying off their debts. The day they mailed that last check, they went straight to the box office and purchased a pair of tickets for the summer music festival—with cash, of course!

This is also a great time to celebrate with the people who've supported you through the last few stormy seasons. Let your imagination soar here, too. Do what feels right to you. The activities can be as elaborate or as simple as you'd like—the purpose isn't to impress anyone, but rather to thank and celebrate with those you love. Perhaps you'd like to mark this time with a symbolic poem, song, or story. It's also a great opportunity to thank each person publicly for their contributions to you and your growth. Your supporters will love sharing in your celebration of the new you.

4. Play!

You've worked hard to reach this point and you deserve to revel in this new sense of freedom. The best way to do this is to *play*. In some ways, this suggestion may seem obvious, but because our work-focused culture tends to downplay the importance of pure enjoyment, few of us know how to play anymore.

Richard Heinberg points out that as cultures moved away from the land, childrearing became more disciplined and structured. As a result, children spend more time competing in games with rules (to prepare them for the rigors of adulthood) than engaging in spontaneous, pleasurable activities. This results in a loss of the ability to express spontaneously their zest for life. As these children mature, their life-force becomes so completely suppressed that they come to see play as a waste of time.

Yet human beings, according to anthropologist Ashley Montagu, are one of the few species that has the capacity to continue to play in adulthood. If we can play, why don't we? Can we relearn how to?

In *Original Blessing*, Matthew Fox quotes Meister Eckhart defining play as the state of being able "to live without a why, to work without a why, to love without a why." The main trick of play is to be completely in the moment. Let your past and future melt away. Use the freedom your confidence and clarity have given you to be irrepressibly spontaneous. Laugh, skip, sing, dance. Feel the energy fill you to fullness. Allow your movements, emotions, and ideas to evolve out of the happenings of the moment. Flow with what comes—ecstasy, joy, gratitude, poignant memories. The richness you feel may transcend words. Don't succumb to the need—for yourself or others—to put your feelings and experience into words right away—or ever. Just give yourself free rein to experience it all.

What Detours Should I Watch Out For?

Icarus and his father Daedalus were being held against their will by King Minos on the island of Crete. Daedalus had been commissioned by the King to build a very elaborate palace with a complex maze in the cellar. After completing the project, King Minos informed the father and son that they couldn't leave the island because they knew the secret of his dungeon. So, while they lived well, father and son were stuck for life in the palace tower.

As he watched the birds fly freely, Daedalus realized the only way they were going to escape was to fly back to the mainland. So the very next morning, he began to save the feathers that dropped on the windowsill. After a year, he'd collected enough to make two sets of wings—one for himself and one for Icarus. After attaching the wings to their backs with wax, they leaped from their window and soared across the sea.

In his last instructions to his son, Daedalus warned him not to fly too high or get too close to the sun. Once Icarus felt the wind under his wings, though, he took off, flying higher and higher. When he realized he had the opportunity to compete with the sun, he decided to push the envelope just a little bit more. But as he got within reach of his goal, the heat from the sun began to melt the wax on his back and the feathers dropped, one by one, into the sea. Daedalus watched as Icarus fell into the ocean, never to be seen again.

1. Raising the Bar

Some people miss having a full experience of Summer because they are forever changing their goals. Just as they are about to reach a key milestone, they raise their expectations and requirements. Like Icarus, who shifted his focus mid-flight from crossing the sea into a life of freedom to beating the sun at its own game, they're always striving and pushing to make that next goal. As a result, they never succeed, and they never get to just let go, have fun, and reward themselves for a job well done. Very often the ultimate result of this detour is burnout, as the Icarus myth demonstrates in mythic proportions.

When I first started my business, I was famous for this kind of sabotage. In my office, I have a board where I track the number of clients I'm working with and my target goal. I remember one particular week I had nine appointments set up. Because it was only Monday, I thought reaching my goal of ten appointments was going to be a piece of cake— too easy, in fact—so I raised my goal to thirteen. Well, as you can imagine, when I did this I cheated myself out of the thrill of achieving a goal. What's scary is that this scenario was just the tip of the iceberg. When I looked into my past, I saw this pattern everywhere. In fact, I remember coming out of my Ph.D. defense thinking, well, that was easy. What's next? The fact that I thought it was "easy" meant that I had conquered great fears, surmounted piles and piles of reading, and learned an awful lot about my field. It wasn't until this insight—six years after I graduated—that I fully acknowledged what I had achieved by getting my Ph.D.

Within many of us, there is a deeply held belief that we haven't succeeded, in the true sense of the word, unless we've struggled and overcome great odds. If we reach our destination due to proper planning and innate skills, we typically downplay the achievement.

Watch for this and catch yourself if you're failing to acknowledge yourself when you've met your goals with ease. If you think about it, reaching goals you set during Winter and Spring, when you were confused and less confident, is a well-earned accomplishment. If the goal looks easy now, that means you really have grown a tremendous amount! You deserve to celebrate!

2. Backing Down Because It's Too Hot to Handle

One of my clients, Cheryl, called me recently to say she'd gotten the job offer she'd been anticipating. I could tell by her voice, though, that she was somewhat less than ecstatic—in fact, shellshocked is a better way to put it. When I asked her what was standing between her and pure excitement, she said, "I'm afraid it's too good to be true." The company courted her consistently for weeks, offering her the extra benefits she requested, and yet she was afraid to go for it. As we talked, I realized she was getting a lot of messages from family and friends to play it safe, stick with what she had, and not push the envelope.

Of course, what they weren't saying, but what Cheryl was picking up, was the fear that too much of a good thing always backfires. With the image of Icarus falling to his death floating through our mind's eye, we become overly cautious and back down from our goals—a dream job, an adventurous vacation, a daring outfit. We believe we mustn't get too close to success or we might lose it all, as stars such as Macaulay Culkin, Robert Downey, Jr., and Oksana Baiul have. Eventually, our fear of success puts a damper on so many of our activities that we end up existing in a very safe but limited world with few options and little excitement.

Take a good hard look at your fears of success. How are they holding you back? What are you missing out on? What events in your childhood or your family background contribute to your fears? Work with your insights and find ways to open yourself up to success. Remember that if Icarus had just focused on the risk to fly across the sea, he probably would have made it. Then we would have learned that risk taking was a good way to get out of a bad situation. So don't turn away from all risks and adventures just because Icarus got foolish and went beyond the capacity of his father s invention!

3. *Waiting for the Other Shoe to Drop*

In the midst of a momentous occasion in your life—a wedding, a celebration, a happy holiday dinner—have you ever felt shivers run up your spine as you wondered when and how your happiness was going to be cut short? It's almost as though you heard a shift in the soundtrack, warning you that the plot was going to thicken at any moment. Sometimes, you even hear people at this point in their lives saying, "I wonder when the other shoe's going to drop." There's a touch of fear in their voice because that other shoe rarely brings good news.

In fact, youth fairy tales and best-selling books by authors like Danielle Steel and Barbara Taylor Bradford capitalize on the adrenaline this kind of plot stimulates. You're familiar with the storyline—everyone is happy, living a full, successful life, when out of the blue disaster strikes. When I was looking for examples of this kind of plot, I didn't have to look very hard. The dust jackets of these books tell it all.

The cover of Danielle Steel's *Daddy*, for instance, reads, "Oliver Watson has worked hard to build a safe, predictable world. But suddenly it seems to dissolve around him." The story summary proceeded with a litany of his losses: his wife leaves him to return to school; his mother is diagnosed with Alzheimer's disease and is later killed in an accident; his grieving father, who is "braver than his son," quickly jumps into several relationships and eventually another marriage; and his seventeen-year-old son impregnates his girlfriend. *Everything to Gain*, a novel and television movie by Barbara Taylor Bradford, tells of a woman whose life was shattered when her wonderful husband and two sweet daughters were brutally murdered in a failed car-jacking. By tapping into the fears of those who see change as a threat to their success, these authors keep us on the edge of our seats. Too much of this kind of fiction trains us to be wary of too much success in our own lives.

Savor the moments of success when they happen, because in time, life will always bring changes. Failing to celebrate by cutting yourself off from enjoyment in anticipation of disaster does nothing but make you a dried up, suspicious negatron.

4. Being a Worry Wart

In this detour, you don't wait for the other shoe to drop, you go ahead and kick it off yourself by passing right through the successes of Summer and moving into the worries of the next Fall. A good example of this is buyer's remorse. When a couple buys a home, for instance, they may celebrate for an evening or the few minutes it takes to walk through their new home, but then they immediately begin to feel anxious about their purchase. How will they pay the mortgage? How will they ever get organized to move? How will they make the modifications they want to make so the home will feel like their own? By asking all these questions right now, the new homeowners move, often in the space of a few heartbeats, from celebrating their purchase to worrying about all the upcoming shifts.

When you start to worry in Summer, stop and give yourself permission to enjoy the moment of attaining your long-sought-after goal. Feel your success in every cell of your body. Fall will come in its own time. When it does, if you've fully celebrated Summer, you'll be ready to embark on another cycle through the seasons to reach an even higher level of self-awareness and fulfillment.

Part III

Finding
Help
Along
the Way

One fine day, Winnie-the-Pooh was out walking through the forest when he came upon Rabbit's hole. Wanting company, he called out to Rabbit and was invited in for a visit. After a bit of pushing and straining, he managed to get into Rabbit's hole.

After a bit of small talk, Rabbit offered Pooh some refreshments— a bit of milk and honey with some bread. Pooh, being Pooh, declined the bread and focused his attention on the milk and honey. Once he finished, he mumbled something about leaving, really hoping Rabbit would offer him more refreshments. But Rabbit was on his way out as well.

So Pooh took his leave. As he climbed out the hole, he had to push and strain as before, but this time, just as his belly should have cleared the hole, he realized he was stuck. He tried going back, no luck. He tried moving forward, no luck. He finally exclaimed, "Oh help and bother!"

About this time, Rabbit, who'd left by the back door, came by and asked Pooh if he was stuck. Of course, Pooh didn't want to admit that anything was wrong, so he just explained he was resting.

Nevertheless, Rabbit offered to help by pulling on Pooh's paws. It didn't take them long to realize Pooh was very stuck. After a discussion about what was to blame—a door that was too small or a bear who had eaten too much—Rabbit set off to find Christopher Robin.

When they returned, the three of them looked at their options. Pushing Pooh back into the hole seemed like a step in the wrong direction, so they determined that the only way out was to wait for Pooh to lose some weight.

They figured it would take about a week—which seemed to Pooh to be an awfully long time without meals. So, in his despair, Pooh asked, "Then would you read a Sustaining Book, such as would help and comfort a Wedged Bear in Great Tightness?"

So all through the week, Christopher Robin read to Pooh. Then when the week had passed and Pooh had shed a few pounds, Christopher Robin grabbed Pooh's paws and began to pull. Then, for good measure, Rabbit and all his friends and relatives joined in as well. For a time, Pooh just made funny noises and then, with a pop, Pooh was free.

After thanking Christopher Robin, Rabbit, and all his friends and relatives, Pooh continued his walk though the forest.

Part III

Finding

Help

Along

the Way

189

This story, "Pooh Goes Visiting and Gets into a Tight Place," by A. A. Milne is not only familiar to many of us from childhood, but we also resonate with it as adults. We know from our own experience what it feels like to be so stuck in a place that it's as impossible to move forward as it is to move back. The gift of this story is that it demonstrates how support can set us free and allow us to continue our journey with a spring in our step.

The next three chapters explain how you too can get the support you need as you move through your transition. In Chapter 10, you have the opportunity to assess your current support network and look at ways you can broaden your base of support. When you get in a fix, you'll have a Christopher Robin to comfort and sustain you, as well as a group of people—both friends and relatives—you can count on to pull together when you need it most. Chapter 11 provides in-depth information about the specific kinds of support you're likely to need as you pass through each season of your journey. Divided by seasons, this chapter gives you specific statements you can use to express your needs so others will understand how to help you.

Chapter 12 offers a different kind of help by describing ways to avoid crisis-driven changes in our lives. If Pooh, for instance, had had this information, he might have taken his rough entry into the Rabbit hole as a warning and not eaten so much. Just think of the time, worry, and effort he would have saved himself and those he loved if he'd learned how to be mindful about the subtleties in his life. This chapter will help you learn what your personal Early Warning System is and how to use it to move beyond crisis-driven changes to make purposeful, mindful enhancements in your life.

Ten

Building Your
Support Network

Whether you're making your first attempts to understand a Fall shift, navigating your way through the "I Don't Know" Land of Winter, taking your first tentative steps into Spring, or having a hard time claiming your Summer success, you're bound to experience times when you need support.

From my own transition experiences and my work with clients, I know that obtaining the support you need when you need it can be difficult. The first challenge is to recognize you really could benefit from assistance. Unfortunately, the moments you most need the support are likely to be the ones when you're feeling the most distressed and the least able to ask for help.

When you do finally understand you can ask for support, you're faced with looming questions: "Who can I talk to?" "Who would want to deal with me right now?" If you have a limited network, these questions might stop you cold, adding more weight to your internal conviction that things really are hopeless. This chapter will help you evaluate your current support system and find ways to strengthen it.

But I Don't Like to Ask for Help

One of the greatest obstacles to creating a good support network is the humiliation many of us feel at having to ask for help. When I was in therapy after my father died, wrestling with this very issue, my therapist said something that has stuck with me ever since: "Being vulnerable is a sign of true strength." Asking for help demonstrates you value yourself enough to get support and that you're strong enough within yourself to share your situation with others. Your disclosure is what allows others to assist you. Over time, you may even discover that your supporters are awed by your authenticity and courage to ask for help.

People also hesitate to make requests of others for fear of being a nuisance or intruding. This tendency can have several roots. You may feel your needs aren't important compared to those of others, or you may be trying to protect or shield them from the intensity of your situation. Very often the stories you make up in your head about why a friend can't or won't help you are just that—stories. Your job is to make a sincere request, and your supporters' job is to determine whether they can or can't fulfill it right now. You might even give them several ways to help you and let them choose what works best for them. Believe it or not, your loved ones may be aching inside to support you—they just don't know what they can do to help. By making a request, you'll provide them the opening they need to make your life just a little bit easier.

How Supportive Is My Current Support System?

Take a few moments to think about the people in your support network right now. What kind of support are you *really* getting from them? Sometimes we get so used to being around a person, we forget to look at what they actually provide us. Although this may be a difficult exercise, especially if you're already feeling isolated and alone, take the time to reflect on the issues raised here. The more you know about the truth of your situation, the more you can enhance it.

Start by jotting down the names of people in your life. Don't be too concerned right now about the number of people on your list. As you'll soon discover, the sheer number of supporters you have is much less important than the quality of the interactions you have with them. If you need to, use these questions to stimulate your thinking:

- Who do you spend time with?
- Who do you talk to?
- Who do you call to get support?

To start with, choose three important people in your life (you can come back later and look at more). Then, using this scale, complete the following questionnaire for each person:

1 = Strongly Disagree
2 = Disagree
3 = Neither Agree nor Disagree
4 = Agree
5 = Strongly Agree

Supporter Questionnaire

1. I can usually get a hold of this person within a reasonable amount of time when I need support.   1 2 3 4 5

2. This person checks in with me periodically, especially when I'm going through a rough time.   1 2 3 4 5

3. This person remembers the details of what I'm going through.   1 2 3 4 5

4. I feel comfortable and safe when I'm with this person.   1 2 3 4 5

5. I trust this person.   1 2 3 4 5

6. I think this person respects my needs and requests.   1 2 3 4 5

7. This person and I have a similar outlook on life   1 2 3 4 5

8. This person is patient with me.   1 2 3 4 5

9. I feel energized when I'm around this person.   1 2 3 4 5

10. I feel heard when I share my thoughts with this person.   1 2 3 4 5

11. This person allows me to take the time I need to talk about
    the issues I'm working through.   1 2 3 4 5

12. I can discuss difficult topics and personal issues with this person   1 2 3 4 5

13. This person is straight with me when giving me feedback and
    holding me accountable.   1 2 3 4 5

14. This person gives me advice only when I ask for it.   1 2 3 4 5

15. I feel comfortable expressing all my emotions around this person—
    from anger, fear, and sadness to hope, joy, and excitement.   1 2 3 4 5

16. This person understands what I'm going through.   1 2 3 4 5

17. This person allows me to be where I am in my transition journey.   1 2 3 4 5

18. This person gives me insights that help me see situations from
    new perspectives.   1 2 3 4 5

19. This person tends to be optimistic and looks for the gift
    in situations.   1 2 3 4 5

20. When something good happens in my life, this person celebrates
    with me.   1 2 3 4 5

21. This person supports my decisions and helps me take the actions
    I need to take.   1 2 3 4 5

22. This person encourages me to learn about myself and explore
    new situations.   1 2 3 4 5

23. This person knows how to be with me when I'm upset.   1 2 3 4 5

Be sure to add up your responses for each supporter separately. Now look at the comments below to interpret the score for each person.

- If the score is between 92 and 115, it's very likely you feel cared for and supported by this person.

- If the score is between 45 and 91, this person may be of moderate help to you. You may not feel totally supported, but you're probably getting something positive from your relationship.

- If the score is 46 or less, your interactions with this person may be doing more harm than good. Take a good look at why you're relying on this person for support. Just because someone is in your life doesn't necessarily mean they're a good source of support for you.

Are you surprised at how your supporters stacked up using this questionnaire? If their score seems too high or too low, make sure you were honest in your answers. Were you too hard on them? Too easy? If your individual responses seem right to you, think about why this person is showing up differently than you expected.

It's not unusual to think you have a lot of friends only to discover that they aren't there to help you in times of need. When Sam lost his home in a fire, for example, the support he received from his large family made him realize just how little his family understood and cared about his situation. Carrie experienced a different awakening. For years she and her best friend had supported each other through thick and thin. At least, that's what she thought. But when Carrie needed her friend's support during a tremendous job change, she discovered, much to her dismay, that her friend really wasn't there for her.

As Walter Mitchell is quoted in *A Gift of Hope*, "A real friend is one who walks in when the rest of the world walks out." Right now, you need to surround yourself with "real friends" who can support you in your journey.

How Can I Strengthen My Support System?

No matter what state your support system is in right now, it is possible to build a network to help you during your transition. From where you sit now, this task may feel overwhelming, if not downright impossible. When my father died, I'd only been in town four months. The few people I knew locally were work colleagues, and it wasn't particularly appropriate to rely on them for the level of support I needed. My mother and I spoke frequently by phone and saw each other periodically, but the support she could offer me was limited by the fact that we were both grieving so deeply. The other people I felt closest to—my brother, friends from school—were scattered all over the country. Although I made plenty of long-distance phone calls that first year, they didn't—and couldn't—fill all my needs.

I remember sitting in the dark many a night, rocking back and forth, crying my eyes out. I felt I had no one I could reach out to. As the intensity of my grief grew, I finally gathered the courage to build a network of professionals—a therapist, bodyworker, and grief counselor—to provide me with the support I needed. And, around that time, a loving golden retriever puppy entered my life. Somehow she knew her job was to shower me with unrestrained affection and offer me constant companionship.

Three years passed before I was ready to reach out to establish a social system of peers. At that point, I joined a church, volunteered, and took classes. Finally, I began meeting people I resonated with. Even today, I marvel at the strength of the network I've created for myself over the last seven years. I know that if I were to experience a crisis of any kind right now, I could contact any one of about thirty people and receive the support I used to crave.

I tell you this story to give you hope. Even if you're all alone now, it doesn't mean you have to live that way forever. Strengthening your support network is a process, just like everything else. If you put in the effort to cultivate this area of your life, it will grow.

In building your support network, the first thing you want to remember is diversity. You want to have different kinds of people you can call upon to help you in a variety of situations. There are six main categories of support you can draw from.

1. *Family and Friends*

If your responses to the Supporter Questionnaire indicate that you have friends and family members who are highly supportive, count your blessings and be sure to nurture your relationships with these people. Thank them, appreciate them, and do what you can to offer them support when they need it.

If, on the other hand, you discovered that some or all of the individuals in your life aren't being particularly helpful to you at this time, you may want to limit your interactions with them until you feel less vulnerable. Although this is a difficult decision that takes some thought, trust your intuition—it's the best barometer you've got. For example, if you always dread interacting with certain people—whether they're family members or close friends—pay attention to that. If you feel completely drained every time you see them or feel you must gather up all your strength to do battle at each visit, it's time to acknowledge that you're not being supported by the relationship right now. Create a way, as some of my clients have, to take a sabbatical from stress-provoking parents, siblings, and close friends in an effort to heal and gain clarity on your change.

By decreasing the amount of time you spend with those who aren't providing you with the support you need, you open up space in your life for new supporters. Although it's true that you can't recreate a new family for yourself, you can build a network that feels like a family should. Of course, this takes some time. Begin by looking at your acquaintances. Are there any you felt comfortable with the moment you met? Do you have shared interests? Reach out to those who attract your attention. Meet for coffee. Go for a walk. Attend a talk together. By extending an invitation, you'll increase the chance that you'll make a good friend. Granted, you may not become best buddies with each and every person you approach, but just participating in the process will help you become more and more comfortable with meeting new people. Have patience. Your network will naturally grow as you have more contact with others.

2. Your Love Relationship

When we're in the midst of transition, the person we most want to count on for support is usually our partner. If your spouse is supportive of you in your time of need, be grateful. Perhaps the reciprocal support skills you both possess have grown through the thick and thin of earlier trials. Although it may be a tough time, be sure to acknowledge yourselves for what you've created between you.

Unfortunately, our expectations are often so unrealistically high that our partners can't possibly fulfill our needs. What's even worse is that in our disappointment we often fail to notice the ways they do meet our needs. Remember that your needs run very deep right now, so it's unfair, to both of you, to pin the responsibility for all your support on your partner. You'll feel unfulfilled and your partner will feel guilty or useless—not a good combination when you already feel vulnerable.

Sometimes partners aren't able to be supportive because they look at the change from a different perspective. Perhaps they see it as a threat and are trying to do the right thing by getting in there and fixing things for you. Or perhaps they don't understand the concept of a transition journey at all. If this is the case, you might want to introduce them to the concepts of The Seasons of Change and where you are in the process, so they can develop a better sense of what your needs are.

Of course when you're going through a transition—deciding to go back to school, getting a new job, grieving the loss of a baby—often your partner is also going through it at the same time. When this happens, you may end up being in two different places in the journey—needing different kinds of support—at the same time. When Sandy and James moved cross-country for her promotion she was ecstatic, albeit a bit nervous, to be in her new job, meeting new people and learning the ropes. Sure, she had some adjusting to do, but it all seemed to be going smoothly for her. James, on the other hand, was having a difficult time of it. He'd left a very good job—the best he'd ever had—and hadn't been able to find anything comparable. So in addition to getting used to a new home and area, he was going through a difficult time trying to piece together a new career. With Sandy in Spring and James in Winter, their needs for support and their capacities to give to each other were stretched thin.

Another potentially difficult time for partners occurs when one person is in Summer—their plans are taking shape, their confidence level is building, and their need to be out in the world is growing. Meanwhile, the other person is spiraling into the depths of Winter. This situation is uncomfortable for both—especially if the person in Summer expects their partner to participate with excitement and joy in all their activities.

Honest, heartfelt communication, trust, and compassion are the key ingredients to navigating this kind of dual transition. Although it's not easy, the process can strengthen and deepen your relationship, making it even more loving than before. Although it's difficult to do, make an effort to keep your partner abreast of where you are in your journey. Write notes. Set up times to check-in with each other. Develop nonverbal ways to express where you are. I once read a story of a couple who put a teddy bear at their place at the table when they were having particularly rough days and needed extra TLC. The beauty of this was that they didn't have to find the *words* to express what they needed; they had only to gather the courage to give the signal.

To get the most benefit from signals like this, it's important to talk about how you like to be supported *before* you need it. When you're both feeling somewhat clear, take some time to think about the things that might signal you're in distress—curling up in a ball on the couch, closing the door to your safe space, crying, leaving the house for a walk around the block. As you talk about these, make a list so your partner has access to them. Then talk about what you'd like your partner to do, or not do, when you engage in these behaviors. By doing this before you're in a crisis, you'll be able to support each other more consciously.

Whether you're in a comforting relationship or not, it is imperative that you diversify your base of support. No one can give you everything you need, especially now. Furthermore, if it's not realistic to expect any kind of compassionate support from your partner, don't. There really isn't any benefit to torturing yourself with expectations that are always left unfulfilled. Devote your energy instead to creating the support you need from other sources.

3. Support Groups

Support groups provide a powerful blend of emotional support, camaraderie, and information. Typically, a support group consists of a number of people who are facing a similar situation, such as grief, cancer, divorce, debt, or recovery from an addiction. One of the most powerful benefits of belonging to a support group is that you get to listen to other people's experiences, which will help you put your own situation into perspective and realize you aren't alone in facing this particular change.

These groups can be informal in nature, started by one of the participants, or more formal and sponsored by an organization, hospital, or therapist. The purpose of most groups is to share experiences and information so that the participants can better handle whatever they're facing. A secondary benefit is that the one-on-one connections you make with other participants sometimes develop into deeper friendships over a period of several weeks or months.

Once you decide you want to think about joining a certain kind of group, you're likely to see and hear references to it all over the place. You can also speed up the process by asking people you trust if they've heard of any groups, by checking the telephone book, reading the calendar section of your local newspaper, calling your hospital, contacting the 800 number of a related association, doing a search on the World Wide Web, or checking with a therapy center.

If you can't locate a group, but find other people wrestling with the same issue you are, think about creating a group yourself. I've done this on several occasions and I know we've all benefited from the experiences we've shared. As a group, talk about your needs and then sketch out an agenda that will support everyone. A mix of sharing, discussing, and brainstorming is often good. After meeting a few times, revisit the agenda to see what's working and what's not. Allow the meeting format to evolve over time as the needs of the group change.

4. Professional Help

Another crucial source of support comes from professionals. Depending on your situation, you may have reason to work with a health professional, bodyworker, lawyer, accountant, financial planner, professional organizer, mediator, life coach, or career counselor.

If you're like most people facing major transitions, your financial situation plays a big role in your decision about whether or not to call on professionals for assistance. Although you probably hate the thought of spending money on something you "should" be able to do yourself, what you may not be taking into consideration are the costs associated with trying to go it alone—costs that can be both financial and nonfinancial.

Frank, for example, finally came to see me after ten years of struggling to find a new career on his own. Although his income had held up pretty well over the years, his self-esteem had plummeted, his health had suffered, and his standing in his field had steadily declined. If he had realized that he needed professional assistance at the end of one or two years, he could have avoided eight long years of misery and had the excitement, challenge, and fulfillment of a new career. So even though he didn't hurt himself financially by staying in his job, he did experience huge losses at a personal level. Indeed, he lost eight years of his life that he can never recover.

Take a moment to think about your situation. Imagine what your life might be like if you continued along the path of fending for yourself. What financial and emotional losses might occur if you lived the way you are now for another ten or twenty years?

Now, imagine how your world might be different if you could hire any professionals you wanted without worrying about the cost. What questions would you ask an advisor if you had one sitting there with you right now? With the help of others, what might you be able to resolve, clear away, or move through?

When you think about it from a broader perspective, what better investment is there than contributing to your own physical, emotional, mental, and spiritual well-being? In the short term, getting the support you need will get you back on stable ground more quickly than if you try to forge through the process on your own. In the long run, you and those you love will benefit from this investment. Your children, for instance, will be profoundly impacted as you release your fears and limiting beliefs because you'll become a better parent, provide them with a better environment, and allow them to grow up with more confidence and self-esteem. Getting professional support may mean you have a pretty tight budget this year, but you'll continue to reap the rewards of your decision for years to come.

Once you decide to invest in yourself, the next step is to discover how to get the best support you can within your budget. Begin by thinking about what you need. Is it emotional, financial, physical, or spiritual support? Perhaps it's a combination of things. As long as you have some idea of what you're looking for, you can begin your research. Then by talking with different people, your vision of what you need and want will become clearer.

With a little investigation, you may find there are some sources of support that cost very little or nothing at all. Check your health insurance policy to see what it covers. Ask the professionals you talk with if they have a sliding fee schedule that will allow you to pay what you can afford. Look for not-for-profit groups or classes that provide low cost or free support that's relevant to you.

If you find the resource you need but still can't figure out how to pay for it, brainstorm who might be willing to help you out. Your parents, siblings, or friends may be willing to invest in your transition. I know this may sound a little farfetched, but a number of my clients have had their entire consulting process paid for by someone else. Get your facts together and be open to receiving a gift!

Although no one can predict just how long you'll need to receive support, you can safely assume that support won't change you or your situation overnight. Depending on your circumstances, it may take several months or even a year or two to resolve your situation. Therefore, it'll be most helpful if you find resources you'll be able to afford over an extended period of time.

To make sure you're making a wise investment, it's important for you to learn as much as you can about the professional, their background, and their expertise with situations like yours. Start this process by gathering as many referrals as you can from people you trust. If they've had a good experience with the professional, you'll have some reassurance that the person provides the services they advertise. Find out if there's a local professional group that provides referrals. Interview several professionals doing the same kind of work so you can get a sense of their different styles. Listen to how they describe their work to increase your own knowledge on the topic so you can ask more detailed questions of the next person you interview. Ask the professional if you can talk with any of their previous clients.

If you intend to have a lengthy connection with this person, use the Supporter Questionnaire to ascertain whether they'll provide you with the kind of support you want. Sometimes it's easy to assume that just because someone has the training and is certified to do the work, they'll be perfectly able to handle all your needs. Although credentials are a good start, it's also crucial that you feel safe with the people you hire to support you. This is true of everyone you work with—from an accountant or lawyer to a therapist or bodyworker. The last thing you need right now is to have to find the strength to fight for your rights with the person you're paying to help you.

The time I spent with Tia during her divorce pointed out the trauma this situation causes. Although the negotiations for the divorce started out fairly well, they soon escalated into a horrific battle. The worst part of her experience was that her own lawyer wasn't telling her the truth, keeping her informed, or completing the tasks he was hired to do. You can bet your bottom dollar that Tia is now very particular about the people she hires to be on her side!

When you first establish a relationship with a professional, you may experience a great sense of relief as you think about putting yourself in their hands and letting them take over. It's easy to think they know best, have all the answers, and will take care of everything for you. Typically, the more authority they have by virtue of their position, the more likely you are to give your power away to them. Their job, however, is not to fix you or remove all your troubles, but to facilitate your movement through the transition you're in.

Your responsibility is to maintain an active role in your own life. Stay involved. Ask questions when you're confused. Voice your concerns and add your opinions. The most important thing you can do is stay true to yourself throughout your work with each professional, whether a doctor, lawyer, or financial planner. If the professional isn't fulfilling your needs in some way, talk to them about your concerns and ask for some modifications. If what they're saying runs counter to what your intuition is telling you, take their advice under consideration. Once you're away from their office, think about their ideas and try them out for yourself. If you still have questions, ask them to help you make sense of what they're recommending. If they can't explain their recommendations to your satisfaction or the agreed-upon changes aren't forthcoming, you've got some decisions to make.

Here are several indicators to suggest when your relationship with a professional is no longer serving you:

- If, at any point, you feel deeply uncomfortable or distrustful of the person you're working with, take notice. If this pattern continues or escalates, you should probably take a serious look at the relationship.

- If you notice the professional isn't giving you the attention you deserve—confusing you with other clients, forgetting what you've said, arriving late for your appointments consistently, or missing appointments altogether.

- If you don't feel the professional is hearing you or understanding your position, realize that it will be very difficult for them to help you.

- If you discover that your philosophies conflict, you may decide not to continue the relationship. This will be especially important if your sense of ethics is considerably different from theirs.

- If you're committed to moving yourself through the entire transition process, be leery of professionals who want you to jump into a quick solution or a solution that's counter to your goals.

Remember, the bottom line is that you hired them. There is no point in continuing to pay for services that aren't meeting your needs.

Sometimes it's hard to let go when you've already invested time and money into building a relationship that now has a history. Recognize how much you've gained from the relationship—what you've learned, how you've changed, how your situation has improved. When, and if, you need to develop a relationship with a different professional, you won't have to start from scratch because you're now in a better position to explain the details of your situation in a shorter amount of time. Actually, you may find that the perspective the new professional has brings new elements to light and allows you to spring forward even faster.

5. Therapists

In certain circumstances, the most important element of your support network will be someone who can help you work through past situations to free you up to move forward. Depending on your situation and where you live, the most appropriate source of support might be a psychotherapist, psychiatrist, social worker, minister, nurse, or hypnotherapist. If you're like most people, just the thought of trying to find a therapist, let alone a good one, may be a bit overwhelming.

Keep in mind that your main objective will be to find someone who is both supportive and professionally qualified to assist you. As you contact potential therapists, remember that you don't have to settle for the first person you talk to and you don't have to stay with one if at any time or for any reason it doesn't feel right. For you to get what you're paying for, you must feel safe and comfortable with the person you choose.

Before you begin, narrow your search by defining the kind of person you'd like to work with:

- Would you prefer to work with a male or female therapist?
- Would you like to work with someone who has a similar world-view or philosophy of life?
- Is it important to you that your therapist have a similar religious or spiritual orientation?
- Do you want traditional "talk" therapy or do you want to explore other options, such as art therapy, hypnotherapy, or dream therapy?

In their book *When Talk Is Not Cheap*, Mandy Aftel and Robin Tolmach Lakoff indicate that it's important to spell out your basic requirements for therapy:

- How much time are you willing to invest in your healing? Think about approximately how long you'd like to work on this issue and how often you're willing to meet.

- What do you want to accomplish? Do you want to find a solution to a current situation, or are you interested in delving into the core issues?

- How do you usually process information—verbally, physically, symbolically? Do you want to work primarily in your preferred mode, or would you get more benefit if you switched to a mode you're less familiar with?

- Do you want the therapist to guide the process or do you want to choose what you address?

- If the issues you're dealing with involve other people, do you want them to be included in the therapy or do you want to focus on your part of the situation?

You may also want to consider some logistical issues:

- How far are you willing to travel?
- What options does your health insurance cover?
- Are you willing or able to pay out of your own pocket?
- When are you available to meet?

Once you've outlined some of your parameters, ask around to see if you can get any referrals from people you trust—friends, other professionals, family members, or through the Employee Assistance Program (EAP). Recommendations are most beneficial when you and your referral source have a similar outlook on life and a similar reason for working with a therapist.

When you've collected a few names, call the therapist for an initial conversation. Begin by giving them a brief synopsis of your situation and your goals for therapy. Find out as much as you can about them to be sure you feel comfortable with them. Ask specific questions about their training, life experiences, way of working, and specialties. See if they've worked with people who have experienced what you're going through. Request copies of any articles they have that describe their work or specific techniques they use. Ask them to tell you how they would work with you specifically. Although they'll need to have much more detail about your history and the background of your specific situation to give you an exact plan, their first assessment of your situation will give you some idea of how they work. If they diagnose you over the phone and settle on a treatment plan immediately, be wary.

If it sounds as if there might be a match, ask them specific questions about their practice: how much they charge, where they're located, what times they work, and whether they're covered by your insurance.

To have a productive relationship with your therapist, it's critical that you agree with and resonate with his/her basic approach. If you tend to be intuitive and see the world from a spiritual vantage point, you might feel rather limited or constrained doing only cognitive work or "talk" therapy. If, on the other hand, you're a logical person, some of the more free-form approaches—dream therapy, role playing, sand tray, art therapy, visualization—may feel uncomfortable to you at first. It's also important to realize that your preferences and the effectiveness of different modes of therapy may change as you move through different stages of your healing journey.

6. Social or Service Organizations

Social and service organizations are also good sources of support as you prepare to venture out of hibernation. They offer the unique benefit of being a ready-made social system. When you feel ready, consider attending a church service, volunteering, joining a club, or taking a class. Like everything else I've suggested, it's important to experiment. Visit different groups over several weeks or months until you find one or two that fit your needs and interests. If you can't imagine going by yourself, ask a friend to tag along with you. Don't force yourself. This is something to allow into your life.

When you find a group you enjoy, get involved. Working on a committee or volunteering for specific activities will give you the opportunity to meet individuals and begin to establish friendships. As you get to know more people individually, you'll begin to feel more comfortable interacting in the group. There's also a good possibility that by just being involved, other social invitations will come your way. Enjoy the process of expanding your circle of friends.

Eleven

Getting the Support
You Need

Once you figure out who to get help from, the next challenge is deciding what kind of support you need. This is rarely a simple process, especially if you've been overly self-reliant most of your life and have a difficult time carving out anything anyone else can do to help you. Furthermore, if you've never before experienced the depths of despair you're feeling right now, you may have no idea how to articulate your needs to yourself, let alone to others.

There's no one right way to support someone in transition. In fact, your preferences may change hour to hour, day to day, and with different transitions. The people around you probably won't be able to tell what you want just by looking at you. They aren't psychic, after all. The best way to get the support you want is to be as specific as you can about what you'd like. If you want companionship, ask for that. If you know you want something, but aren't sure how to verbalize it, at the very least, initiate a conversation with someone who can help you figure out what you want. As storyteller Susan Gordon writes, "Healing is about receiving and nurturing. There is a bounty and it is necessary to ask for it," for only then "the walls between people can crumble."

If you think back on the Handless Maiden's journey, you'll remember several points along the way when things looked pretty bleak—when she could see the pears but couldn't get to them, when she entered the forest with her baby bound to her breast, when her baby fell into the well. In all these cases, she asked for help and it arrived in the form of the Spirit in White, who opened up new options either by aiding her directly or by guiding her to help herself. Whether your request is a silent prayer or a verbal statement, the better you are at articulating your needs, the more support you'll receive.

Of course, your needs for support will change as you move through different phases of your journey. This chapter outlines how people can support you in each season. Because it's so hard to ask for help, I've suggested specific requests you can take word for word from the book if you need to. As you learn more about your own preferences and how to read your emotions, you'll be able to fine-tune the suggestions given here so they'll fit your unique situation even better.

Fall

As you recall, Fall is a time when shifts occur signaling that your future will be different from the past. Your main focus during this time is to acknowledge that a change is actually happening and do what you can to prepare. You may want to ask the people around you for the following types of support.

1. Give You Moral Support

One of the most painful parts of Fall is waiting—for test results, telephone calls, information, decisions, or for others to take action. Of course, with the waiting comes the worrying about what will happen next. If you're waiting and worrying right now, what do you want most? What would comfort you best? Do you want someone to:

- Sit with you while you wait?
- Reassure you?

- Field all the calls you're getting?
- Check in with you several times a day?
- Hold you?

You may also want some moral support if you're facing a frightening or frustrating task. Do you want someone to:

- Be available if you run into trouble?
- Go with you to a meeting?
- Sit with you while you tackle the task?
- Do the task for you?

You might request support by saying: "I'm really having a hard time right now. I could use some moral support. Are you available to help me out?"

2. Encourage You to Create a Refuge

To prepare for Winter, it's critical that you develop a place where you can go to let down your defenses. There are several ways you can utilize your supporters help in this:

- "Can you help me figure out what makes me feel safe?" Your supporter might ask questions about when you last felt safe, what brought you feelings of safety as a child, or what you imagine might feel safe. He or she might also point out remembered situations or stories you have told to help you create a sense of safety.
- "Would you help me brainstorm the best place for my safe space and what I might put in it?" Sometimes it's a challenge to locate a good spot for your refuge. Some joint thinking may illuminate new ideas for you. A conversation might also bring items to mind that you might not have thought of on your own.
- "Will you encourage me to create my safe space this week?"

In my experience, constructing a safe haven is a very private process. If that's true for you as well, you may want your supporter to encourage you to take time away from all your other activities to do this. If you'd like your supporter to help you during the process, ask for that specifically.

- "Will you guide me through a visualization process so I can create an inner sanctuary for myself?"

See the Fall chapter for more specific ideas on this.

3. Assist You in Looking at Your Options

Sometimes Fall shifts require us to make decisions at a faster pace than we're ready for. Usually, this occurs with an emergency of some sort—you lose your home in a natural disaster, a loved one has to have immediate surgery, or you're in a car accident. In these situations, you *can't* wait until you feel calm enough to make a decision; you must respond now. If you're faced with this kind of crisis situation, ask your supporter to assist you by:

- Helping you ask the right questions.
- Noticing aspects of the situation you don't see.
- Identifying options beyond those that are obvious to you.
- Helping you weigh the pros and cons of the various options you're considering.
- Clarifying which decisions must be made now and which ones can be put aside for a time.
- Helping you choose which actions to take.
- Brainstorming new ways to handle the financial aspects of your situation.

Your supporters will most likely come to these situations with a clearer mind and a different, if not more objective, viewpoint. Although you need to make the final decisions yourself, the sense of perspective you receive from these people will be most beneficial.

Special Note to Supporters

Because the person you're supporting may not be able to verbalize what he or she wants, you may need to find ways you can offer support. One of the most important things you can do is help the person acknowledge that a change really has happened. Sometimes it's hard for someone *in* the situation to grasp the extent of what they're facing. Depending on their openness, your observations might trigger their healing process or be met by a wall of denial that can't be overcome. Know that you have at least planted a seed of awareness.

Keep your eyes and ears open for information—a therapist, a support group, a television show, an article, a Web site—that may be relevant to the transitioner. Who knows? The piece of information you provide may lead your friend in a new, life-changing direction.

Keep the transitioner focused on finding the long-term solution that fits them and their circumstances best. If the person is panicked and in chaos, he or she may well try to jump at the first option that presents itself. Your reassurance and reminders that quick fixes aren't usually the answer may help them delve into Winter so they can make a true, lasting change in their life.

Early Winter

This is the part of the transition journey that our society understands the least. As you descend into the darkness, ask your supporters to:

1. Help You Slow Down and Renew Yourself

Request that your network help you see:

- When you're staying frenetically busy in an attempt to bypass your emotions. Don't brush them off when they try to give you feedback—they really are trying to help.

- When you're worn out physically and emotionally. In some traumatic situations, you may not be aware of how run down you really are. If you're hearing comments about how tired you seem or how on edge you are, take notice. Their perspective is probably more objective than yours is right now.

In addition to having your supporters notice what state you're in, you might ask them to encourage and support you in slowing down. Request that they honor your need to rest by allowing you to change plans or turn down offers at the last minute if you don't feel up to doing something.

If you're stumped as to how to renew yourself, ask your friends to help you brainstorm ways you can nourish yourself. Their ideas will be especially useful if you have a limited budget, overwhelming responsibilities, or other factors influencing you. Sometimes the best support someone can offer is to give you permission to take the afternoon off for a nap, a walk, or a bath.

2. Help You Create More Quiet Time

- "Would you sit down with me and help me look at ways I can incorporate more quiet time into my schedule?" Sometimes someone else can see possibilities you can't.

- "Would you be willing to help me with _____ so that I can take some time by myself?" Perhaps you need someone to take care of your pets while you go out of town for the weekend, or to take your children for a few hours so you can have some uninterrupted time to yourself.

- "Will you please give me some space?" Your supporters may think you want their companionship, and at certain times you may. But occasionally you'll need time to focus all your energies inward. If you're not used to making such requests, it may feel selfish to ask people to stay away. You must remember that to heal, your process must be your first priority. Explain to your loved ones, either in person or in a note, that you've been feeling out of sorts recently and need time to move through it. If it's true, you can reassure them by adding that you're not mad at them for anything. In fact, you're quite thankful to have had their help along the way.

- "Would you be willing to go with me to _____?" If you're uncomfortable going places alone at this time, your supporter may accompany you on a retreat, to a church service, or to a park. Sometimes, just being with someone is the best support in the world.

3. Help You Deepen Your Reflective Process

You may find that you get into an infinite loop in your thinking—no matter how you look at the situation, the answers always come out the same. Get some outside perspective by asking your supporters:

- "Do you see a pattern between this situation and other situations in my life?"
- "Can you see any angle that I'm missing?"
- "Have you seen me respond this way before? In what situation?"
- "I'm stuck with this situation. Can you ask me some questions that might jump start me into thinking in a new direction?"
- "I feel like I'm missing something. Can you see where my blind spot is?"
- "Do you see any beliefs I have that are getting in my way?"
- "Can you reflect back to me what you're hearing?"

If you're using any of the insight tools mentioned in the Winter chapters, it sometimes helps to talk with other people about what you've found. Their ideas can bring richness and new depth to your thinking.

- "What connections do you see between my situation and this card, dream image, or object?"
- "This is how I interpreted this. Do you see anything else?"

Consider others' insights, but remember that your interpretations of symbols, dreams, and events are what count the most. When people tell you in no uncertain terms that your interpretation is wrong and theirs is right, thank them for their ideas and let them know you'll think about it. Don't let yourself get hung up on someone else's doomsday interpretation of a dream you thought was uplifting and full of hope.

Special Note to Supporters

Early Winter is the darkest, loneliest, most confusing place to be. Yet transitioners *must* experience this place before they can move on. The most important thing you can do is be compassionate:

- Allow your loved one or friend to be confused. Be willing to just listen as they share their foggy chaos.

- When asked to help interpret a dream or make sense of a situation, offer suggestions and ideas, but encourage the transitioner to use your ideas only as a catalyst to stimulate more insights rather than as the truth.

- Encourage the transitioner to express their feelings. If they're afraid to feel anything, help them express emotions in small doses and safely. Don't be too surprised if they express conflicting emotions within a fairly short span of time. Remember, they are confused to the core of their being.

If you become concerned with the depth of their feelings, encourage him or her to get professional help. If you're a professional yourself but find you're out of your comfort zone, refer your client to another professional who's better equipped to handle the intensity of the situation.

Winter Solstice

Now that you've set the stage for your Winter Solstice insights, your only objective is to stay open enough to receive them when they flash through you. You might want to ask your supporters to:

1. Give You Extra Space

For the most part, you probably feel a deep urge to be hibernating in your refuge right now. Voice your desires:

- "I'm processing through a lot right now, and I'd appreciate it if you'd let me have the day to myself."

- "I feel like something is brewing deep inside me. I don't want to lose it so I'm going to take some time for myself today."

2. Help You Ignite the Sparks

If you have a supporter who understands the importance and magic of the Winter Solstice, and if you'd like a companion during this precious time, invite him or her to serve as a catalyst or a witness.

- "Will you help me brainstorm all the ways I've benefited from this transition?"
- "Will you serve as a witness as I draw a line in the sand and say, 'Enough is enough'?"
- "Will you help me perform some completion rituals? I could really use your support."
- "Will you listen to me as I tell my new story for the first time?"

Special Note to Supporters

Aside from supporting your loved one or client in the magical wonders of the Winter Solstice, your main role may be helping him or her see a blind spot. If the transitioner's been spending time in their safe space and still isn't making the progress you'd expect, it's possible there's an issue they can't see for themselves. Remember that progress in this season isn't in quantifiable actions but in subtle shifts of awareness and perspective. It's time to suggest, somewhat strongly if you must, that the transitioners invite others to help him or her unlock their past so they can move into their future.

Late Winter

Like a watched pot that never boils, your passage into Spring may feel interminable. The more work you do, the fewer results you seem to see. That's because you're becoming one with your new ideas and visions. Your supporters can help you keep the faith that something really is happening. Ask them to:

1. Help You Integrate Your Insights

If you discover you're having a difficult time making sense of all your new ideas, ask your supporters to help you in any of the following ways:

- "I've got all these ideas floating around in my head. Do you have some time to sit and listen to me?"
- "I've come up with some new ideas based on the insights I've been getting over the last few months. I was wondering if you see any connections or patterns I've missed."
- "I just had this fantastic dream. Can I tell you about it? I'd love to hear your thoughts."

2. Assist You in Clearing Out

You may want some moral support as you make you way through your boxes, piles, and closets. Start by asking your supporter, whether a friend or a professional organizer, to help you determine which part of your home, office, cabinet, or closet you'd like to begin work on. Choose something that feels doable and that will feel good when done. By getting a few successful sessions under your belt, you'll feel more motivated to tackle the harder parts.

If you still can't seem to make any progress, ask your supporter to help you separate items into several piles—definitely want to keep it, definitely want to toss it (garbage, giveaway, donate), and definitely don't know what to do with it. This last category gives you a safety valve so you won't feel paralyzed by having to make absolute decisions on everything. Ask your supporters to help keep you focused on the three piles rather than on the story and emotion attached to every item. I'm not saying you shouldn't reminisce during this process, but what I am suggesting is that it helps to have someone around who can steer the process back on track when necessary.

If your life seems to be cluttered with outgrown friendships or old commitments, ask your supporters to help you sort out which ones really aren't serving you. For instance, they might ask you if you're giving more than you're getting from any relationships these days. Or if you're dreading the time you must spend meeting certain responsibilities. When you find a relationship that's not working, brainstorm with your supporters to discover how you can pull away gracefully, keeping your integrity intact.

3. Help Create a Cohesive Plan for Your Future

Because you're so close to your plans, it may be helpful to ask other people to review them with you:

- "Do you see any holes in my plan?"
- "Can you help me break down my long-term plans into steps that I can achieve?"
- "When I put my plans together, I find I'm going in so many directions I can't possibly move forward. Can you help me identify my priorities and set up a timeline?"

Special Note to Supporters

By this time, your loved one or client is feeling as though he or she will never get out of Winter.

- If the transitioner is frustrated with their progress, help them see that they really are moving forward. Point out the glimmers of Spring you see—new attitudes, new behaviors, new images surfacing in dreams, new ways of handling situations. Remind them how far they've come.

- If they're rushing into a solution without really thinking it through, do what you can to persuade them to wait until they have more information, until the time is right, until others can help out, or until they further clarify their vision.

- If they don't seem to be making any progress consolidating their ideas into a plan, encourage the transitioner to look at what's getting in the way.

Spring

If you're like many of my clients, you may have assumed that Spring would be easy. In some ways, this is true. In other ways, however, you may need just as much support now as you did in the other seasons. Ask your supporters to:

1. Give You Permission to Trust Your Own Sense of Timing

As you learn to interpret signs from your environment about when to move forward or when to hold back for a time, ask your supporters for their thoughts. Remember they can provide you only with their opinions. The ultimate decision about your timing rests with you.

2. Encourage You to Find Ways to Stretch and Grow

From the time the birth in your life is imminent to the point where you have completely integrated the new element into your life, you are bound to need various kinds of support from your network:

- "Can you help me outline what I need to do to prepare for the new _____ in my life?"
- "I'm trying to figure out how I can experiment with this part of my plan. Would you help me brainstorm where I might be able to do this, how I might check this out inexpensively, or who I might talk to?"
- "Would you go with me as I try something new?"
- "Now that I've tried several experiments, I feel good about certain aspects of my plan, but I also realize that this won't work the way I thought it would. Do you have any time to help me look at other alternatives?"

During this process, have your supporters remind you that you're still just exploring options and not yet wedded to any one outcome.

3. Support You in Putting Your Plan into Action

Just because you're now ready to take action doesn't mean you don't need support. Be sure to request the help you need from your supporters during this season as well.

- "I'm feeling very overwhelmed with all these new tasks. Can you help me prioritize them?"
- "Do you have time to listen while I talk through the various steps I need to take? Perhaps together we can find a way to streamline the procedures."
- "I'm trying to come up with a way to do this task that fits my personal style better. Can you ask me some questions to stimulate my thinking?"

Special Note to Supporters

Although people in Spring are likely to be excited about their new prospects, few expect to run into turbulent storms on their journey. You can provide a great service by being close at hand when these emotional storms hit from out of the blue.

One way Spring storms manifest themselves is in the emotional roller coaster people experience in this season. It's very important to reassure the transitioner that the stormy emotions they're feeling do not signal that they're back at the beginning of Winter.

Your loved one or client may also experience a great deal of fear as he or she delves into new arenas. Show them that because fear is a natural response to situations that feel unsafe, it can help them see when they are and aren't yet ready to move forward. By seeing fear and other emotions as tools rather than weaknesses, they're easier to handle.

Sometimes if the internal emotional roller coaster is too intense, you may notice the transitioner ignoring their own wisdom and making no movement whatsoever. This is an indicator that some deeper issue needs to be handled before they can proceed.

Summer

You've arrived at the destination you've been striving toward for months. Depending on your nature, you may love Summer or you may feel a great sense of discomfort. Either way, your supporters can play an important role during this season. Ask them to:

1. Participate in Your Celebrations

This is a great time to give back to your supporters and thank them for all their support, wisdom, and time. Don't be surprised if they turn the tables on you by thanking and acknowledging you for how you've enriched their lives and how you've served as a powerful model for consciously going through life changes.

2. Help You Learn to Enjoy Your Success

If you're uncomfortable taking credit for your successes, being in the limelight, or being happy, ask your supporters to help you:

- "I'm having a hard time fully grasping my success. Can you help me look at why I'm blocking this?"
- "I want to spend the day having some spontaneous fun. Would you like to join me?"
- "Will you help me brainstorm ways I can begin to let in and receive all the good things in my life?

I know it may seem funny to be asking for this sort of support, given that you've just "made it." Take heart. You're definitely not alone in lacking the skills to enjoy your success fully. However, like so many things, once you learn how to receive, you won't forget it.

3. Help You Stay in the Moment

You've worked long and hard to bask in your success. Recruit your supporters' help by saying:

- "I keep worrying about the future. Will you stop me when you hear me talking about it?"
- "Will you remind me to breathe when you notice I'm starting to worry?"

Special Note to Supporters

Although the person you've been supporting has "made it," he or she still needs your support while they get used to their success. It's not always as easy as it seems.

- Help build their confidence level—especially if they're having a difficult time claiming success. Compliment them, make comments about how far they've come, and share how proud you are.
- Ask questions to help them define their fear of success. Assist them in seeing that they have choices they can make to welcome success on their own terms.
- When life begins to shift again, be available. Your presence alone may give your loved one or client the strength to notice the need for a slight adjustment in their life. Having had the experience once, they will probably have a much smoother trip the next time around.

Twelve

Making Change
Your Ally

After years of observing people going through major transitions of all varieties, I've noticed a disturbing pattern. Due to our conditioning, we usually hold fast to our lives no matter what, even as everything is falling apart around us. The part of us that's sensitive to the pain we're experiencing, and might act to reduce it, is numb. Because we've been under duress for so long—pushing ourselves too hard trying to be perfect, fulfilling others' needs at the expense of our own, pretending we're satisfied with our lives when we're not—we've lost our internal radar which alerts us to trouble. As a result, we're so out of touch we don't notice when our heart dries out, we begin to limp, or our vision blurs.

At some level, we take great pride in persevering. Perhaps it comes from our training—religious and otherwise—that it's noble to suffer. That the only way to get reward is through hard work and struggle. With this thought, we keep our heads down and push forward toward what we hope will eventually be a better life.

In the process, we put up with situations, homes, relationships, jobs, and churches that are detrimental because whatever is wrong isn't bad enough to motivate us to change. We saw this dynamic with the Handless Maiden, who didn't argue with her father when he was about to chop off her hands. We tell ourselves, "I can take it," "I can put up with this for a while," "It's not so bad." Somehow, we believe that the known chaos and pain is better than the unknown created by change. We hold onto any shred of hope we can find, no matter how remote, and tell ourselves that life will change and get better somehow, someday.

What strikes me most is that the circumstances people are wrestling with are rarely new—in fact, often they've been facing these or similar issues for years, sometimes even decades. For some reason, they've just never found a way to make the changes required to alter their lives significantly. When I listen to people tell their stories, I hear several explanations for why they can't resolve their situations:

- They don't think they can make a change because something is wrong with them. For example, they feel they're too old, have too many responsibilities tying them down, don't have the education, or aren't creative or strong enough.

- They don't think they can make a change because the shifts are just too big and will require too much risk, time, energy, money, or effort.

- They don't think they should change because it would be too much of an imposition on other people. Others won't approve of them or their actions, won't like their changed priorities, would be jealous of their new success, or would be forced to change in their own right.

The pain, anguish, and struggle these people—and that's most of us—endure is frequently overwhelming. It takes incredible amounts of time and energy to remain in a desperate situation—always protecting yourself and climbing out of one crisis after another. Then when change is forced upon us—from an illness, a death in the family, a job loss—the despair, stress, and futility create such a tremendous drain on us that it shows up in our pocketbooks, health, relationships, mind, emotional state, spiritual well-being, homes, and work. The toll is just too high.

Crisis-Oriented Change

Eventually, after years of holding our lives together with grit and toothpicks, the bottom drops out. As Clarissa Pinkola Estés says, we're "finally and suddenly" pushed "over the edge and into the rapids" of life. It's almost as though we've been waiting for a traumatic event to release us from our pain and suffering. Just like the soon-to-be Handless Maiden, who sits nonchalantly for three years waiting for the Devil to come take her away, we sit detached from ourselves and our world, watching as our crisis, looming in the distance, draws closer each day. All the while, we hope and pray the devilish crisis will dissipate like a spent tornado. It isn't until the crisis hits, and we lose our hands and everything else, that we're forced on the journey.

It doesn't have to be this way. We can actually befriend the change process and learn to be prepared for the changes that will occur. When I first share this idea with people, they often explain, "Well, some changes just happen." In their voices I hear indignation that I would dare to suggest that we create our own crises. I agree that some traumas do come out of the blue and strike in unexpected ways, and we have no means to control or even avoid these kinds of changes. Natural disasters such as earthquakes, hurricanes, floods, and tornadoes, major accidents, and acts of violence and abuse certainly come to mind. But even in these cases, if we're conscious enough of the potential that these events may happen, we *can choose* to take appropriate precautions and be prepared to mobilize after an event occurs.

If we look at some examples of changes people tend to think just happen to them, we'll begin to see what our stupor really costs us. Sam, for instance, had a heart attack. He tells you he had no warning whatsoever, but when you look at his lifestyle you see the words "high stress" written all over it: busy with appointments from sunup to sundown, key business trips scheduled back to back with only enough time in between to pack another suitcase and kiss his wife hello and good-bye, his habit of bringing two or three caffeinated sodas to every meeting. Who says there was no warning?

By taking a moment to collect her thoughts and talk herself out of flinging open the exit doors and bolting from the church, Susie finally got it together enough to start down the aisle with her father. Two years later she divorced the man she married that day. Everyone was stunned and asked, "What happened? They looked so happy together!" The real surprise was that the wedding had happened at all. As it turns out, there were ample warning signs the weekend of the wedding: the bride and groom shouting at each other over the phone right before the rehearsal dinner, the couple swearing at one another as they parted that night. The signs were so blatant, in fact, that the entire wedding party knew the score but no one wanted to speak up because it would have been awkward to call off the wedding at that point. Everyone bought into the idea that the show just had to go on.

If we look back even further, we can see that signs of discord were there months before the wedding. Susie, however, just assumed they were the jitters "everyone" gets when they're about to be married. So the divorce that seemed to come out of the blue had actually been brewing, unattended, since a week after the engagement. I'll bet if we looked at even subtler signs we could find reason to suspect that even the engagement was doomed from the start.

Think about some of the shocks you've experienced in your life—an illness, a divorce, a layoff, abuse. Is there any reason to believe there were some subtle signs of trouble brewing before the crisis hit? In some cases, you may have to look beyond yourself for signs. With abuse, for instance, the warnings that signaled trouble may have actually begun several generations back and were never dealt with by those involved. Over the years, the subtle warning signs escalated, erupting into a hurtful or often violent situation.

Over the years, as I've watched my clients, read about people in the paper, and seen stories on television, I've found myself saying, "There just has to be another way." I couldn't believe we had to struggle so much to improve our lives. Finally, I asked the question: "Must we wait until we have a crisis on our hands to muster up a sufficient amount of strength, courage, and motivation to make the changes we need to make?"

I don't believe we do. Furthermore, with the ever-changing world we live in, I don't believe we can. We must move beyond the reactive method of responding to changes in our lives and learn how to make change by choice, with purpose and intention. As storyteller Susan Gordon points out, even though we may be handless on occasion, we're not helpless. We all have the ability and the option to make choices.

Clearly, if you've been conditioned to fear change because you believe it threatens your chance of success, the idea of approaching change from a place of choice can be a very frightening proposition. If, however, as a result of the transition you're working through right now, you're beginning to see that changes can be a catalyst to improve your life, you may be in a better place to entertain the idea of using change as an ally.

Choosing to Change

What if we all had the inner strength to make needed changes as soon as we noticed something wasn't working in our lives? How would our lives be different if we took this proactive approach to living? What if we were so fully in touch with our essence and personal cycles that we, as Clarissa Pinkola Estés said, could enter change "by a graceful dive from the cliff?" Yes, you heard me—we can actually choose to embark on the transition journey rather than being pushed, forced, or kicked into changing.

Joseph Campbell tells us in *The Power of Myth* that we have a choice—we can transform our consciousness "either by the trials themselves or by illuminating revelations." Both paths get us to change the way we think; the latter is just a lot less painful and costly once we learn how to do it.

Indeed, *pleasure* can also create change! To develop a case for this in *Original Blessing*, Matthew Fox quotes a couple of important thinkers: Fritz Perls, a Gestalt psychologist, states, "The organism does not move by will, but by preference." And thirteenth-century theologian and philosopher St. Thomas Aquinas "taught that people are changed more by pleasure than by anything else." Finally, Fox concludes that one day "pleasure and blessing will indeed change people and structures" and when we do learn to savor pleasure "we will learn what simple living means."

So think of it. By catching situations early on, before they reach crisis proportions, we would:

- Experience less stress—physically, emotionally, mentally, spiritually.
- Spend less time and energy handling full-blown crises.
- Cut crisis-spending.
- Have more time to identify and think about underlying issues.
- Have choices about how and when we respond to situations.
- Spend more time and energy enhancing our lives.

Certainly sounds like a simpler, more enjoyable life to me. By acting with purpose in this way rather than waiting for disaster to strike, we can make a series of small but significant mid-stream course corrections that ultimately add up to a more manageable and enjoyable life. Are you ready to dive in?

Making Purposeful Changes

If you've successfully navigated the journey through The Seasons of Change or are now in that process, you're already learning the skills you need to make purposeful changes in your life. Using this framework of the seasons you can, depending on the situation, run through the entire transition process in a matter of minutes, days, or weeks.

First, let me lay out the five phases again so you can see them clearly:

- Notice something isn't working (Fall).
- Think about your situation (Early Winter).
- State what you want (Late Winter).
- Take the appropriate action (Spring).
- Enjoy your results (Summer).

There's really nothing magical about these steps. In fact, I would guess that you already use some version of this process every time you notice that a house plant needs water, your leftovers need to be tossed, or the garbage must be taken out.

Imagine walking through your home and noticing a slightly wilted plant (Fall). Within a few seconds, you ascertain that the plant needs water (Winter), so you get a pitcher of water and give the plant the drink it needs (Spring). Within a short period of time, the plant revives and you get to enjoy the results of your actions (Summer).

Because all this happens in such a short time, you may never have noticed the process you went through to resolve the problem at hand. But you can use these five steps in any situation:

- Deciding when to go to the dentist or doctor.
- Facilitating a meeting.
- Figuring out how to spend your vacation.
- Deciding to leave your job or relationship.
- Bringing up issues with your spouse.
- Streamlining your work flow.

The only thing that sets this approach to change apart from the larger-scale journey is your ability to notice the subtle indicators that something isn't working and your capacity to attend to it as soon as possible. The earlier you catch a problem, the easier it is to work with the situation to improve it—often in a matter of minutes or days rather than months or years.

Granted, the scenario I've just described is rather mild. In most cases, we probably wouldn't go into crisis if we forgot to water a plant. But take a moment to think back on the situations in your life that did reach crisis proportions. How might they have been different if you'd been able to notice and act on the early warning signals that something wasn't right?

Early Warning System

The key to making purposeful changes in your life hinges on developing an Early Warning System (EWS). At first, this may sound preposterous. How can you possibly notice something you aren't yet able to see?

Imagine for a moment that you're an aboriginal tracker in the Australian outback. Someone is lost in the arid desert, and it's up to you to find him. Because you're so "at one" with the earth and wildlife of this area, you see signs of his presence—the places he stumbled, spent the night, stopped to drink, and brushed up against a tree for support. By reading the signs carefully, you can retrace his journey, step by step, to find him. To the casual observer, however, none of these signs would be noticed, let alone acted upon.

By birthright, you are as at one with your life as the tracker is with the outback. Unfortunately, most of your innate ability to read your surroundings has been discounted and squashed by society and those you grew up with, who said, "You couldn't possibly know that, you must be making it up," or "You mustn't be so emotional," or "Keep your harebrained ideas to yourself."

It's time to dismiss those limiting comments and rediscover how attuned you really are to all that goes on around and within you. Be patient. At first you may be able to see only bold footprints and other obvious signs that something's happening. As you reawaken your inner senses, though, you'll become more and more skilled at grasping the need for change when it's incredibly subtle. In fact, your time in Winter has already made you more attuned to ideas that float by, the sense of being drawn somewhere, and your gut feeling that something needs attention. After a while you'll be able to resolve situations as they occur.

Your EWS has six different channels of information—Physical, Emotional, Mental, Intuitive, Behavioral, Vocal. These channels provide you with continuous information about when things are and aren't working in your life. You could call them Stop and Go Signals. As you read about them, see which channels fit your personal style and past experience best. Let's start with the Stop Signals:

1. Physical Channel

Your body provides you with a wealth of signals all the time:

- Pain—sore throat, bursitis, indigestion, a headache.
- Illness—heart attack, ulcers, the flu.
- Body Sensations—tension, shakiness, jumpiness.
- Energy Level—tired, exhausted, low energy.

Start becoming aware of how your body responds to situations. If this feels like a foreign concept to you, you may have disconnected from your body after some emotional or physical trauma in your life. Explore ways to become more conscious of how your body is experiencing the world. Try doing t'ai chi, yoga, dance classes, or expressive movement.

As you become more in touch with your body and how it responds when things aren't going well, you can use this information to identify aspects of your life that need attention. Leann, for instance, was frequently bothered by headaches. She eventually realized that her headaches usually started during long meetings at work. At first she thought they might be from tension or hunger, but then she noticed they occurred when she sat for long periods of time in chairs that weren't suited to her body—at the movies, in her car, on airplanes, in conference rooms. After some experimentation, she found that if she propped herself up so she sat at a right angle, she didn't experience the headaches as frequently. Now, as soon as she senses that her neck is out of alignment, she readjusts her seating arrangement and avoids headaches.

2. Emotional Channel

Because emotions happen in the moment, they can be a tremendously important part of your alert system. The spectrum of feelings and emotions is wide, but they tend to fall into certain categories. I've listed several possibilities of each here.

- Anger—mad, furious, annoyed, outraged, frustrated.
- Fear—scared, terrified, intimidated, panicked, fearful, dreading.

- Hurt—abandoned, lonely, left out, ignored, defeated, crushed, in pain.
- Sad—tearful, grieving, despairing, miserable, weepy, heavy.
- Oppressed—intimidated, trapped, pressured, imposed upon, cornered, powerless, pushed.
- Uneasy—nervous, distracted, distraught, vulnerable.
- Overwhelmed—agitated, anxious, suicidal, on edge, in crisis.
- Numb—no feeling, empty, apathetic.
- Jealousy—envy.

Another helpful signal to notice is those times when your emotions are inconsistent with your words, thoughts, and actions. For instance, if you laugh when you tell someone about an abusive situation, your emotions and words are incongruent.

Joanne recently noticed that every time she became furious with someone, she could trace it back to a situation in which she felt cornered into doing something she didn't want to. By becoming aware of this, she was able to speak up for herself in the moment, thereby avoiding a number of angry outbursts.

But what if you aren't able to feel your emotions in the moment? Know, first of all, that you are not alone and, second, that you can learn to do so. There may be any number of reasons you're reluctant to feel. Perhaps you weren't encouraged or allowed to express your emotions as a child, or perhaps something happened to you that was just too much for you to handle at the time. In any event, you're probably afraid of the sheer depth, intensity, and range of your unexplored emotions.

I certainly experienced this fear after my father died. By using the expressive drawing activity described in Chapter 5, I explored my intense fear of my emotions. One of the first pictures I drew was a brick dam, holding back enormous amounts of water. In the face of the dam, there were several individual bricks that were loose or missing, and small streams of water were already spurting forth with great force, threatening to burst the dam. No wonder I was afraid of my emotions! Get the support you need to start finding safe ways to feel your emotions so that you can use this powerful part of your Early Warning System.

3. Mental Channel

The way you think about situations can also be very telling. If you've been cut off from your body and/or your emotions for any length of time, you may need to start learning about your EWS here.

The mental signals that something isn't working tend to fall into two groups at the extreme ends of a continuum.

- Overactive Mind   obsessing, worrying, "should ing," plan ning constantly.
- Inactive Mind—being ambivalent, dull, confused, bored, disas-sociating.

George had a tendency to review conversations for days after they occurred. Working with a therapist, he learned that this thought pattern usually meant that he wasn't feeling complete because he hadn't expressed all his feelings or ideas about what had transpired. By learn-ing to recognize when he was obsessing, he was able to spot problems before they became crises.

Lucy had once been very excited about finishing her degree in accounting. Then, all of a sudden, she found she was bored in class and very ambivalent about how she wanted to apply her degree in her career. After a lot of soul-searching and informational interviews, she realized that as her classes had become more detailed and technical, she'd lost contact with the more strategic, big-picture side of accounting. By making some adjustments to her plan of study, she was able to grad-uate with a double major that enabled her to combine her interests. Now she's excited about entering the workplace.

4. Intuitive Channel

Intuitive signs are often hard to catch because they occur deep within you. Here are several examples:

- Images—dreams, nightmares, recurring images, synchronistic events.
- Inner Feelings—a knowing, an instinctive tug, a gut feeling.

- Messages—internal information that comes from sources you can't see.
- Energy—sensing energy in a room, situation, person, group, interaction.
- Connectedness—a sense of connection or lack of connection, "spacing out," leaving your body energetically, disassociating.

Let me say a bit more about disassociating. Have you ever felt extremely scattered or easily distracted in a certain situation? Chances are that something jarred the connection you had with your higher self, and you became ungrounded or uncentered. It's important for you to become familiar with what this sensation feels like so you can tell when you disassociate. You can enlist the help of a trusted friend: set up a signal—a touch of a hand on your shoulder, a tap on your legs—so your friend can help you reconnect with your body even when you're with a group or in conversation. As you become familiar with the sensation of disassociating, you'll learn to notice when you're getting out of focus and how you can stay present. You might also find it helpful to ground yourself daily using the exercise described in Chapter 5.

Sarah felt so uncomfortable in certain situations that she'd concluded long ago she was not very good at socializing. As she became more in tune with herself through her transition journey, she realized her discomfort occurred when she picked up on undercurrents of conflict in social situations. Now that she understands how to use her discomfort as a warning signal, she can choose when she wants to tap into the energy and when she doesn't.

5. Behavioral Channel

Your behavior can be an easier source of clues about how your life is working because these signals are so visible.

- Overdoing It—overeating, over-sleeping, over-drinking, over-medicating, overworking.
- Underdoing It—undereating, not exercising, not doing anything, being a couch potato.

- Avoiding—being late for appointments, having trouble getting out of bed, forgetting to accomplish tasks, procrastinating, hesitating.
- Pushing—rushing about, forcing things to work, skipping steps.
- Unpredictable Behavior—being clumsy, tripping, dropping things, being scattered, having accidents.
- Cluttering—keeping outdated papers, things, relationships, or commitments in your life.

Leslie worked long hours because she loved her job. What she didn't realize was that she tended to work more feverishly to avoid an issue in her personal life. Her deadlines gave her a way to escape the emotions that tugged at her when she was home alone. Although it took a fairly big health crisis for her to see this connection, Leslie now takes notice when she feels compelled to work several evenings in a row or all weekend.

6. Vocal Channel

Our voices can also provide a wealth of signals when we can interpret them. For some people, this is a difficult skill to develop. It helps to have a trusted friend use an agreed-upon code word to signal you in the moment your voice shifts. By getting immediate feedback, you'll begin to hear and feel your voice shift. These vocal shifts can provide you with clues in the following ways:

- Regressing—your voice takes on the higher, quieter, and thinner qualities of a child's voice; you use words and phrases from a previous stage of life. (When this happens, notice the age the voice represents to discover any link between the current situation and past circumstances.)
- Changing Content—whining, swearing, gossiping, complaining, blaming.
- Losing Your Voice—can't speak for physical reasons such as laryngitis or jaw problems, don't speak up, defer to others' desires.

- Raising Your Voice—yelling, screeching, shouting, screaming.
- Difficulty Communicating—losing words, skipping words, mispronouncing words, not finishing sentences, jumping around from one topic to another.

Offhand comments from several friends alerted May to the fact that every time she was upset about relationships in her life, her voice started sounding like a four-year-old's. Although she knew a little about her family history, it wasn't until she had a hypnotherapy session that she came to understand that when she was four she'd been sent to live with her grandmother for about nine months. By talking with other family members, she learned that during that time her mother had a very sick child who eventually died. After healing this childhood experience of abandonment, her voice rarely regresses anymore. If it does, May knows to pay attention and go right to the source of the hurt.

Seeing the Early Warning System in Action

Let me take a moment to illustrate how all the channels of your EWS work together to alert you to difficulties in your life. Aside from my father's death, the biggest crisis to hit my life occurred when I became physically burned-out during my stint in the corporate world. There were numerous signals that, if noticed, might have allowed me to catch the situation sooner than I did. Looking back, I can identify signs from each of the channels:

Physically, I was exhausted and had been for months. My muscles ached constantly, my back hurt, I was frequently sick, and I experienced headaches on a far-too-regular basis. Furthermore, my energy was so severely depleted that I really had to limit my work and social activities.

Emotionally, I was constantly on edge. Tears and angry words were always lurking just under the surface. My manager even commented on these displays of emotion that were totally "out of character."

Mentally, I was completely overstimulated by incessant comments from my inner critic. I planned obsessively, came up with excuses before I did anything wrong, and worried constantly.

Intuitively, I was bothered by frequent stress dreams. I also had the constant desire to curl up in a fetal position under my desk. (A clear sign I was not feeling safe.) Furthermore, each day after work, it took me about three hours to feel as though I'd come back to being myself.

Behaviorally, I had to battle with myself every single morning just to get out of bed. I tended to be about five to ten minutes late to work every day, even though I lived very close to the office. I dropped things like my keys and papers constantly. Once I even dropped my wallet in front of my house. I didn't even know I'd lost it until the local post office called to say it had been deposited in a mailbox. Another time, I left the front door of my house wide open as I left for an evening meeting. (Thank goodness I have observant neighbors!)

Vocally, I experienced several terrifying signs. For about a week or two, I would scream at the top of my lungs every time I went to work. On top of that, I would lose words or use the wrong word several times a day in memos and conversations. Often I couldn't finish sentences. I also did a fair amount of complaining during that period—always seeing everything in a negative light. Usually I deferred to others' desires rather than voicing my needs.

Looking back, it's so easy to see that my life was completely out of control. At that time, however, I don't think I could have acknowledged the signs because I didn't see any other options. From my point of view, I had a good, secure job in a reputable company making a dependable salary, using my hard-earned training and building my retirement fund. Why would anyone ever think of leaving that kind of long-term security? The turning point came when I realized job security meant nothing if I lost my health. I now believe my healing process would've been much shorter if I'd been able to see and act upon the signs a year or two before they'd reached crisis proportions.

Creating Your Own Early Warning System

Because this is such a crucial part of making purposeful changes in your life, I want to take the time here to help you begin to build your own EWS. Find a safe way to keep track of your discoveries during this

Figure E: Your Early Warning System
_____ Channel

Go Signals	Extreme	
	Moderate	
	Subtle	
Stop Signals	Subtle	
	Moderate	
	Extreme	

Note: Make six copies of this template, one for each channel.

process, because you'll be able to add to them for some time to come. Begin by making six copies of the template in Figure E. Label each page with one of the six channels we've just discussed. Then lay these charts out in front of you for the next part of this activity.

Knowing Something Needs to Change

Now, take a moment to think about a situation in your life that isn't working for you. How do you know it's not working? What are your Stop Signals?

Each time you think of a clue, ask yourself whether it's an extreme, moderate, or subtle sign that something isn't working. What's your gut response? Think about other times you've felt or sensed this sign. What quality did it have then? Jot it down in the lower half of the chart for that channel, according to its degree of intensity. If you're not accustomed to being aware of yourself, you may realize that you don't notice signs of change until they're quite extreme. You may not even be able to identify any subtle indicators at first. That's fine for now.

The following chart illustrates Stop Signals of various intensities for each channel to give you some guidance. If you think of a sign that isn't used as an example, just do the best you can to categorize it in one of the channels.

Stop Signals

Channels:	Subtle Signs:	Moderate Signs:	Extreme Signs:
Physical	Sore Throat	Exhaustion	Heart Attack
Emotional	Nervousness	Tears	Rage
Mental	Being Bored	Worried	Endless Obsessing
Intuitive	Ungrounded	Gut Feeling	Nightmares
Behavioral	Tardiness	Procrastinating	Having Accidents
Vocal	Raising Voice	Regressing	Screaming

It's important to realize that each person's EWS is unique. What's extreme to one person might be subtle to another. For instance, a person who has not cried in thirty years might see tears as an extreme indicator that something's wrong, whereas another person who cries during a touching commercial might think tears are a subtle indicator. The person in the latter example might also know that different kinds of crying provide different kinds of information.

Spend some more time thinking of various situations, past or present, to help you flesh out your EWS. This is just the first pass, so don't be concerned if you're coming up with only extreme or moderate signs.

The next step is to uncover what happened just prior to the signs you've already identified. What did you experience right before each signal? Recognize that more subtle clues may come from an entirely different channel than the original clue. For instance, you may notice that your sore throats are often preceded by situations in which you were shocked or disappointed. By recognizing this pattern, you can identify ways to limit the impact of the shocks or to feel the appropriate emotions so they don't have to be expressed through your body. Again, you may find it useful to think about several different situations to help you expand your lists. At this point, you may be able to bring to the surface some fairly subtle signs. Jot them down on the appropriate places on your sheets.

Now, take a look at the sheets for all the channels. Do you notice any patterns? Which channels do you tend to rely on the most? Are there any channels you aren't very comfortable with? If you notice any holes, see if you can dredge up any signs from that channel. Look at the descriptions of each channel earlier in the chapter to see if they spark new ideas.

Knowing You're on Track

So far, we've talked about the EWS as a way to spot things that aren't working. You can also use your EWS to help you recognize when you're on the right track. These are your Go Signals.

Think about a time in your life when things were going extremely well. What signs told you that you were on track and should proceed with what you were doing? Use the same six channels to stimulate your thinking: Physical, Emotional, Mental, Intuitive, Behavioral, Vocal.

When Jo and I talked about Go Signals, she immediately remembered a project she'd worked on a year ago. With a big grin on her face, she told me that she'd jumped out of bed with enthusiasm every day during that project because she knew she was making a difference in the lives of the children she worked with. She was energetic, full of ideas, and had a sixth sense about which children needed special attention. She also recalled laughing spontaneously throughout the day. As she talked about this time, she practically glowed with passion.

In some ways, these Go Signals may be even more unfamiliar to you than your Stop Signals. How many times have you really experienced life working extremely well? Just as we cut ourselves off from the bad things that happen, we also limit our experience of the truly ecstatic moments of life.

Take some time to jot down your Go Signals according to whether they're extreme, moderate, or subtle signs of your flow. Here are some examples:

Go Signals

Channels:	Subtle Signs:	Moderate Signs:	Extreme Signs:
Physical	Energetic	Healthy	Tingling
Emotional	Confident	Excited	Ecstatic
Mental	Present Focus	Clear Thinking	New Connections
Intuitive	Connected	Intuitive Hits	Prophetic Dreams
Behavioral	Eating Well	Coordinated	Effortless Projects
Vocal	Speaking up	Articulate	Full Voice

Putting It All Together

Now that you're becoming familiar with your EWS, your job is to pay attention to it! When you sense something isn't working in your life, acknowledge it as soon as possible. This is the key to making purposeful changes and minimizing crisis-driven ones. Learning to use your EWS is like learning a new language which is full of subtle nuances. Be patient. It may take you a while to learn which signals are meaningful and which are just random anomalies.

1. Notice Something Isn't Working (Fall)

When you notice a signal that something's amiss, take some time to interpret what it means. Watch for a pattern of events or several signs pointing in the same direction. Try to recall when the sign has happened before. Ask yourself what preceded the signal in previous situations and what transpired as a result. By combining all your observations, can you tell which element of your life isn't working? If you're coming up with several possibilities, look at the situation from as many angles as possible to come to a clearer conclusion. Let's look at an example.

Suppose you find yourself sick with the flu. One explanation might be that you had a meeting with a colleague just hours before he went home sick—a purely biological explanation that may be the whole story or only a part. If you want to examine the situation more closely, you might look at what else was going on in your life right before you got sick. Did you experience any emotional upsets, overwhelming stress, or an underlying desire to avoid a situation? The point of asking these questions is not to blame yourself for being ill, but to take notice of any issues that could be cleaned up before they escalate even further.

2. Think About Your Situation (Early Winter)

After identifying that something's out of alignment, take a moment to look at your situation. Although this situation is likely to be less extreme than the ones that led you to read this book, put yourself back in the reflective mode of Winter to uncover what's going on. Begin by asking, what's working in this situation? What's not? Give yourself some time and space to think, and then be open to new ways of looking at the situation.

3. State What You Want (Late Winter)

Next ask yourself, "If I could have anything I wanted in this situation, what would it be?" Really give yourself permission to answer this question from an ideal perspective. If, after defining your ideal, it becomes clear that your ideal is way out of line with your current reality, try to put the essence of your desire into words. How can you incorporate this essence into your life today? Is there any way you can make a first step toward this ideal? What one thing can you do today to move closer to your goal? Use the answers to these questions to put your plan together.

Let's look at an example. Suppose your EWS is screaming that you need some time away—from your job, your kids, the household chores, and maybe even your spouse. Or, on second thought, maybe you and your spouse need to get away together for once!

When you think about this dilemma ideally, you immediately picture a bungalow on a white sandy beach with palm trees, a private cove, and a wonderful hammock for two. Before you even solidify the vision, you begin to hear your inner critic's commentary about how it'll never work—you don't have that kind of cash, who do you think will take care of your kids, and what about that big project at work everyone's depending on you to complete. Although there may be truth to every one of these barriers, there's also truth to your discovery that you need to get away and soon!

Before you take the next step, turn down the volume on your inner critic and turn up your imagination. What's the essence of your desire? Do you want to be in the tropics or just somewhere warm? Do you want to be alone with your spouse? Do you want time to do nothing? Really search through all the messages you're getting from your EWS to identify the Go Signals that highlight your true wishes.

Now, look at the other side of life—reality—to begin defining the parameters of what you really can do. How much time could you squeeze out of your schedule? How much money can you really spend? How far do you want to travel?

Then start blending the two kinds of information—your reality and your desires. Perhaps the interim answer is a weekend away at a bed and breakfast. Or perhaps it's swapping homes with a friend in another city. If you find that nothing will truly do except a trip to Hawaii, brainstorm ways to make that happen. Price the trip, start a savings account, search for special deals that will enable you to live your dream.

Review the tools described in Chapter 5 for some reminders about how to find creative solutions to tough problems. Remember you can't get very far in changing your life if every time you come up with an ideal solution you tell yourself it's impossible to proceed.

4. Take the Appropriate Actions (Spring)

Once you have a clear idea about what your next step looks like, take it. As before, it's important to trust your own timing when you move forward with your plan. Because you've caught this situation early, the actions you need to take to implement your plan will probably be fairly subtle.

Keep tuned into your EWS because it can tell you whether your plan is working or not. If you become aware of any Stop Signals, acknowledge you've hit a snag. Take a step back, reassess your situation, and refine your plan. If, on the other hand, your Go Signals show up, you'll know you're on the right track.

5. Enjoy Your Results (Summer)

After you've put your plan into place, allow the results to ripen and mature. Give yourself an opportunity to really relish the new level of success you've created for yourself.

The beauty of learning how to read your EWS to discover what is and isn't working in your life is that you can use this skill in any situation. Let me share one last example about how to do this.

Jessie came to me because she'd been focusing so much time on chores and other "have-tos" she'd completely lost track of her passions. Our first goal was to help her free up her time. As we talked, she realized that grocery shopping and meal preparation were the biggest drains on her energy. She never found the time to plan ahead, and had to scramble to get food every night after work when she was exhausted already. Once we identified the problem, I asked her what she'd like to have happen—ideally. She came up with some wonderful options, including having a live-in cook! Then we started looking at combinations that might actually work. In the end, she decided to shop once a week for staple ingredients her family uses all the time, to dedicate a particular time to make her weekly shopping run, to sign up for an organic vegetable service that delivers each week, and to create a list of quick and easy meal concoctions her family likes so that she doesn't have to rack her brain every night to reinvent meals she's already discovered. By the time we finished, her voice had lifted, and she was excited about her ideas. Now she can devote more time to discovering her passions!

Once you get the hang of this process, you'll use it every chance you get because you'll realize just how much more satisfying and effective it is to change when you're in a place of choice. Just imagine the joy you'll feel each year as you look back and see how far you've come. Savor each and every step of your journey.

Tools for Your Journey

Whenever we take a journey in life, it's helpful to have the appropriate resources at our side to guide us, reassure us, and teach us new skills. In preparing this section, I scanned my own bookshelves and talked with others who have been through major transitions.

Facing Your Transition

• Sarah Quigley and Marilyn Shroyer, Ph.D., *Facing Fear, Finding Courage: Your Path to Peace of Mind*. (Berkeley, CA: Conari Press, 1996).

Fear is an emotion that will surface regularly throughout your journey. This book, written by two women who have faced their fair share of fear, assures you that "It's okay to be afraid" and offers comforting suggestions about how to face, feel, and transform your fear.

• Robert L. Veninga, *A Gift of Hope: How We Survive Our Tragedies*. (New York: Ballantine Books, 1985).

• Melba Colgrove, Ph.D., Harold H. Bloomfield, MD, and Peter McWilliams, *How to Survive the Loss of a Love: A Different Guide to Overcoming All Your*

Emotional Hurts. (Los Angeles: Prelude Press, 1993).

If you've suffered a severe loss—the death of a baby, the loss of a love, a disaster—these two books will help you make sense of what you're experiencing and give you practical suggestions on how to start your healing process. Best of all, both books assure you that what you're feeling is perfectly normal.

Handling Financial Hurdles

• Amy Dacyczyn, *The Tightwad Gazette: Promoting Thrift as a Viable Alternative Lifestyle.* (New York: Villiard Books, 1993).

In this book, and two others like it, Amy Dacyczyn reprints articles from her newsletter "The Tightwad Gazette" which provide hundreds of creative, sometimes wacky, ideas to help you make ends meet. As each tidbit illustrates, Amy firmly believes that "tightwaddery is about not hardships and deprivation, but fun and creativity."

• Joe Dominguez and Vicki Robin, *Your Money or Your Life: Transforming Your Relationship with Money and Achieving Financial Independence.* (New York: Penguin Books, 1992).

As you progress through your journey, you may find yourself questioning the alignment of your values and ideals with the actions you must take to live in today's world. Whether or not you choose to work through the authors' nine-step program to achieve financial independence, their discussion of the meaning of money is both eye-opening and behavior-shifting.

Taking Time and Slowing Down

• Elaine St. James, *Simplify Your Life: 100 Ways to Slow Down and Enjoy the Things That Really Matter* (New York: Hyperion, 1994); *Inner Simplicity: 100 ways to Regain Peace and Nourish Your Soul* (New York: Hyperion, 1995); and *Living the Simple Life: A Guide to Slowing Down and Enjoying More* (New York: Hyperion, 1996).

In the midst of your transition, are you realizing that your life is more complex than you'd like? In these three easy-to-read books, St. James offers hundreds of suggestions about how to cut out activities, chores, relationships, thoughts, and things that no longer feed us so we can devote our precious time and energy to deeper, more rewarding parts of our lives.

• Jack Kelly and Marcia Kelly, *Sanctuaries*. (New York: Bell Tower, 1996).

Sometimes the best way to clear your mind for Winter Solstice insights is to go on retreat. Even if you think going on retreat is out of the question, check out this guide to more than 250 centers throughout the country. Who knows, you may find a quiet retreat house, abbey, or monastery in the next town that has surprisingly reasonable prices. In the introduction, Jack and Marcia Kelly say they found "an open door, welcoming smiles, a quiet chapel, a secluded path, or a lakeside beach" at each location.

• David Kundtz, Ph.D., *Stopping: How to Be Still When You Have to Keep Going*. (Berkeley, CA: Conari Press, 1998).

A useful book if you're having a difficult time carving out time to reflect. While taking into account the overwhelming pace and complexity of our world today, Kundtz teaches, in a simple, approachable way, three ways of stopping: Still Points, Stopovers, and Grinding Halts. He also devotes a section of the book to helping you deal with any resistance or fear that surfaces when you stop and do nothing for periods of a minute to a month.

Reconnecting with Your Personal Style

Psychological Systems

• David Keirsey, David Bates, and Marilyn Bates, *Please Understand Me: Character and Temperament Types*. (Del Mar, CA: Prometheus Nemesis Book Company, 1984).

Keirsey and the Bates believe that each of us is as unique in our temperament as we are in physical appearance. By giving you a way to understand your own style using the Keirsey Temperament Sorter, you will have the opportunity to claim your uniqueness more fully and to see how your style shows up in your relationships, career choices, interests, strengths, and frustrations. These types are constructed using the same Jungian principles as the

Myers-Briggs Type Indicator, so your results will give you a fairly good approximation of how you'd score on the Myers-Briggs.

- Helen Palmer, *The Enneagram: Understanding Yourself and the Others in Your Life.* (San Francisco: Harper, 1991).
- Renee Baron and Elizabeth Wagele, *The Enneagram Made Easy: Discover the Nine Types of People.* (San Francisco: Harper San Francisco, 1994).

Another commonly used method for understanding your own personal style is the Enneagram, described by Helen Palmer as "an ancient Sufi teaching that describes nine different relationship types and their interrelationships." By determining your own type, you'll have a clearer understanding of your preferences, goals, style of interacting with other people, and much more. If you're a visual learner, you may find it easier to learn about the Enneagram using the lists, personality inventories, and easy-to-grasp cartoons in *The Enneagram Made Easy.*

Esoteric Methods

Another way to explore your personal style is to step out of modern logical methods into any of several esoteric systems. Although often touted as New Age techniques, each of these tools can be traced to ancient cultures in many parts of the world, including Egypt, Greece, China, and India. For some of you, exploring these tools may feel like too much of a stretch right now; others may feel it's just the right time to expand your horizons. Trust your intuition on this!

Numerology

Numerology uses simple calculations based on your birthdate and birth name to give you information about your main lessons, gifts, cycles, interests, and traits. With the help of either of the books listed below, you can learn to do the calculations and then read about your numbers to gain more understanding about who you are, where you've been, and where you're headed.

- Juno Jordan, *Numerology Romance in Your Name.* (Marina Del Rey, CA: Devorss and Company, 1977).
- Lynn Buess, *Numerology for the New Age.* (Sedona, AZ: Light Technology Publications, 1978).

Astrology

Based on your place and time of birth, an astrological chart provides you with in-depth information about life lessons, tendencies, traits, and patterns. Although it's possible to learn to interpret your own chart after years of study, start by having a reading done. If you'd like to learn more about astrology in general, refer to the following resources.

- Linda Goodman, *Linda Goodman's Sun Signs*. (New York: Bantam Books, 1990).

Although astrology takes into account far more than just your sun sign, this book describes the qualities commonly associated with each sign and some of the basic terminology used in astrology.

- Lance Ferguson, *Skywatch: A Daily Astrological Timing Guide for All Signs*.

This informative monthly newsletter describes the daily astrological highs and lows as well as longer-term patterns that are impacting you and everyone around you. If you'd like to receive a sample copy, send a business-size self-addressed stamped envelope and $1.00 to Skywatch, P.O. Box 100754, Fort Worth, TX 76185.

Mythical Sources

In your quest to understand your personal style, you may also be exploring what it means to be a man or a woman in our rapidly changing world. I heartily recommend the following three books. While reading them to research ideas for this book, I was swept away by the personal reveries they evoked on a number of occasions.

- Allan B. Chinen, Ph.D., *Once Upon A Midlife*. (Los Angeles: Jeremy P. Tarcher, Inc., 1992).
- Clarissa Pinkola Estés, Ph.D., *Women Who Run With the Wolves: Myths and Stories of the Wild Woman Archetype*. (New York: Ballantine Books, 1992, 1995).
- Samuel Keen, *Fire in the Belly: On Being a Man*. (New York: Bantam Books, 1991).

Enhancing Your Reflective Time

• Jonathan Robinson, *The Little Book of Big Questions: 200 Ways to Explore Your Spiritual Nature.* (Berkeley, CA: Conari Press, 1995).

If you're searching for new ways to look at yourself and your life, use the 200 questions listed in this book to stimulate your thinking about life's mysterious ways and your deeper truths.

• Betty Bethards, *The Dream Book: Symbols for Self-Understanding.* (Rockport, MA: Element, 1995).

Sometimes in the midst of Winter, you'll notice that your dream life becomes quite active—sometimes in disturbing ways. But, as Bethards puts it, "There is no such thing as a bad dream symbol. The most frightening dreams have the most positive insights once they are worked out." In this book, you'll learn about the various kinds of dreams and how to interpret them using your own intuition and this extensive 150-page dream symbol dictionary.

• Jill Mellick, *The Natural Artistry of Dreams: Creative Ways to Bring the Wisdom of Dreams to Waking Life.* (Berkeley, CA: Conari Press, 1996).

If you're drawn to explore your dreams in even more depth, you'll be interested in learning to work with dreams using several creative methods, including journaling, sculpting, composing poetry, miming, and painting. Once you're familiar with these techniques, you may want to use them to explore other symbols in your life: signs from nature, situational dynamics, or insight flashes.

• Madeline McMurray, *Illuminations: The Healing Image.* (Oakland, CA: Bookpeople, 1988).

If you want to explore using drawing to illuminate insights and dream images, you can unleash your "inner artist" with the help of this book. In addition to describing the basic guidelines for using this method, McMurray offers a number of simple yet profound exercises to deepen your experience of this process.

Turning the Corner

• Dawna Markova, Ph.D., *No Enemies Within: A Creative Process for Discovering What's Right About What's Wrong.* (Berkeley, CA: Conari Press, 1994).

Starting with the premise that each of us is the "ultimate healer of his or her own condition," Markova offers a powerful process for turning internal demons into allies and for "discovering what's right about what's wrong" in our lives. She also includes a questionnaire to help you understand how you perceive and process information at the conscious, subconscious, and unconscious levels—providing one more piece to your personal style puzzle.

• Patricia Montgomery, Ph.D., *Mythmaking: Heal Your Past, Claim Your Future.* (Portland, OR: Sibyl Publications, 1994).

Acknowledging that the myths of our youth just don't fill the bill any more, Montgomery introduces a step-by-step process to help you discover and write your own myth. By reviewing your life, you're not only able to "heal your past," you're also able to "claim your future." This book offers a powerful way to write your new story.

Using Your Body, Your Home, and Your Experiences as Messengers

• Louise Hay, *You Can Heal Your Life.* (Carlsbad, CA: Hay House, Inc., 1987).

Although Hay's idea that the problems in our lives are the result of our beliefs may be a little too extreme for some, her exercises, techniques, and affirmations can still be profoundly healing. The part of her book I find most useful is the sixty-page list of physical ailments which helps me understand the possible meaning underlying my illnesses, aches, and pains.

• William Spear, *Feng Shui Made Easy: Designing Your Life with the Ancient Art of Placement.* (San Francisco: Harper Collins, 1995).

According to *feng shui,* the Chinese art of placement, your home is a reflection of your psyche. By being mindful of the way you arrange your furnishings and decorations you can improve your relationships, finances, and health. Using this instructional manual will help you determine how the life energy flows—or doesn't flow—in your home and what you can do to "cure" the blocked energy.

• Clare Cooper Marcus, *House as a Mirror of Self.* (Berkeley CA: Conari Press, 1995).

Through over twenty years of research, Clare Cooper Marcus recognized that our home environment is as much an expression of our unconscious as our dreams. Indeed, "the state of reconnection with soul is best described by the metaphor of *coming home.*" By exploring your relationship with "home"— your childhood home, special places, homes you've shared with partners, homes you've lost—you will tap into a powerful method of becoming more fully yourself.

• Denise Linn, *The Secret Language of Signs: How to Interpret the Coincidences and Symbols in Your Life.* (New York: Ballantine Books, 1996).

According to Linn, "Whether we are conscious of it or not, the universe is communicating to us through signs." If you'd like to learn where to look for these signs, how to ask for a sign, and how to create the best conditions for receiving one, you'll be intrigued by the fascinating examples in this book. To serve as a starting point in interpreting the signs you receive, Linn has provided an extensive 200-page dictionary of signs.

Finding Intuitive Tools

• Carol L. McClelland, Ph.D., *Nature's Wisdom Deck: A Powerfully Insightful Guide for Exploring Life's Changes.* (Palo Alto, CA: Transition Dynamics, 1993).

I created this deck to help people to access nature's wisdom even when they can't get outdoors. Each card in the ninety-card deck taps one of the nature metaphors used in The Seasons of Change: "Tree Branches Grow," "Young Born," "Leaves Fall." The accompanying guidebook outlines nine different ways to use the cards—from one-card readings to more complex multi-card layouts. Although you will probably have your own experiences with most of the images in the deck, there's a description of each card to help you get the most out of the metaphors.

See page 273 of this book for information on how to order *Nature's Wisdom Deck.*

• *Osho Zen Tarot* (New York: St. Martin's Press, 1994).

This is my favorite Tarot deck because it incorporates Zen notions: "The Zen attitude towards life is that of laughter, of living, of enjoying, of celebrating . . . It accepts all that is." Whether you're in the depths of despair or just having a hard day, you'll find the cards and the descriptions to be soothing, healing, and thought-provoking. A great way to nudge yourself to see life from new angles.

Other tools you might be interested in looking into include the *I Ching*, Runes, and other intuitive card decks. Before you purchase any tools, be sure it suits you. You may even discover that you prefer to use different tools or decks for different purposes.

Afanas'ev, Aleksandr. *Russian Fairy Tales*. New York: Random House, 1973.

Aftel, Mandy, and Robin Talmach Latoff. *When Talk is Not Cheap: Or, How to Find the Right Therapist When You Don't Know Where to Begin*. New York: Warner Books, 1986.

Bateson, Mary Catherine. *Composing A Life*. New York: Plume, 1989.

Berry, Thomas. *Dream of the Earth*. Scranton, PA: Harper Collins, 1993.

Bradford, Barbara Taylor. *Everything to Gain*. Accord, MA: Wheeler Publications, 1994.

Bridges, William. *JobShift: How to Prosper in a Workplace Without Jobs*. Reading, MA: Addison-Wesley Publishing Company, 1994.

_____. *Transitions: Making Sense of Life Changes*. Reading, MA: Addison-Wesley Publishing Company, 1981.

Buscaglia, Leo F. *Love*. Greenwich, CT: Faucett Books, 1972.

Calvino, Italo. *Italian Folktales*. New York: Pantheon, 1980.

Campbell, Joseph. *The Hero with a Thousand Faces*. Princeton, NJ: Princeton University Press, 1968.

Campbell, Joseph, and Bill Moyers. *The Power of Myth*. New York: Doubleday, 1984.

Chinen, Allan B., Ph.D. *Once Upon A Midlife*. Los Angeles: Jeremy P. Tarcher, Inc., 1992.

_____. *Waking World: Classic Tales of Women and the Heroic Feminine*. New York: Jeremy P. Tarcher, Inc., 1996.

Dery, Mark. *Escape Velocity: Cyberculture at the End of the Century*. New York: Grove Press, 1996.

"EMDR: The Breakthrough Therapy for Overcoming Anxiety, Stress, and Trauma." *Publishers Weekly*, March 3, 1997, 69.

Estés, Clarissa Pinkola, Ph.D. *Women Who Run With the Wolves: Myths and Stories of the Wild Woman Archetype.* New York: Ballantine Books, 1992, 1995.

Fadden, John Kahionhes, and Carol Wood. *Keepers of the Earth.* Golden, CO: Fulcrum, Inc., 1988.

von Franz, Marie-Louise. *Problems of The Feminine in Fairytales.* Irving, TX: Spring Publications, Inc., 1972.

Fox, Matthew. *Original Blessing.* Santa Fe, NM: Bear & Company Publishing, 1983.

Gordon, Susan. "The Powers of the Handless Maiden." *Feminist Messages: Coding in Women's Folk Culture.* Edited by Joan Newlon Radner. Urbana, IL: University of Illinois Press, 1993.

Grimm, Jacob, and Wilhelm Grimm. *The Complete Grimm's Fairy Tales.* New York: Pantheon Books, 1972.

Heinberg, Richard. *Celebrate the Solstice.* Wheaton, IL: Quest Books, 1993.

Jackson, Ellen. *The Winter Solstice.* Brookfield, CT: The Millbrook Press, 1994.

Johnson, Robert A. *The Fisher King and the Handless Maiden: Understanding the Wounded Feeling Function in Masculine and Feminine Psychology.* San Francisco: Harper San Francisco, 1993.

Keen, Samuel. *Fire in the Belly: On Being a Man.* New York: Bantam Books, 1991.

Kelly, Jack, and Marcia Kelly. *Sanctuaries.* New York: Bell Tower, 1996.

Korda, Michael. *Success!* New York: Ballantine Books, 1978.

Kotre, John, and Elizabeth Hall. *Season of Life.* Boston: Little Brown, 1990.

Longman, Robin. "Creating Art: Your Rx for Health, Part I." *American Artist,* May 1994, 64–69.

McCaughrean, Geraldine. *Greek Myths.* New York: Margaret K. McElderry Books, 1993.

McClelland, Carol L. Ph.D. *Nature's Wisdom Deck: A Powerfully Insightful Guide for Exploring Life's Changes.* Palo Alto, CA: Transition Dynamics, 1993.

Milne, A. A. *The World of Pooh.* New York: E. P. Dutton & Co., Inc., 1957.

Montage, Ashley. *Growing Young.* New York: McGraw Hill, 1981.

Montgomery, Patricia, Ph.D. *Mythmaking: Heal Your Past, Claim Your Future.* Portland, OR: Sibyl Publications, 1994.

Moore, Robert L., and Douglass Gillette. *King, Warrior, Magician, and Lover.* San Francisco: Harper, 1990.

Naisbitt, John. *Megatrends: Ten New Directions Transforming Our Lives.* New York:

Warner Books, 1982. New York: William Morrow and Company, Inc., 1990.

Naisbitt, John, and Patricia Aburdene. *Megatrends 2000: Ten New Directions of the 1990s.* New York: William Morrow and Company, Inc., 1990.

Our Amazing World of Nature: Its Marvels and Mysteries. Pleasantville, NY: Reader's Digest Association, 1969.

Perkins-Reed, Marcia. *Thriving in Transition: Effective Living in Times of Change.* New York: Touchstone Books, 1996.

Ray, Paul H. *The Integral Culture Survey: A Study of the Emergence of Transformational Values in America.* Sausalito, CA: Institute of Noetic Sciences, 1996.

_____. "The Rise of Integral Culture." *Noetic Sciences Review,* Spring 1996.

Rigoglioso, Marguerite. "Living Your Dreams." *New Age Journal,* November/December 1996, 76–81, 154–159.

Robinson, Jonathan. *Book of Big Questions: 200 Ways to Explore Your Spiritual Nature.* Berkeley, CA: Conari Press, 1995.

Saltzman, Amy. *Down-Shifting: Reinventing Success on a Slower Track.* New York: HarperPerennial, 1991.

Steele, Danielle. *Daddy.* New York: Delecorte Press, 1989.

Stepanich, Kisma K. *The Gaia Tradition: Celebrating the Earth in Her Seasons.* St. Paul, MN: Llewellyn Publications, 1991.

Stocker, Sharon. "Seven Signs of a Good Therapist: A Guide to Help You Make a Perfect Match." *Prevention,* August 1995, 80–86.

The Student Bible. Grand Rapids, MI: Zondervan Bible Publishers, 1986.

Toffler, Alvin. *Future Shock.* New York: Random House, 1970.

Veninga, Robert L. *A Gift of Hope: How We Survive Our Tragedies.* New York: Ballantine Books, 1985.

Wheatley, Margaret. "The Heart of Organization." *Noetic Sciences Review,* Spring 1996.

Wilhelm, Richard, and Cary F. Baynes. *The I Ching: Book of Changes.* Princeton, NJ: Princeton University Press, 1977.

Index

Bold entries indicate an anecdote relating to that topic

Acknowledgments

Looking back, there have been many individuals who have enhanced my connection with nature. I wish to acknowledge them for their part in guiding me on a path that none of us knew existed at the time. Thanks to: my third-grade teacher Julie Bretz, for introducing me to Pagoo the hermit crab, assigning me my first reports on nature, and awakening in me my love of books. I know your presence in my life did much to propel me on my path. And to Dr. David Hamilton, for persuading me to venture out of California to pursue my graduate studies. Little did either of us know how important my years in the Midwest would be.

My interest in transitions was galvanized by a series of changes that occurred in my own life between 1985 and 1991. For their support and guidance throughout my long Winter, I thank Dr. Virginia Dennehy, Susan Sparrow, KARA, Leslie Buffard, Hope Hospice, and Joan Alford, RN.

Others have played a significant role in bringing my connection with nature and my interest in transitions together. Tina Anderson saw the power and richness of my work long before I did. My clients and those who have attended my workshops have greatly enhanced my work by sharing their questions, their successes, and their resonance with my ideas.

During the past five years, I've been blessed to meet weekly with Ginger Bennett, Suzanne Keehn, and Carol McDonald to meditate, find meaning, and hone our intuitive skills. Although the journey has occasionally been rocky, I treasure the time we've spent together and the wisdom I've gained from each of you. I also thank Charlene Littau for her guidance and support over the years.

From the moment I met my publicist and agent Carol Susan Roth, my life changed. She has been instrumental in building my confidence, boosting the professionalism of my materials, developing my presence, and manifesting a way to publish this book. I can't thank her enough. I'm also grateful to my editor Mary Jane Ryan, for her instantaneous understanding of my work on seeing the *Nature's Wisdom Deck.* Her faith, vision, and clear guidance have greatly enhanced my work. I appreciate all that she and the Conari Press team have done to help me birth this book.

I want to thank many others who have contributed to this book: Carol Susan Roth, Maria Remboulis, and Maria del Cioppo for their constructive comments and heartfelt reactions to earlier drafts; Ellen Silva, for her help with creating the figures; my brother Thomas McClelland and Clyde Lerner, for using their technical expertise to do some Internet research and for spending many hours one weekend nursing my computer back to health after it spontaneously erupted; and Diana Dieck, Fran Fisher, Matt Griffin, Margo Keeley, Ted Lafeber, Joan Lederman, Deborah McCallum, Willow Million, Sylvia Neal, Crystal Ruocchio, Emmah Smyth, Janice Summers, Leslie Wolber, and Julie Woolway for taking the time to review the Supporter Questionnaire.

During the writing of this book, Sunrise, my ten-year-old golden retriever, has been my constant companion. Her hugs, her invitations (pleadings) to go for walks, and her presence brought much joy to the months I spent writing. Thanks, girl! I also want to bless the trees outside my window, which waltzed with me through the seasons as I wrote.

As always, my mother Margaret McClelland has been there to celebrate with me, commiserate with me, encourage me, discuss ideas with me, and, most certainly, to laugh with me.

And to all of you who have helped me keep body, mind, soul, and home humming throughout the past year, I am most grateful. I couldn't have done this without your thoughtful encouragement, interest, and caring. I count you all among my blessings.

A Personal Note from the Author

In the year I spent writing this book, I reviewed the journey I've taken since 1983 when I first learned about transitions. What a journey it has been! I am quite thankful it has brought me to this point where I am able to share this hopeful and helpful approach to growing through life's inevitable ups and downs with you.

I would love to hear how The Seasons of Change has touched your life.

To Learn More About the Seasons of Change, visit

www.seasonsofchange.com

Online you can:
- Subscribe to the free Seasons of Change eNewsletter
- Find sources of support for your transition
- Purchase a copy of the *Nature's Wisdom Deck*: the essential companion for The Seasons of Change
- Become certified to use The Seasons of Change model in your work with clients in transition
- Contact Carol

About Carol McClelland, Ph. D.

Carol McClelland, Ph.D., founder of Transition Dynamics Enterprises, Inc, provides hope, insight and a sense of direction to people who are in the midst of transition in their personal lives and their careers. As the author of *The Seasons of Change, Nature's Wisdom Deck, Your Dream Career for Dummies* and the *Career Clarity Program*, Carol McClelland, Ph.D. provides clients with unique tools, refreshing perspectives, and powerful insights to help them transform their confusion into clarity. In addition to her work with clients, Carol trains coaches, therapists and other Transition Professionals to incorporate The Seasons of Change and Career Clarity Program into their work with clients.

Conari Press, an imprint of Red Wheel/Weiser, publishes books on topics ranging from spirituality, personal growth, and relationships to women's issues, parenting, and social issues. Our mission is to publish quality books that will make a difference in people's lives—how we feel about ourselves and how we relate to one another. We value integrity, compassion, and receptivity, both in the books we publish and in the way we do business.

Our readers are our most important resource, and we appreciate your input, suggestions, and ideas about what you would like to see published.

Conari Press, an imprint of Red Wheel/Weiser, LLC
665 Third Street, Suite 400
San Francisco, CA 94107
www.redwheelweiser.com